Praise for Herding Smart Cats

"Readable and accessible."

— *Jeffrey Seglin*

Director of the Harvard Kennedy School communications program, author of "The Right Thing" syndicated column and numerous books, speaker, and senior lecturer

"I could not speak more highly about the book. Suzanne has done an exceptional job highlighting project management's joys and tribulations. The book is loaded with practical advice that makes it a must-read."

— *Gurpreet Dhillon*

PhD, G. Brint Ryan Endowed Chair of AI and Cybersecurity, University of North Texas

"A highly useful and practical guide on how to effectively combine traditional project management practices with what modern technologies and techniques have to offer. Especially in times of rapidly increasing complexity and uncertainty, with projects becoming more than ever crucial vehicles for change and innovation, this book is a valuable contribution to a much-needed critical review of existing project delivery practices."

— *Marcus Glowasz*

Project leadership coach, executive coach and facilitator

"Suzanne's first book presents the merger of traditional and agile ideas in project management. Its title suggests that project managers are still herding cats when they try to align stakeholders with various backgrounds to collaborate and team on a project. It can be challenging to give the team a common purpose and a joint vision but also agree on the way to go forward. Especially when people on the team do not talk the same language, come from different cultures (like business and IT) and have different contexts and experience. But this diversity is also required to find a range of solutions to problems arising. The question is how to instill discipline.

Suzanne is looking at her modern concept of project management to tackle this tension between diversity and discipline and provides the reader with aspects and perspectives useful for daily situations. Worthwhile read."

— *Thomas Walenta*

PgMP, PMP, PMI Fellow, mentor and wisdom builder

"A wonderful work for our turbulent and unstable times. It is a reminder of the inevitable advent of new digital technologies that can completely revolutionize the principles and approaches to project management based on big data science."

— *Sergey N. Batiuk*

CEBA, researcher on blockchain, AI / ML, and project management

"Suzanne's book is easy to read and very practical, and she provides a thoughtful approach to project management in the dynamic and fast-moving technical era. Not just a book, it's a toolkit that we should all embrace when running complex projects."

— *Pindy Bhullar*

ESG CTO, PhD Researcher, sustainability in software projects and innovation in bio-diversity solutions

HERDING SMART CATS

Project Management *Reimagined*

Suzanne S. Davenport

Smart Projex, Inc.

6134 St. Andrews Lane

Richmond, VA. 23226

www.smartprojex.com

Library of Congress Control Number:

ISBN: 978-1-7356354-0-8

Printed in the United States of America

Ordering Information:

Quantity sales. Special discounts are available on quantity purchases by schools, teams, associations, and others. For details, contact the publisher at the address above, or by email: info@smartprojex.com

Contents

Introduction

Complicated. Complex. Chaotic. Workforces today face ambiguity, rapid change, and uncontrollable global effects. Increasingly, they need to experiment, fail, learn, and adapt. Success isn't coming without a big fight. Across the world, businesses, professional organizations, governments, and nonprofits are using projects to enact the changes that are sorely needed, and to improve profits and performance. Sadly, many of these projects will not produce the anticipated results or will do so at an excessive cost or much later than desired.

After years of exploring why this is true, dissecting project management methodologies, and revisiting age-old assumptions, I built a working project management software solution. I continue to work with clients and colleagues on all kinds of projects, and write extensively on the subject.

This book is an exploration of my project management journey and my frustration over the amount of wasted time and money. Work has undeniably changed dramatically in the last 50 years and in *Herding Smart Cats*, I reimagine how we could better manage projects throughout businesses, governments, nonprofits, and professional organizations.

I chose the title *Herding Smart Cats* because I often find that managing projects with teams of businesspeople, especially creative and innovative individuals, is like herding smart cats. People working today often have strong wills, even stronger opinions, and are more likely to question authority than they were fifty years ago. They can't always control their schedule. They juggle the needs of multiple bosses, commitments, and priorities. Just as cats cannot be herded, neither can smart, dynamic, and innovative individuals.

The term "smart cats" is not a commentary on IQ – it is a commentary on the need to creatively outsmart the competition and deliver value for your customers. When I use the term "smart people," I'm not talking about people with higher intellect – only people who use their brains, rather than machines, to accomplish tasks. Some people use both. More and more, people are being called upon to use their heads and creatively look for better ways to accomplish their objectives.

When I was researching the herding smart cats metaphor, I spoke with Pam Merritt, author of *The Way of Cats*. According to her, cats are not easily herded because they are not pack animals, genetically. They don't particularly respond to hierarchy. She describes them as "communal egalitarians" who form social communities and divide up responsibilities. Cats will do almost anything for the people they love but they don't respond particularly well to discipline.[1]

Merritt has written about the kinds of techniques that can be used to train cats, and her saying "training is communication" reminds me so much of good project management. Her insights on the importance of developing trust and how to divide up responsibilities aligns surprisingly well with my Smart Projex methodology – a fundamentally different approach to project management that I have been working on for years. It blends the flexibility that traditional methods do not easily provide with the reliable data analytics that executives and project leaders need to make sound decisions. When I first began exploring this need to reimagine project management, I felt like a lone voice.

And now, it feels like change is occurring. For all the talk of project failure, I see more and more project experts talking about bridging communication divides, identifying strong visions, abandoning approaches that don't work, and finding better ways of working together with respect and appreciation. Also, I hear people talking about using the project disciplines, that experts have been tweaking for years, to manage all kinds of work – from projects to products to operations. And yet, we still have a long way to go.

Want to guess how much money we are losing on projects? Back in 2012, a *Gallup Business Journal* post noted, "One estimate of IT failure rates is between 5% and 15%, which represents a loss of $50 billion to $150 billion per year in the United States."[2] While that statistic was limited to IT failures, the same article noted that a "study by PricewaterhouseCoopers, which reviewed 10,640 projects from 200 companies in 30 countries and across various industries, found that only 2.5% of the companies successfully completed 100% of their projects."[3]

Fast-forward almost a decade and according to the Project Management Institute's 2020 *Pulse of the Profession* report, "11.4 percent of investment is wasted due to poor project performance. And organizations that undervalue project management as a strategic competency for driving change report an average of 67 percent more of their projects failing outright."[4]

Translate whichever failure rate you choose into dollars and swallow that bitter pill. For every $1 billion that we spend on projects annually, we are irrevocably losing somewhere between $114 million and $670 million a year. To pull an example from today's headlines, let's ask: as the US prepares to spend mega billions on President Biden's infrastructure projects, can it afford that kind of waste?

Our inability to significantly improve overall project performance is not due to a lack of trained project managers. The Project Management Institute, a leading global professional organization, began issuing the Project Management Professional (PMP) certification in 1984; by mid-2020, there were over one million certified PMPs.[5] One might expect that with so many highly trained project managers, we could be doing better. I wonder if we are wasting time and money on efforts that don't matter that much and not spending enough time on the work that *does* drive project success.

Many people, including Amazon's former CEO Jeff Bezos, argue that we *need* some level of project failure. "If the size of your failures isn't growing, you're not going to be inventing at a size that can actually move the needle."[6] Innovation and experimentation are essential, I agree; and that means some waste. Yet, Bezos goes on to say that "multibillion-dollar failures are actually a good thing."[7] The reality is that few companies can afford multibillion-dollar waste. And at Amazon, are all of those wasted dollars a necessary cost of learning and innovation, or could we reduce that waste and more wisely spend some of those billions?

In this book, I explore that question. Could we reimagine project management to improve collaboration and communications, empower productive and engaged teams, expedite the delivery of customer value, and reduce project waste? Do twenty-first-century technologies offer us an opportunity to reduce the mundane; track production, project assets, and expenses in real-time; use artificial intelligence-enhanced simulation technologies to improve our decision-making; and even use virtual and augmented reality to visualize the inner workings in our organizations?

With all that we have learned from modern brain imaging techniques and studies, could we better empower people, working as highly functioning teams, to deliver results to the client more frequently and at less cost? Or will we stay locked into thinking that the tools and approaches of the past need to be those of the future?

This book, written for busy business leaders and project management thinkers like you, is about reimagining project leadership and work management in organizations that are relying on teams of smart people to make transformative change. The change may be a company's need to restructure the organization or its product line to increase profits, a struggling nonprofit's wish to organize its annual fundraiser, a pharmaceutical company's attempt to develop an effective pharmaceutical, a USAID project to get aid to starving souls in another land, or a law firm's obligation to manage a complex piece of litigation that involves multiple parties. The book is organized into four parts: Analytics, Leadership, the Smart Projex Methodology, and The Future.

Analytics

After explaining my journey to understand project management, one that you may be on as well, I begin with analytics because you, as an executive, first need to understand what is happening in your organization. Where are the problems? Are your projects aligned with your strategy and producing the planned benefits? What should you be doing now and in the future?

Businesses today operate in a complex world of global forces, ambiguity, evolving work trends, and rapidly changing technologies. Projects rarely fail in a vacuum, and yet they are often managed that way. You likely don't want to hear this, but the project data analytics that you have relied on for years can be badly flawed. I explain how and why, and propose some new data analytics that I believe add value and can inform your business decisions.

Leadership and Methodology

From there, I move to leadership, where I offer my thoughts on what is working best and how to improve team efficiency. Thanks to improving brain imaging capabilities and mounting neuroscience research, we are accumulating good data on what works and what doesn't.

And in Part 3, I discuss a project methodology that I've been working on for over a decade, and why it works. Some of these ideas may seem new to you. They are drawn from a variety of project leadership approaches. Some are based on old-fashioned common sense, and some are drawn from evolving brain science. Our world is vastly different from the world in the 1950s – when there was a greater respect for hierarchy and authority and people didn't multitask to the extent they do now. What might have worked then doesn't work quite so well now, which is why we need to reimagine project management for the twenty-first century.

The Future

In the book's fourth section, I discuss the future and the opportunities that artificial intelligence, blockchain, and other twenty-first-century technologies offer the business world. I propose Smart Projex 2.0 – a project software tool infused with the latest technologies – and explain what that could look like, its value, and the challenges.

I explore how a software tool that allows teams to manage products, projects, and operations together, using the best project management disciplines, and enhanced by twenty-first-century technologies, would help us collaborate more effectively, rapidly spot problems, adapt quickly, and deliver solutions. I ponder how it might help us address problems in global collaboration, supply chain management, environmental upheavals, and business disruptions.

I know that too much time and money is wasted on poorly managed projects. New and evolving technologies offer the opportunity to build a solution that gives us the project controls that are needed for effective leadership, together with the agility that is needed for our rapidly changing world. Blockchain offers us a path to building trust among disparate groups of stakeholders, and artificial intelligence is already improving the insights that we use to make decisions throughout our organizations.

In *Herding Smart Cats*, I delve into how we could reimagine project leadership and work management to improve your bottom line. While this book contains a wealth of information, it is not a project management training manual. It is meant to be a quick read; hopefully, it will make you think. Thank you for reading.

Part 1
Analytics

"Some of the best theorizing comes after collecting data because then you become aware of another reality."[8]

— *Robert J. Shiller*

Chapter 1

The Light at the End of the Tunnel

In the Introduction, I discussed the high cost of failed projects and why I believe part of the problem is the dramatic shift in how we work, at a general level. I also talked about why it feels like we are herding smart cats. And I'm not alone in believing that there has been a sea change in business. In 2016, Colin Mayer of the British Academy published a study on *Reinventing the Corporation*, where he discussed the evolution from transnational corporations, heavily invested in tangible assets (i.e., plant, property, and equipment), to mindful companies, which primarily consist of intangible assets (ideas and the people who can turn them into cash).[9]

In this chapter, I describe the difficulties I have had in making the traditional project management methodology work for me. I have wondered if part of the reason for the high failure rate is a change in the way people work, combined with the difficulties of using the traditional methodology when change and ambiguity are so prevalent. As I mentioned, I became so frustrated that I created working software. It wasn't perfect, but it did offer the agility needed to execute during rapid change and ambiguity, as well as some pretty good project controls. After you finish this chapter (or the book), if you are curious about my software creation endeavors, check out Appendix 1. This book is not about the software, but about reimagining project leadership and work management for the future.

Sometimes, when managing projects, I have felt like I was traveling in a tunnel and living with the fear that one of the cars in the tunnel would depart from its lane, causing an accident that would keep me from reaching my destination on time, or worse.

I have struggled with traditional project management methodologies more than I have succeeded. The widely accepted approach to project management is the Waterfall method, which relies on a tool called the Gantt chart. The approach favors linear thinking. I don't think particularly linearly; more importantly, I would argue that linear thinking doesn't work well when the world around us is changing rapidly.

Yet, when introduced to alternative approaches, such as Scrum, that offered more flexibility, I could not completely abandon the need for some cost, scope, and schedule controls. I remember an "aha!" moment, years ago. Let me explain it to you, first with a bit of background.

Some years back, the executive director of one of my favorite charities asked me to organize a project for her; this was before I had studied project management. The local nonprofit was less than three months away from a fundraising event and had barely begun planning the details. My designated contact at the charity was critically injured on her way to our first meeting to discuss their needs. The organization had hired an expensive band and caterer, but had no venue lined up, no invitations or guest list, no media or financial sponsors, and no raffle donations.

Fast-forward to the post-event meeting with executives. The event was a sellout, but I sat in that room sweating bullets as I waited for their assessment. I had submitted a comprehensive report on the event, but I was largely unprepared for one question that awaited me. One of the executives asked me where my schedule was.

I was completely taken aback. There was no schedule, as such. I was brought into a crisis; they were about to cancel the event. I had agreed to resuscitate the event and was pleased that the event netted a whole lot more money than anyone projected before I was hired. Things had been changing so fast during those three months that creating a schedule would have been a complete waste of my time. I knew the deadline well. I knew what needed to be done and when. There was no way I was going to miss that deadline! And yet, this older and supposedly wiser man was asking for a schedule *after* the event. I scratched my head and wondered why he wanted a schedule at this point.

That conversation launched my project management education. One of the first courses I took was on schedules, where an instructor went over Gantt charts - the traditional schedule creation and management tool - and gave us several examples. All the examples were construction projects, and they seemed to make sense when he was explaining them.

But then, my classmates and I were asked to create some schedules for our own work projects. As I sat with my group, we all discussed the projects we handled in our different jobs. None of us worked for building contractors. We were busy with nonprofit events, an insurance product development project, a pharmaceutical drug effort, and a marketing campaign.

We struggled mightily. But when that course was finished, we all understood how to build and use a Gantt chart. And yet, I was still frustrated. The tool, when applied on more creative projects, didn't work well for me and a lot of others in the class. I continued to question this, took more project management courses, and went on to get several project certifications as well as my MBA. And still, I struggled whenever a business or nonprofit client asked for a detailed Gantt chart.

And as my frustrations mounted, I began to ponder what project management, if done well, meant. I went back to basics, dissected every process I had learned or thought I knew, and questioned everything – for a very long time. Finally, a light bulb went off, and I figured out why many project managers still struggled with schedules.

Many of my classmates and I were working on *complex projects* at our day jobs. But the course instructor had given us a tool that was designed for *complicated projects*. At the time, I was unfamiliar with this distinction. The words themselves – complex and complicated – seemed almost synonymous to me. But are they? They probably are if you are relying on a dictionary definition. But in the project world, they are sometimes used to refer to two different types of projects.

Complicated or Complex?

Complicated projects, like building construction projects, are typically linear and predictable. You can logically map out a sequence. Complex projects, on the other hand, have too many factors involved to be predictable and often evolve in response to real-time decision-making; that is, they progress based on what has most recently happened. Building a bridge is a complicated project. Designing a bridge is a complex project.

Make no mistake. Complicated projects can be quite large and complex, using that dictionary definition. But the point here is that they can be sequenced. There is enough historic data to estimate how long the activities will take. And you can reasonably estimate progress. Complex projects are too unpredictable to be handled in the same manner.

Think about this in simple terms: If you are building a new house, that's a complicated project. You dig a hole before you pour the foundation. You put in the studs before you staple in the wiring. And you put up the sheetrock before you paint. You can estimate how long each of these activities will take, the number of people needed, and the supplies and materials that are required. From that you can calculate the costs and estimate how long the entire project will take.

And at the end of each month, you can walk around the site, observe the progress, and estimate how much has been finished. In a business project, the process is not as straightforward.

Complex projects, such as organizational change projects, product development projects, or strategic initiatives, are not as linear and predictable as construction projects. Project teams are flying by the seats of their pants. At the end of the month, they look back on what they have accomplished and wonder if they have made any real progress or not. And all of this was true long before the COVID-19 pandemic took the world by storm.

Suppose, for example, you are writing the user manual for a new piece of scientific equipment that your company is developing. When a team of smart people must approve any major deliverable, it is not unusual for smart minds to delay completion, because new and improved information is always emerging. It may be as simple as someone deciding that the manual needs to be produced in multiple languages, or the developers may still be tweaking the equipment – necessitating a change in the instructions.

And so, if you try to estimate how much work you have finished, you may not know.

And there is another factor. We work in a rapidly changing knowledge economy. And now we are increasingly working from home. We have smart people toiling away on several complex projects at a time, with multiple bosses; and these people have families and other personal commitments. They can't peer into the future and tell you exactly when they will be available to work on your project, because they don't know. And yet, managing people using the traditional Gantt chart approach requires that team members commit to a schedule of their availability well in advance.

Daily, construction workers show up on the job, clock in, go to work, and then clock out. It's relatively easy to track their work. In the business world, people move back and forth between multiple projects, often with frequent interruptions, during the day. It's far harder to know how much time has been spent on any one project or activity.

If we can't reliably estimate how long our project activities will take, predict exactly when people will be able to work on those activities, and accurately measure how much time has been spent on those project activities, how can we have the controls that Gantt charts offer? And do we *need* project controls?

Is project management in the twenty-first century about controlling or leading? I argue that project management today is much more relationship centric; it is about leadership rather than control. It's about engaging your teams, building awareness about risks and challenges, sensing trends and patterns, learning from doing, and continually improving.

Time to Give Up the Gantt Chart?

The Gantt chart tool that is at the heart of controlling projects is about 100 years old. It doesn't work easily when change is rapid, when innovation is important, and when projects need agility. And on complex projects, it doesn't always produce reliable data on which to base decisions. Aren't we at the point in history when innovation is essential, collaboration and communication are critical, and speed is required? Is it time to let go of the traditional Gantt chart and find a new way to work in the twenty-first century?

Many challenges face us today. Whether it's global pandemics, the fight to survive your neighborhood competitor, or rapidly changing technologies that are hard to embrace, we all struggle. How do you increase revenues or market share, or decrease your costs? How will you finish this project on schedule when some people on your team may be fleeing wildfires or hurricanes? How are disruptions to the supply chain, from a ship stuck in the Suez Canal, impacting your scheduling? Many of us are exhausted. And yet, I believe we are in a period of great promise. Others agree.

According to Klaus Schwab, founder and executive chairman of the World Economic Forum, "We stand on the brink of a technological revolution that will fundamentally alter the way we live, work, and relate to one another. In its scale, scope, and complexity, the transformation will be unlike anything humankind has experienced before. We do not yet know how it will unfold, but one thing is clear: the response to it must be integrated and comprehensive, involving all stakeholders of the global polity, from the public and private sectors to academia and civil society."[10]

This so-called Fourth Industrial Revolution is characterized by massive and rapid technology breakthroughs in fields as diverse as quantum computing, nanotechnology, energy storage, biotechnology, artificial intelligence, robotics, and more – all of which are "blurring the lines between the physical, digital, and biological spheres," according to Schwab.[11] The ethical challenges are hard to fathom.

Also, according to Schwab, executives today are "too often trapped in traditional, linear thinking, or too absorbed by the multiple crises demanding their attention, to think strategically about the forces of disruption and innovation shaping our future."[12]

Technology, that light at the end of the tunnel, will offer us capabilities that I can't begin to envision. Our future rests on our ability to innovate and execute, and on our people, projects, and values. Will we continue to waste time and money on project techniques that don't work? Will we create systems that put people first or will we build technologies that make many of us irrelevant? We owe it to ourselves, our children, our grandchildren, and our planet to actively seek solutions that empower teams, raise up individuals as valuable members of our societies, and use the best aspects of project management as an organizing principle behind all work in our businesses. This book offers a way to do that.

Chapter 2

Executives Need Reliable Project Data Analytics

For years, business leaders, Wall Street analysts, and investors have sought to understand the success drivers in the business world. We desperately want to know the answer to the question: if I take this action, will revenues rise, costs drop, profits increase, or market share improve? Unfortunately, many identified causal relationships are often flawed. There are simply too many dependent variables in the business world. Businesses operate in a complex world of global market forces and rapidly changing technologies. Companies and their executives cannot be put into petri dishes and analyzed like cancer cells. We simply cannot always understand cause and effect in our complex world.

Yet business leaders are routinely called upon to make critical business decisions that depend on reliable analytics. For years, the Gantt chart schedule has been a primary vehicle through which project leaders understand whether their projects are on schedule, on budget, or at risk of failing to meet identified targets.

Yet, as I've discussed, for many projects, I question whether building a detailed schedule that will change frequently is the best way to spend valuable project time. Could we find a better way to move projects forward so that we can rapidly innovate, collaborate, and communicate effectively? Could we reimagine project management and achieve the reliable project analytics that benefit executives and project teams?

Before I go further, I should note that I am using the term "reliable" in a general way, to indicate that the data are both valid and reliable, so that executives can confidently rely on the data for critical decision-making.

Analytics Drive Decision-Making

How many times have you tried to make a good decision and wondered if your decision was based on reliable data? In spring 2020, as I watched state governors making decisions about whether to close schools in a global pandemic, I thought about early data that suggested that young people were at much lower risk. And then, the data changed. That's the problem with data. It changes. It's open to interpretation. It can be misleading.

In the earlier days of mapping software, a daughter, then a junior in college, was returning from a trip to Morocco. Her flight had landed in Atlanta during a blizzard that would be dubbed "Snowmageddon 2014," and with almost no juice remaining on her cell phone she called me, practically in tears. She was exhausted, having not slept in about 36 hours. She was stuck with hordes of people in an airport with no place to sleep, no way to charge her phone, and no place to safely store her valuables so that they would still be there if she dozed off.

For a few long minutes, my husband and I discussed ways to get her back to her college in South Carolina. That problem belonged to the college, but we were trying to help – and we felt so sorry for our daughter.

At some point, I logged on to a map site and tried to

figure out how long it would take a car to get her back to school, if we could find a car, or a bus – since there were lots of kids in her predicament. A map inquiry reported that it would take a car 8,336 hours to get her back to her school, which we knew would be just a three-hour drive under normal, moderate traffic conditions. Clearly the algorithm behind the calculation didn't factor in the fact that snow melts. Common sense is required. Unless we know the assumptions and algorithms behind the reported data, we must question it.

Reliable analytics are critical to the decision-making process. Yet, I wonder what is going on in the minds of even the best executives. And I'm not alone. Many are discussing the short-term thinking that Wall Street demands. And Clayton Christiansen says in *The Innovator's Dilemma* that "there is something about the way decisions get made in successful organizations that sows the seeds of eventual failure."[13]

In 2017, a group of McKinsey analysts studied the supposedly great, excellent, and enduring companies that are spotlighted by Tom Peters in *In Search of Excellence* and by Jim Collins in *Built to Last and Good to Great*. The companies were analyzed over specific time frames to make results more comparable; the results today show a situation even worse than McKinsey reported in 2017. According to the 2017 results, only eight of the fifty companies outperformed the S&P 500 index by more than five points. Fourteen underperformed the S&P. Today, at least seven are no longer operating: Wang Labs, DEC, Data General, Dana, National Semiconductor, Circuit City, and Amdahl. Kodak filed for bankruptcy in 2013 and several others have received government help, have huge lawsuits pending, or are often cited in the news for management problems (Boeing, Wells Fargo, General Electric, IBM, and Kmart).

According to Chris Bradley, who reported on this McKinsey study, "Great companies were more likely to do really badly than really well."[14]

I wonder how many of our "great" companies are being run by people who think they are playing a finite game, the kind of game that Simon Sinek defines as one with established rules, winners, and losers. I discuss this more in Chapter 8 (on people). For now, consider these questions. Are businesses operating to beat the competition and deliver superior results this quarter, or this year? Or are businesses playing the long game – to operate relatively successfully over the long term? Those objectives require radically different strategies.

From what I continue to hear, many executives still rely on their key project leaders to provide analytics manually. This is often a one-page report on open projects, with red, green, and yellow indicators, typically based on input from project leaders throughout the organization. Provided those key leaders are getting reliable insights from their teams, that approach may work. But as I read about the problems in project management, I increasingly think that people don't love admitting that there is a problem. And when people know that information is going all the way to the top of the organization, they like such confessions even less. Perhaps they optimistically believe that they are positioned to resolve the delay or cost overrun if they just continue on the current trajectory.

No one likes admitting that a particular activity or milestone is behind schedule or about to exceed the budget; but figuring that out early can save your project. That's because figuring it out early gives you time to understand what's happening and why, and time to adjust. In many cases, the problem will be with the original estimates.

We work in a rapidly changing world on all sorts of

complex projects, many of which have never been done before. Terms such as "innovation projects," "strategic initiatives," or "organizational change projects" are sometimes used. Whenever project leaders are venturing into uncharted territory to create a new product, service, or process, there will be many unknowns. The work will not be linear or predictable. And you won't be able measure progress like you can on a tangible construction project. In this environment, can we still develop reliable analytics that inform better executive decision-making?

There are several areas where analytics can provide help for executives and project teams. These include work efficiency, project profitability, risk management, project selection, and continuous improvement projects. Part 1 of this book devotes a chapter to each of those.

There are other traditional metrics that work well in some industries but are less valuable in the kinds of business projects that I talk about in this book. For example, project leaders and executives love to talk about earned value and return on investment.

Simply put, earned value is the value of work that has been performed on a project or group of activities, measured against the budget for the project or group of activities. It's a measure of project performance that factors in schedule, costs, and scope. It considers partially completed activities. And when the metrics are reliable, it helps us understand the value of work completed on a project to date. But what happens when we can't measure or observe the progress on partially completed activities? What happens when we can't trust the estimate of what percentage of the work is completed?

Return on investment, often called ROI, is another popular metric in the business world and is the benefit of a proposed change divided by the cost of making that change. It is usually measured by dividing the forecast net profit from completing a project by the projected cost of the project. While the math isn't hard, some assumptions go into the calculation, and thus the result depends on the quality of those assumptions.

ROI typically doesn't factor in any social benefit to an investment, and it doesn't give any weight to legal requirements. If a regulatory authority requires that your project be done, calculating ROI is hardly worth the effort. But, achieving the regulatory authority's mandate as cost-effectively as possible should be a key objective.

If these metrics are not reliable in today's world, should we give up on building portfolio metrics that improve executive decision-making? If we want meaningful metrics across a diversified portfolio of project investments, we must reinvent our entire approach to project management. To do this, let's first explore the human, economic, and technological factors that will influence how we approach redefining project management for the twenty-first century.

Human Factors Are Changing Organizations and Work

Smart people want to enjoy working with other smart people on meaningful projects. In my experience, smart people generally prefer to self-manage and be accountable for results, are frequently in high demand, and want some level of autonomy.

Traditional oversight structures, as well as traditional project management methodologies, aren't particularly good at accommodating autonomy.

Organizational structures are evolving – with some companies moving, quite successfully, to flatter organizations. Perhaps one of the best examples of a flat organization is the Internet Engineering Task Force (IETF). This huge body now governs how the internet evolves, with no one in charge. And in these flatter organizations, people seem to be thriving on the autonomy.

In recent years, we've seen younger people arrive in our organizations, often with stronger technology gifts than previous generations, and begin to use social media to push for changes in how work is done. Many want more flexibility and rapid feedback.

Transparency shines a spotlight on failure and success. Creating a culture where teams can be accountable without fearing failure will result in earlier identification of problems and better solutions. But who wants to admit failure? What can we do to create a more collaborative culture that promotes early disclosure of problems?

Well-run meetings are still a formidable way to communicate, despite the many protests about meetings. Poorly run meetings waste time and suck the life out of your teams. I discuss some suggestions for conducting better meetings in Chapter 13.

Our organizations are staffed by people who are as individual as their fingerprints. We do them and our organizations a great disservice when we don't recognize that. From the highly detail-oriented introverts to the unpredictable and charismatic extroverts, we need to understand what makes people tick as individuals. Some people will never be able to sit still and focus for an hour – while others will never be able to comfortably speak in public, and that includes *your* large meetings. Some people are highly task oriented and will be frustrated when you spend the first five minutes of your meeting having a check-in. And others are more people oriented and need that check-in time.

Additionally, people come with biases and fears that can greatly impact their ability to make sound decisions. I discuss this in greater detail later in the book. As you begin to think about what kinds of systems will work in your organization, remember that some of your folks will always prefer a paper to-do list, while others will never be able to function without their laptops or cell phones attached to their hands. We need to learn to meet people where they are and communicate with them in a language they understand.

Economic Factors Dictate the Need for Analytics

We have moved from a machine economy to a knowledge economy, though technological advances seem to be moving us in the direction of a high-tech economy. High-tech machines, replete with artificial intelligence, increasingly feature prominently in the workforce. But for now, people, not machines, still plan and execute your projects. Despite increasing high-tech investments, companies need smart people to work on these projects.

Change is a constant. Our increasingly mobile world is moving faster, and we are accumulating massive amounts of data – some valuable and some flawed. There is a tendency to think more is better, but that is not always true, and we are left with the challenge of spotting the difference between reliable and unreliable data.

Another challenge is to figure out what to measure. People are smart, and they will quickly play games with your metrics. You will get what you measure, so be careful about measurements. We've all seen situations where a focus on the wrong key performance indicators led to bad decisions.

This is particularly evident in compensation structures. If you reward people for individual accomplishments to an extreme, your people may not work well on teams. If you pay rainmakers absurd amounts to produce new clients or customers, don't expect them to help you redefine your processes. If you reward short-term thinking, your long-term results may fail you.

Is your organization a conglomeration of individuals sharing resources? Many law firms and professional partnerships fall into that category. These companies, and many other businesses, simply do not have the cash buffer to weather storms when they blow without cutting partner or employee compensation, which few people enjoy.

Technology Factors Make Analytics Possible, But Challenging

Technology plays an increasingly larger role in our lives. Most of us go nowhere without our smartphones. Legal concerns mount each day, as companies collect more and more data and wrestle with what constitutes appropriate use. For example, we have read that Microsoft, Amazon, and IBM have decided to ban police departments from using their facial recognition technologies, for now.[15]

With COVID-19, we have experienced what a pandemic feels like. Even the companies that were not well-suited for remote work before the pandemic are having to learn how to do that. In organizations that are not well-suited for remote work, the novelty will probably wear off soon if it hasn't already by the time you read this. And while working remotely may be better than not working at all or not getting paid, many jobs simply cannot be done remotely. Yet remote work reinforces the need for good data analytics on your projects. When we aren't around our colleagues in person as much, it is hard to build trust. We find ourselves looking to the data analytics to understand how projects are evolving.

When we purchase goods and services, we increasingly have higher expectations. Thanks to the internet, we frequently find that they can be met. We look for faster, better, and cheaper, and gradually find it. Companies making those goods and services are increasingly challenged to remain competitive and find that moving to the low-cost provider model may not improve profits. How can you distinguish your company in other ways?

While I don't discount the importance of gut instinct, or perhaps you want to call it divine inspiration, I also believe you need great analytics to make good decisions. Yet, we all must cope with the security, technological, educational, legal, workspace, and human challenges that continue to develop and impact our ability to find those reliable analytics that we so desperately need.

As mentioned in the Introduction, I discuss in Part 4 of this book how a software solution that manages all work, using proven project management principles and an approach that offers agility along with reliable project data, could dramatically improve performance. To get there, we face some big questions. Let's discuss four of them here.

Four Big Questions We Need to Consider

With human, economic, and technological factors in mind, creating software that allows us to glean useful (i.e., reliable) project metrics in real time requires that we consider many issues. Here are four:

1. Should project baselines be changed, mid-project?

In traditional project management, teams go through a process of estimating the costs and schedule. They establish a baseline, or a projection of the final costs and completion date. The project is then measured against that baseline. In some high-profile projects, those baselines become public information, contractual agreements, or other ways of holding teams accountable. Arguments continue about how, whether, and when projects should be re-estimated mid-project. Earlier in this book, I offered my thoughts on the difficulties with estimating costs and durations on complex projects. Yet, some estimating is necessary – particularly to manage costs.

How and when should we allow teams to revise estimates? Is there a better way to measure project progress and hold teams accountable than through a baseline? Are baselines important?

2. What is the purpose and value of a schedule?

In a rapidly changing world, we need to rethink the purpose of a schedule and the value that schedules add to a project plan.

In 2001, an independent group of seventeen software practitioners created four premises for software development on which they agreed. The resulting Agile Manifesto of twelve principles has formed the basis for discussions, project methodology development, and a growing community of Agile proponents. Scrum is perhaps the best-known methodology to grow out of this community. (Note that throughout this book, I use a lowercase "a" in agile to indicate flexibility and an uppercase "A" in Agile to mean a specific approach to project work.)

Many Agile and Scrum proponents argue that a detailed schedule is the outcome of a well-managed project. This is the antithesis of traditional project management, which places a priority on creating a schedule in the early days of the project, often by assigning best-guess durations and sometimes arbitrary dependencies (links between activities) so that the software can "calculate" the most effective sequence of activities and provide deadlines against which the results can be measured.

Experts have developed sophisticated techniques to help project managers manage this somewhat arbitrary schedule, but these efforts take time away from other tasks that will move the project forward or improve the bottom line. If the critical deadlines are met, why do we need a detailed Gantt chart schedule, with dependencies? Are there better ways to understand critical dependencies? I discuss schedule management in more detail in Part 3 on methodology.

3. How can we balance the need for cost management against the need for agility?

Cost management has long been a significant part of traditional project management. A Gantt chart with costs assigned to individual activities allows the project manager to forecast cash needs by time period. Using earned value, the project manager can track progress against costs. If we move away from a schedule to a more agile approach, we lose the ability to forecast cash needs by time period. If business executives can be open with teams about cash resources, can we trust teams to execute in accordance with available cash flow? I discuss cost management in more depth in Part 3.

4. Is constant transparency misleading?

There is no question that project teams and executives benefit from well-designed dashboards. But consider this. As many project teams enter data, there can be other balancing data that has not yet been entered. It can be as simple as marking a complex activity "done" and waiting until the next day or week to record the amount of time worked. Or it might simply be that you are in the process of updating the risk log but not yet finished. Data metrics at those times might be misleading. Perhaps it would be more helpful to set a specific time every day or week by which all important data would be entered, and then produce dashboard analytics from that data. For now, however, we are still dependent on people entering data on a timely basis.

Are Gantt Charts Required?

Frequently, particularly in the government world, we get locked into contracts with cost and schedule estimates on which we will be assessed. Keep in mind that the federal government was involved in the development of earned value management (EVM) back in the 1960s and so EVM is often their default. It's completely logical that governments need accountability and controls, particularly when they are spending taxpayer dollars.

Finishing a project, especially a large government project, over budget or behind schedule may tarnish the record of the project manager, often with little understanding of what caused the problem until the experts study it later. I would argue that when estimates are seriously flawed from the outset and progress cannot be reliably estimated, we need to find a better approach.

When project managers are contractually obligated to use Gantt charts and earned value metrics, they will spend a lot of time using sophisticated techniques to manage the schedule and costs. Since earned value analysis correlates the amount of money spent and the value received to date, it makes perfect sense – except that the data may not be reliable. And all that time and effort to build and track those controls don't move the project forward.

I remember an organizational change management project that I was involved in years ago with a government agency. There had been some recent news articles about irresponsible project efforts that had tarnished every agency's reputation to some extent, and when it came time to negotiate the contract it took considerable work to convince the agency that an Agile approach was in its best interest on this project. Fortunately, the IT folks in the agency had set the stage for using Agile. But it can be challenging to overcome the default project management technique of Gantt charts and earned value management, particularly on federal contracts. To replace a default management structure, we need an alternative that offers solid controls and reliable analytics. Before I move on, what are you and your clients planning to do with all the data you collect?

I laugh at the notion that Mark Twain reportedly said: "Data is like garbage. You'd better know what you are going to do with it before you collect it." Who knows whether he said that? But whoever did say it is right. Data collection takes resources. It behooves us to understand *what* we plan to do with data that we want to collect and to understand what our clients plan to do with that data. As I read the *Wall Street Journal*'s report that Amazon was using proprietary data on third-party sellers to create competitive products, it was clear to me that there are ethical issues, and perhaps legal ones, involved as well.[16]

In the remainder of Part 1, I discuss some ways that I believe we can build reliable metrics and controls while still achieving agility in the face of change, complexity, and ambiguity.

Chapter 3

To Improve Efficiency, Start by Tracking Complexity

When a business improves the efficiency of its project teams, it improves its bottom line. But it can be challenging to accurately measure work efficiency. This chapter introduces Complexity, a Smart Projex concept, as one approach to measuring efficiency. Throughout this book, I use a capital C when referring to the name of the Smart Projex metric that measures how complex an activity is. I use a lowercase c when discussing complexity as a general concept, or the Scrum concept of complexity.

What is Efficiency?

Before we go too far, let's make sure we're clear on what efficiency is. Efficiency is getting the best results with the least time, effort, and costs. Said differently, it's about saving resources. If we can find a way to measure what has been accomplished against the resources used, we can then begin to improve efficiency. This chapter discusses an approach to measuring efficiency and the metrics we can calculate. Part 2 of this book covers many leadership suggestions that will improve your teamwork efficiency.

In traditional project management, estimating durations plays a large and important role. Project managers are sometimes encouraged to go so far as to videotape someone doing an activity to estimate how long that activity will take. This may have been a valuable exercise in a machine economy, but we now work in a knowledge economy. When we have fully arrived at whatever next high-tech economy hits us, I doubt that will be necessary. At this point, estimating durations on complex projects feels like a waste of time and effort.

Any writer can tell you that there are days when the words flow easily and there are other days when they don't. Research experiments work one day, and the next day, they don't. A software developer may write 1000 lines of bug-free code one day, and the next day, things fall apart in the code. The marketing intern may spend a day finding hotel arrangements for a promotional seminar in one city, but that same task may take three days when the seminar moves elsewhere. And that PowerPoint presentation that the CEO is giving next week was almost finished, until the CEO looked at it and decided to start over and talk about something else.

What Is Complexity?

Are there any metrics worth capturing? For now, I'll recommend "Complexity," a term loosely borrowed from the Scrum world but used somewhat differently in the Smart Projex world.

To begin with, Scrum is an Agile framework – and began as a method to manage software development. In the Scrum world, simply put, story points are one measure of the effort that a particular task or feature requires. In Scrum, they are relative within the project. I'm not going to delve into the Scrum world debates over complexity, effort, relative complexity theory, or story points. Instead, my point here is to recognize that when estimating is done in a Scrum world, it is typically done relative to the other work within the project.

In the Smart Projex world, estimations are more related to time, and not relative to other activities within the project.

In both the Scrum world and the Smart Projex world, there can only be a limited number of choices (5 to 8), since estimations grow less and less reliable as complexity increases. Also, people have a hard time with decisions when there are too many choices.

There was a simple reason for setting up Complexity so that estimates are relative to time, rather than the other activities. It allows you to compare projects across the organization.

For example, in a complex business project, the least complex item on your list might be to create a document that you think will take a week. And the most complex activity might be to create a new compensation structure for the organization that will take three to six months to complete. In different projects, the least complex item might be writing a document that will take only a day to finish, or digging the foundation for a house, which might take a few days to a week. By treating Complexity as an absolute, rather than a relative estimate, we can compare Complexity across the board – from innovation projects to more structured construction projects. It will not be perfect. We must let go of perfection to make progress.

To explain the Smart Projex approach further, Complexity is a number that estimates the length of time an activity will take one reasonably skilled person to complete, based on the difficulty of what is involved. (There could be some flexibility on this within organizations, but the definition must be consistent within the organization.)

As a possible recommended approach, think about your choices of Complexity as a 1, 3, 5, 10, 25, and 100. A 1 represents a low level of complexity, i.e., one skilled person could do that activity in a day. A 3 or 5 represents something that might take that person three or five days. As the level of complexity gets higher, it's harder to estimate reliably and you need to spend more time clarifying the activity requirements before you begin execution. A 100 is a level of complexity that is so undefined that you don't know what to expect.

Your job, as you continue to plan and execute the project, is to quickly gain clarity on these activities *before* too much work is done or time is wasted. I would argue that subdividing the larger activities into smaller activities that can be accomplished in one or two sprints (well-defined blocks of time during which the team focuses intently on a subset of work) is more effective than working for months and months on a large activity without clearly understanding the requirements.

Perhaps I should explain that, in the Smart Projex world, I distinguish between activities and tasks. Activities are more akin to work packages. Tasks are the smaller items that are just part of the process, but not estimated. I will discuss this later, when I get into decomposing the project and building a work breakdown structure.

There is always the question of how granular to be in defining your project and the answer depends on the type of project. How much detail do you need? For now, know that you can estimate Complexity on your activities and compare those Complexities across an entire project portfolio.

Benefits of Using Complexity to Measure Efficiency

Once the team estimates the Complexity of each activity on its projects, it can compare the total Complexity in the project portfolio by looking at work assigned to individual people or teams, work that hasn't been done, work that has been completed during different time periods, and a host of other possible comparisons.

Over time, it will become clear when individuals don't have sufficient work or are hoarding work. Teams and individuals will be able to compare the amount of work that is being done and seek to improve efficiency levels.

For example, if one seven-person team is regularly producing work that has an aggregate Complexity of 200 during two-week periods, and another team of the same size is producing work with an aggregate Complexity of 400 or 600, one might question what is happening. If one team always has a large backlog of work and another doesn't, we might think about moving some more work to the team without the backlog. If we used such a tool for managing all work, not just projects, this creates even more opportunities for shifting work.

Keep in mind that in the business world, apart from the technology projects, many people are working on multiple projects at the same time. And in professional partnerships, it is not unusual for some partners to hoard work, believing they are the best person to do it. However, that may or may not be true. Wouldn't it be nice to know more about what is happening?

In the Smart Projex world, teams work in sprints, also known as time blocks, during which they commit to accomplish (i.e., finish) certain portions of work. When the composition of the project team and the sprint length both remain the same, a team that is building its efficiency should be able to increase the total Complexity completed in succeeding time blocks.

In some business projects, teams will change over time, and an analysis of total Complexity in each time block is less helpful than in a project where the team and sprint length remain constant. If time blocks are consistently the same duration, the total Complexity completed in each time block can still be a meaningful indicator of whether the project completion date is achievable. Complexity analysis for individuals could spawn even more insights.

Analyzing the Complexity of work completed to date, versus the work in progress, versus work that has not been done, allows the team to better understand whether it is on track to finish the project on schedule, and what needs to happen to meet the final deadline. Figure 1. shows a bar graph that illustrates this concept.

Figure 1: Complexity Bar Graph

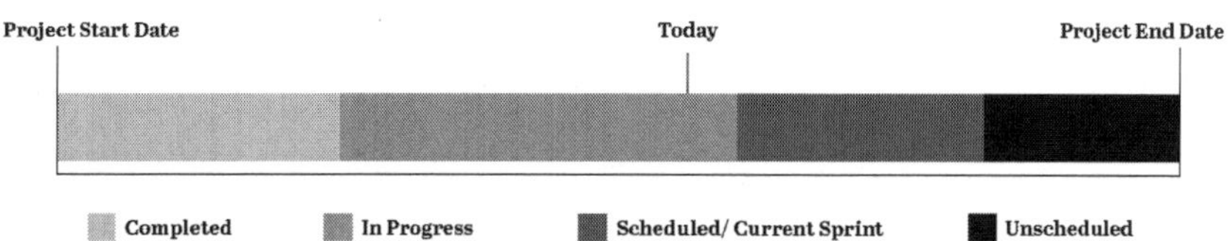

When estimating Complexity, it is essential to understand the activity requirements and the quality of work needed. For example, if the activity is to create a PowerPoint, Keynote, or Prezi presentation for the CEO to give at the annual stockholders meeting, it is helpful to understand the medium, and whether the slides will present six key words, raw numerical data, or bar graphs. Or should a graphic designer create slide pictures that tell a human-interest story? The more you understand an activity, the more closely you can reliably estimate Complexity.

For example, suppose you are working in a small start-up on a team of eight people. You have agreed to do three activities at this time. You have been asked to test a new feature that a group of developers has built. You have been asked to create PowerPoint slides for the company founder to use at an upcoming pitch competition. And, finally, you are supposed to create some new copy for the company website to explain a product change that is coming with this new feature.

To complete these activities, you might need to answer some questions like these: Are you supposed to do simple testing, running the code through a bunch of automated tests to see how it performs, or are you supposed to do more elaborate user testing and try to break the code? How many PowerPoint slides are you supposed to make? Is there a format to follow? Are the slides just for the talk, or will they be given out to the audience as handouts? Who reviews your slide presentation when you are finished? Does it go to a committee or to the founder? And is the website copy supposed to include a full-fledged demo, or is it just three lines of attention-grabbing copy?

There are many questions you could ask, and you won't get answers to all of them. You should pick your battles, so to speak. But when you assign a Complexity of 1 to the pitch slides activity, for example, the founder may come back and say, "Wait, I need high-end slides and that sounds low to me." Or the reverse could happen.

The more clarity you have on the expectations, the better you can estimate Complexity, prioritize your work, and direct your efforts. In the next chapter, I take the concept of Complexity farther and discuss project profitability and cost management. But until you have clarity, you cannot hope for reliable estimates, a profitable project, or effective cost management.

Chapter 4

Do You Understand Project Profitability?

When we combine Complexity data with money data, we unlock several helpful insights. On external projects, or those done for paying clients, you may want to understand profitability. On many projects, you will want to keep a close eye on costs. In this chapter, I discuss some possible metrics for assessing money matters on both internal and external projects, address the question of why and whether you should measure project profitability, and examine some related challenges.

Why Should You Estimate Costs or Track Profitability?

That's two different questions but the answer to both is, maybe you shouldn't. That is a question that only you can answer. About ten years ago, I was reading an older PMBOK (*Project Management Body of Knowledge*) guide, widely thought to be one of the definitive guides on project management. I was surprised that there was no focus on project profitability. The guide spends considerable time talking about cost management, but there is no focus on income. The question is, does estimating costs and tracking profitability offer you value on your own projects? Or are there easier and better ways to manage your money?

In thinking about the profitability question, the answer depends on your business. For the law firm that is doing fixed-price legal matters, tracking profitability is hugely important. Are you making money? In the billable-hour world, it was easy for law firms to make money. But you cannot assume that your fixed-price matters are profitable for the firm.

The next question is how much flexibility you have on your pricing. If your client simply will not pay anything more, you must decide whether to continue working with that client. It makes sense to understand your profitability.

On the cost management question, it may depend on how you are compensating your teams. Take, for instance, a clinical trial being done in a hospital. Suppose a large pharmaceutical company has engaged you to run a trial on a drug that is in development. You may or may not be required to track the hours spent on that trial. But even if you aren't required to track the time on this one, you may be required to track time on other such trials. You may have people working on multiple trials. How will you or they know if their time is being spent wisely?

On the other hand, if you are doing an internal project where your management team is the client, there are other factors. If you have engaged independent contractors to work on it, you must track those costs. If you are using salaried employees, you may decide not to spend the time tracking these costs. But consider this: Your salaried employees may be drawing hefty wages and unless you are tracking where they spend their time, do you or they know how much value they are providing? Does anyone know whether they are focusing their time where it makes the biggest contribution?

What Metrics Can You Measure?

Before I delve into the metrics, let's ask, what does the traditional Gantt chart approach do for us? It connects project costs (and by extension, resources) to the project schedule. This means that to have a complete Gantt chart, together with the traditional metrics — such as an estimate to complete the project, an estimate at project completion, the schedule and cost variances, and performance indexes — we must nail down a schedule. We can change the schedule, and the metrics will adjust, but all that requires some time and attention.

If we want to encourage innovation and accept the reality of a quickly changing landscape, is that the best use of our time and attention? Using the Smart Projex approach, and by combining money data with the concept of Complexity that I discussed in Chapter 3, we can still have some meaningful and reliable metrics. We need to understand that some of this data will only be reliable and useful *after* the project is finished, thus offering you some perspective. Here are some examples of useful metrics.

1. Budget to actual dollars

Comparing budget to actual dollars is not a new concept. Businesses have been doing that through earned value management for years, both during the project and after the project. With the traditional approach, there is a strong correlation between the schedule and costs. What happens when we use a more Agile approach and give teams no credit, so to speak, for unfinished activities?

For starters, it simplifies cost management. No longer are we spending time calculating earned value concepts. We can still track the budget to actual dollars by activity, related activities, activity leader, project manager, project sponsor, or money manager at the end of every sprint, when there are, hopefully, no partially completed activities. (Remember, I said that teams commit to finish a block of activities during each sprint.)

Wouldn't it be helpful to know that Mary Jane's team historically comes in under budget while Joe's team often comes in over budget? If you are working with independent contractors, it can be particularly critical to know when someone is throwing your activities into the red.

I'm aware that Agile practitioners don't like the idea of comparing teams against each other. And in a true Scrum environment, you can't, since story points are relative within the project, not within the organization. I'm inclined to believe that if we can identify inefficiencies by comparing teams, that we can work on improving those inefficiencies. It's not about pitting teams against each other in a mean-spirited way. It's about identifying ways and places to improve.

2. Activity and/or project Complexity compared to income generated

Why might this metric be helpful? To some extent, it will depend on how you are billing the project. Are you billing for time worked, by the month, or for work that has been completed? There are various ways that you could set this up.

In comparing activity and/or project Complexity to income generated, we can better assess project profitability and identify our most and least profitable clients. This might help you make better marketing spend decisions or analyze your aggregate streams of revenue. You might be able to assess which employees are producing the most client value with the least effort. It is essential that the team fully understands the work that is needed, the quality that the client (or management) is expecting, and how the team will know when an activity is finished.

3. "Profitability" by client, project manager, or sponsor

It still astounds me that many firms are not tracking this kind of data. And I do understand that many firms aren't doing projects to make money. But when you are, wouldn't you want to know who your profitable clients are, and who is working on lower-profitability clients?

4. Budget, actual dollars, or Complexity by general ledger and/or other customized code

When I built the original Smart Projex software solution, I included a field that would ultimately interface with the client's accounting system. I wanted to be able to filter budget, actual dollars, and Complexity by a general ledger number or a customized code – such as the UTBMS codes used in the legal profession, or the CPT codes used in the medical insurance world. Are there questions that a customized code might help you answer?

5. Estimates on when revenues and costs are predicted to occur

For many businesses, cash flow management is a necessity. In a traditional Waterfall project management approach, the scheduled sequence of project activities allows for a more reliable cash flow forecast. Think about it. In the traditional approach, you estimated costs and timing and you could build reports about what would occur. In the Smart Projex world, we've only estimated costs, and perhaps income. We have deliberately left timing open so we can execute with flexibility. It might be that you need to execute in accordance with cash flow. Or, it might be that you want to execute so that you create the highest value for your client in every sprint.

Once we move into a more agile execution, which is so desperately needed on projects being done in a world of rapid change, we lose the ability to accurately forecast cash flow. What we can do is to schedule our project activities in accordance with available cash flow or seasonal cash flow trends. Simply put, if we know that an activity has significant costs associated with it, and we project a shortfall of revenues in March, we will avoid scheduling that project activity around that time, unless necessary.

From a client retention standpoint, the prospects of making money and still helping a client better control costs are remarkable. We all have different gifts to bring to the table and it's time to recognize that. To know, for example, which of your team members can produce a well-written training document in the fewest hours will help you better price your services. Improving the speed with which software development teams can create software will help your clients control costs and still allow you to make money. Understanding when and why activities have stalled will help you know when to involve your client in the conversations. And having the option of allowing the client to do some work on the project may provide other cost savings without negatively impacting your own bottom line.

What Are the Challenges of Assessing Project Profitability?

To assess project profitability, you begin with estimating costs and revenues. Then you track your costs. This may sound easier than it is. First, you will need to figure out how you plan to estimate costs. Here are four suggestions.

1. Develop a granularity plan based on the project.

   Estimating a budget for business projects requires

that firms decide how granular to be. I have wrestled with the trade-offs here for years, but the reality is that you will need more granularity on some projects than you will on others. Let's think about a simple in-house project – planning a company-wide sales conference in Florida to connect and motivate your sales team. Much of your team, including operations folks, will be there because sales are thought to be the lifeblood of your company. You've decided that you want to understand your conference costs in the following categories: transportation, housing, entertainment, food and drink, education, and personnel.

With the proper vendor communications, it's easy to track most of those costs. One challenge comes with personnel. Will you track the time that Suzy spends trying to negotiate your hotel contract? Will you track the time that your salespeople spend at the conference? And if Suzy and Bob visit three fancy resorts to decide where to host this event, how will you track those costs? Do you create another category to track site selection costs? If you've never been involved in a project of this nature, I can tell you that thousands of administrative hours can go into planning one. How will you track that time?

The problem gets even greater when you are dealing with fixed-price software development or legal projects. When a project involves highly paid people, it can quickly slide into the red if you are not careful. Independent contractors may not understand your challenge. And when it's your own team doing the work, there are always cost-benefit trade-offs that people make. Should your $500K-a-year vice president be spending her time on activity A, B, or C?

Unless you are allocating all the time that people are working, you can't properly assess the profitability of the project. That may or may not be important to you. You need to have a policy. Some firms may decide, for some projects, and not for others, that tracking money is unimportant. Some firms will simply assign a person to one project full-time, and his/her costs are easily assigned to the project. More frequently, in the business world, team members are splitting their time between projects, so how is their cost allocated among projects?

One approach to estimating labor costs is to estimate an aggregate cost for each activity. For revenue-generating projects, a separate set of activities can be set up to account for client billings. You will want to talk with your client to understand the data that it needs. Perhaps an aggregate billing rate can be used for some activities. By including labor billings and cost rates, you can assess the profitability of the project and compare the profitability of different clients. It won't be perfect, but over time, you can get more clarity on the best use of your time and resources.

2. Be clear about estimation expectations.

Executives need to be clear with their project teams about their estimation expectations. This is particularly true on projects where a partial delivery will not suffice, and thus, it's hard to stop the project in midstream and realize any value. And it's particularly true on large projects with a lot at stake.

For example, in a software project, you might well produce value if four of the ten features are built and deployed and then the rest of the work is cancelled. But what good is a new house without the roof, walls, wiring, and appliances? In construction work, we simply must complete the project, and cost overruns and schedule delays are rarely received well.

And don't make the mistake of thinking that all software projects have value when some parts are cancelled.

The author of a 2019 *Dallas Morning News* article entitled "After $367.5 million, Texas gets no new child support computer software – just painful lessons," reported that the state legislature pulled the plug on a 12-year project and the state got nothing in exchange for its sizable investment. Nada.[17]

In addition to understanding the necessary level of granularity, teams need to understand how much accuracy is needed. What are the options for estimating a project? Here are a few approaches.

- **Expert judgment.** This method is simply the use of an expert(s) to subjectively estimate based on provided criteria. It is used frequently, and often quite successfully. I'm cautious when this is the first answer I hear and when no other useful guidance is provided. The outcome depends entirely on how much of an expert the estimator is. And it can be hard to get team buy-in on a project estimated by an outsider.
- **Parametric estimating.** This approach uses formulas to calculate estimates based on historical data. A simple example might be that new construction in a particular neighborhood typically runs $200 per square foot. So, a 3,000-square-foot house would cost $600,000 to build. Parametric estimating is often a starting point, but depending on the type of project, it may or may not be accurate.
- **Analogous estimating.** Often used when estimating is done by a pricing expert, this method is typically a high-level approach for estimating a project based on the historical experience with a similar matter.
- **Bottom-up estimating.** This method can be more time consuming, and much depends on the needs of the client or the executives. It starts at the activity or work-package level and estimates the cost and/or dura-

tion of each activity in the project. Typically, estimating activities that are smaller and better scoped is more accurate than estimating larger and more ambiguous pieces of work, but it does take more time. The client or the executives must decide on how much accuracy is needed. Be sure to communicate that to your teams.

- **Three-point estimating.** This approach often begins like bottom-up estimating – at the activity or work-package level. It is used to improve the accuracy of a single-point estimate. The most frequently used technique is the PERT formula. For those unfamiliar with the PERT formula, it is a weighted average of three estimates – the most optimistic (O), the most pessimistic (P), and the most likely estimate (L) of how long something will take. The basic equation is Estimate = (O + P +4L) / 6.
- **Agile group techniques.** Group decision-making techniques have been introduced by the Agile community over the years. Most of these techniques are used for estimating complexity or story points, but again, management should communicate its expectations. Many of these techniques have been designed to reduce gridlock caused by multiple opinions and cut the time spent on estimating. To some extent, they also reduce the bias that occurs when we estimate our own work.

Many teams will combine aspects of these various approaches to create something that works for them. I'm not suggesting that executives need to be overly involved in the estimating process or dictate how teams do their estimating. However, I am recommending that you be clear with your teams about how much time you want them to spend on their estimations and how accurate you expect them to be. It helps to understand what executives will do with these estimates in the long term, and no one likes being beaten over the head with a flawed estimate.

3. Get buy-in from the team on the estimate.

My third recommendation on estimating costs relates to the idea of getting your teams committed to the idea of working within a budget. In today's world, with smart people working on projects, it can be easy to slip into the habit of overthinking the work at hand or seeking too much perfection. How much preparation time does that report require? How perfect does the new website need to be before it launches?

Does your company expect your teams to pay attention to cost estimates? Or is the estimate done and then forgotten? Much depends on the type of project you are working on. And one question is: who is doing the estimate?

While it's usually best done by the team, some firms and industries have had good experience with using a professional estimator or pricing expert. The problem with this approach, which I noted earlier, is that getting buy-in may be harder. Think about it. If you are being asked to create the literature for a new kitchen appliance that your company is about to launch, and someone from the corporate office tells you to do it in 15 hours or less, and you think it will take twice that long, how receptive will you be? It is so easy for team members to go off on tangents that don't directly benefit the project. Getting the entire team committed to the budget reduces that tendency. And letting teams know that they will need to explain any cost overruns may help.

Let's revisit that project example of planning a sales conference. Anyone who has attended one of these conferences will attest to the fact that the entertainment and recreation opportunities and the food and drink options are key. The salespeople I know like to have a great time. If you are planning one of these events with no historical precedents, it is critical that you get some input from your team, including a few salespeople, and get buy-in from them.

And when your project involves expensive contractors, it is critical that they understand the need to work within the budget provided unless legitimate pitfalls surface. The sky cannot be the limit on every activity.

4. Solve the challenges of tracking actual costs.

If you do cost estimates, then you must track actual costs. One hurdle that often arises is getting the cost of labor accurately and promptly entered into the time-tracking software. Knowledge workers don't often work in a time-card environment, working on one project all day long. They get interrupted, sometimes frequently, and they flit from project to project at irregular intervals. At the end of the day, they may have to calculate or review how much time was spent on individual projects and/or activities.

Timekeeping software may be useful when people are focused on one activity for an extended period, but it often fails for those who multitask or work in environments that are particularly prone to interruptions.

There is also the question of when to bill the client for time spent learning. Any client can reasonably expect the firm it has hired to employ people who know how to use Word. Yet, when the writer of a product training manual spends hours trying to figure out how to get an extraneous black line removed from within a document, should the client pay for that? It may be considered professional development, or it might be a bug in the software or an incompatibility issue. Who pays for that time?

It can be challenging to get busy people to enter time stats daily, but it's the only way to accurately monitor costs on any project. When business owners are lying awake at night worried that employees or contract workers are going to throw a project under the bus, something is wrong.

Good judgment and honesty go a long way towards helping firms accurately assess the amount of time that it took to complete the project activities. And now, with some ability to estimate income (if any), develop a budget, and track hours worked, you have a basic ability to manage costs and determine how profitable your external projects are. The metrics outlined earlier offer reasonably reliable ways to analyze money across your entire project portfolio. What's next? We need to step back and discuss risk management.

Chapter 5

You Positively Need to Focus on Risk Management!

Every organization needs to understand its risk tolerance and prioritize risk management. In this chapter I talk about what risks are, why you need a risk strategy, and then outline the three basic steps of risk management: identify, analyze, and monitor. I talk about risk management in Part 1 on Analytics because good data analytics allow us to prioritize risks, so that we know where to focus our efforts. Especially without the controls that Gantt chart schedules provide, risk management is so important that it needs to become a core value of your organization, particularly when facing uncertainty, volatility, and rapid change.

I'm not the only believer in the importance of standardized risk management practices. In its latest *Pulse of the Profession*, the Project Management Institute (PMI) reported that 2020 saw notable improvement in project performance, primarily due to an increase in pivoting, significant business changes, and more "gymnastic enterprises," due to the COVID-19 pandemic. One key was standardized risk management practices. The report refers to "gymnastic enterprises" as those that focus on empowering changemakers, boosting human performance, and delivering value.[18]

It's important to understand that risk happens at many levels, from the environment to the organization, to the project, and to the people. Traditional project management training focuses extensively on project risk management – from risk identification to various forms of risk management, including sophisticated techniques for monitoring risks and risk mitigation strategies. The hardest part can be ensuring that you have considered everything that's important. If you've ignored weather risks, for example, and a hurricane hits when you are trying to convert a data center, your project management career may be doomed.

And we need to accept that innovation comes with risk. You simply cannot innovate without taking risks. There are ways to reduce that risk, but to a large extent innovation requires us to embrace risk. One way to manage that risk is to adjust the length of your sprints. If you are involved in an innovation project and trying to create something new, you will have failures. You will have to try things, see what works, and learn from those experiments. Ask yourself how much investment you need to make in a given activity before you declare defeat. If you want to experiment faster, cut your sprint length, and reduce the time estimates that you are allowing on certain activities. Work towards completing the activities in less time.

It's also important to understand that people come with biases (see more in Chapter 8). This makes risk management particularly difficult.

What Is Project Risk?

From a project management perspective, a risk is any uncertainty that will impact a project positively or negatively if it materializes. Time spent managing risks should be commensurate with the level of risk, which depends on the size of the project and the number of stakeholders. These same risk management concepts can be applied to the operations of your company, the products you are developing, and all the many activities that you undertake within your organization.

For example, if you have a machine that is heavily used in your daily operations, have you created a plan for how you will manage unplanned machine downtime without negatively impacting operational results, as well as your open projects? Or, if you are a start-up and your business is the ongoing creation of a software product, is there a risk that you will lose funding or a key player soon? Don't think that there aren't risks that need to be managed in your world.

Taking the time to identify and manage risks reduces the financial consequences of negative risks and helps you cope with uncertainty. It also allows organizations to maximize the benefits of a positive windfall. For example, suppose you are planning the annual sales conference, historically held in Miami. One of your risks is a specific concern about the location. The risk could be general, perhaps related to hurricane season in the Atlantic, or it could be related to rumors about management at the resort. Perhaps in thinking about that risk, you should consider it an opportunity to rethink the conference. Does moving it somewhere else allow you to save money? There is a tendency to look at risks as negative, but risks can represent opportunities as well.

If you are in leadership at your company and you want your project teams to take risk management seriously, you need to talk with them about the risks. It's not that different from raising children. If you believe that ethics, religion, honesty, or family time are important, you need to talk with your children about these values. Risk management essentially becomes a value that your company holds dear, or it doesn't.

Teams that are not used to a process that includes risk management may present a cultural challenge. Team members may balk at having to do risk management or question why they need to spend time on something that doesn't move the project forward. Let's consider why having a risk management strategy is so important.

Why You Need a Risk Management Strategy

Innovative companies can invent and experiment and, because they have a risk management strategy, they can weather storms and economic disruptions, and pivot when it makes sense. For these companies, risk management is a core value of the business. They have defined their risk management strategy and process. They know how much risk they are willing to assume and have a strategy for ensuring that they stay within that boundary.

It is easy for smaller companies, start-ups, and nonprofits to think that risk management is unimportant. Absent project management training, the people who are working on your projects may not have a clue how to do project risk management. But in your tiny company, even a small project failure may result in bankruptcy. Ignoring risk management can be a costly mistake, since you don't have the depth of resources that larger companies have.

For example, if you are opening a new location of your small business, have you focused on the risk of contractor delays financially strapping your company? If your project is to develop a new strategic plan for your organization, have you focused on the risk that discussing a large staff reorganization plan with your company may scare employees into thinking that they need to hunt for a new job?

Innovation requires us to take risks. It forces us to experiment, fail, learn, and adapt. But the faster we do that and the better the process for learning from those endeavors, the less risk we undertake when innovating. It is also critically important to establish a culture that doesn't punish teams for failure. It has to be okay to fail, provided teams are failing quickly and learning from the process. In fact, perhaps you should consider celebrating failures? After all, you accomplished something, you learned valuable lessons from it, and now it's time to apply those lessons learned to your next experiment.

Begin by Dedicating Time to Identifying Your Risks

For years, I've heard that writing and editing are two different steps and require different parts of the brain. The left brain is the analytical side that handles editing, while the creative right side is better for writing. I suspect that the same is true of risk identification and risk assessment. I do know that emailing team members who are running in circles and simply asking if there is anything new on risks will not yield results. It takes focused time.

Think about the identification piece and the assessment piece separately. Set aside time on a regular basis to stop running in circles and focus on risk identification as a team. This is not a step that can be done by one person in a vacuum. The entire team should be involved. Sometimes, you will want to bring in some knowledgeable outside people, but don't make the group so large that it becomes unwieldy. You want everyone to feel like they are important to the process, not superfluous among the crowd.

The team needs to commit to periodically taking time away from regular work to sit back, think, identify, assess, and manage risks. Things change over the course of any project and new risks will arise. Risk identification is the first step, and it's one that teams often miss. According to a 2012 *Harvard Business Review* article, a US investigation commission looking into the explosion of BP's *Deepwater Horizon* oil rig "attributed the disaster to management failures that crippled 'the ability of individuals involved to identify the risks they faced and to properly evaluate, communicate, and address them.'"[19]

It starts with knowing what your risks are. Identifying risks requires a team to make the time to sit down and think. We make the mistake of thinking that work is just about "doing." In today's knowledge economy, work is also about *thinking*. Create a risk register or log and enter your identified risks. You will use this log to record your assessments over the life of your project.

Think, in a focused and disciplined way, about what could go wrong. If you stay the course, what unintended consequences might arise? What assumptions must be true for this project to be successful? Consider the threats, as you might define them in a traditional SWOT (strengths, weaknesses, opportunities and threats) analysis. And ask yourself if there are any strengths that might be properly thought of as a positive risk. In his book *When: The Scientific Secrets of Perfect Timing*, Dan Pink recommends that project teams consider a premortem. Hold a meeting. Fast-forward the discussion to the project closure. Assume it was a dismal failure and ask why.[20]

One reason for tackling the challenge of risk management as a team, rather than simply assigning it to one person on the team, is that to some extent, it helps compensate for an optimism or overconfidence bias, which can lead to an understatement of risk. In Chapter 8, I briefly discuss biases and what evolving science is teaching us about how people work and think. But for now, recognize that we all hold biases that can impact our ability to assess risks.

Analyze Your Risks – Key Questions to Consider

Risk assessment involves the analysis, evaluation, and documentation of several factors. The extent to which you spend time on risk assessment will depend on the complexity of the project, the dollars at stake, the length of time spent on the project, and the numbers of stakeholders and risks involved.

Once you've identified risks, the next challenge is to analyze each risk. The analysis begins with developing a strong understanding of each risk. Ultimately your goal is to create a numerical ranking system that helps you clearly identify your top-ranked risks, so that you can focus your efforts there. But it's only going to be as effective as you make it.

There are several reliable ways to analyze risks. The challenge is to be consistent in how you do this. Pick a simple approach. You might consider having the same person or risk team assign the numeric values to all your risks, to reduce the inconsistencies and errors that will skew the rankings and help you develop more consistent rankings throughout your organization. Take steps to avoid groupthink as you debate your risks.

Your risk log, also called a risk register, needs to be highly searchable and filterable. It's essentially a database; and the systems in place in your organization will determine whether you use a simple Google spreadsheet or something else. If you track risks at the organizational level, you will be adding to this for years. The advantage of doing so is that you can begin to interface risk management at the project level with what is needed in operational efforts. The goal is to learn from your efforts over time. A warning: if you make it hard to quickly identify helpful information, people will not think of the risk log or register as a useful resource.

To complete the risk register, answer these questions:

1. Who is the risk expert?

Institutional knowledge is great; but we live in a world with frequent employee turnover and job moves. Identify and document the person who is the most familiar with the details of each risk. It may not be the same person that you assign to manage the risk.

2. Who is going to manage the risk?

As projects unfold, someone should be watching each risk. This may or may not be the project manager. While larger companies may have risk management departments, smaller companies typically do not. The team has the option of putting one person in charge of monitoring all risks or assigning a risk manager to each individual risk.

3. What is the financial impact if the risk materializes?

A risk that impacts only one small deliverable will have less impact than a risk that could potentially impact an entire event. How much money is at stake?

4. What is the chance that this risk will materialize? (Likelihood of occurrence)

For example, the chance of a hurricane occurring in Florida during the summer is higher than it is in winter, or in Massachusetts. If you are working on a technology data center conversion in Florida that is scheduled for February and months of delays occur, the risk of the project being impacted by a hurricane will increase and should be managed with more attention.

5. What is the likelihood that the risk can be detected early enough to mitigate the risk? (Likelihood of detection)

For example, hurricanes have a high likelihood of detection, while tornados have a lower likelihood of detection.

6. Are there any trigger events?

A trigger event is an event that, if it occurs, is likely to result in a risk materializing. Trigger events can be used to predict when a risk may occur. Document your trigger events in a format that you can use when things are chaotic. Knowing that your Florida office is relocating during hurricane season is meaningless unless someone is paying attention to that risk log.

7. Do you need a risk mitigation strategy?

A risk mitigation strategy is a plan to reduce any negative impact or increase any positive impact from a materialized risk. Sometimes risks can have a positive outcome, and the team must be poised to exploit the risk. Top-ranked risks should have a mitigation strategy, such as purchasing insurance to cover you in case that risk materializes. The higher the risk is ranked, the more important the risk mitigation plan becomes. The effort to develop risk mitigation plans should be commensurate with the amount of risk to the project.

Monitor and Manage

All projects have risks. Monitoring them may be easier with software that automatically ranks your top risks. Software or no software, the key is to periodically reassess your risks. Just as you set up a time to identify risks, you need to set aside time to periodically reassess your risks. Because change can be constant, this means regularly analyzing the financial impact, likelihood of occurrence, and likelihood of detection, and it may mean developing a risk mitigation strategy for a risk that has suddenly escalated as a concern, or thinking through whether any triggers have materialized. For lower-ranked risks, you may choose to simply accept the risk.

Managing risks is more than producing a neat report that can be submitted to management at the end of every week or month. The purpose is to minimize any adverse impact from a risk that materializes and capitalize on any positive risk that occurs.

In later chapters, I provide more discussion of the Checkpoint Meeting (a Smart Projex concept) held at the end of every sprint, usually about every two to three weeks. This meeting is a good time to review risks. Prior to the meeting, have the risk manager(s) review their risks. Reanalyze and rank them numerically, as rankings can change. Again, review top-ranked risks to ensure that any possible trigger events have been identified and a mitigation strategy is in place, where needed.

We decrease overall risk when we regularly review our organizational strengths, weaknesses, opportunities, and threats. And we decrease that risk when we can effectively experiment, quickly fail, try again, sometimes succeed, and understand when to quit and move on. Because we can rarely trust one person to do this alone, we need to put systems in place that help us manage the risks in our organizations and understand where risk fits into our project selection strategy (which is covered in the next chapter).

And if you doubt the importance of risk management on your work efforts, consider the case of the Build-A-Bear sales campaign that was too successful. In 2018, Build-A-Bear announced a campaign to provide the $20 stuffed bear-building experience for the discounted price of a young customer's age. Imagine the number of young children who lined up in malls around the country to take advantage of this opportunity to build a bear for $5, $6, $7, or $8. There was no contingency plan developed, no thought given to risk management, and a clear failure to understand the demand that this campaign would create. With the chain's overwhelmed 400 stores all shutting down the campaign within hours of the start, the cost of launching the campaign was completely wasted and the bad will generated was incalculable.[21]

I can't overemphasize that risk management is a value that your organization needs to take seriously. For any project, risk management needs to align with the size of the project and the riskiness of that effort. The riskier the endeavors, the more time and energy you need to put into managing your risks. But it's a mistake to think that you can ignore risk. Embrace risk and a process for managing risk, just as you embrace change.

Most classically trained project managers view risk management as a responsibility of the project manager, and I don't disagree with that view. I also believe that it needs to be a core value of the organization that feeds into how we select projects. And that's the subject of the next chapter.

Chapter 6

How Are You Selecting Projects?

With agreement on the need for reliable data metrics; a plan for improving efficiency, managing costs, and evaluating project profitability; and solid risk controls now in place, you are better positioned to think about project selection. In this chapter, I discuss some strategies for selecting projects, how to ensure strategy alignment, and how to evaluate the business case for a project.

Some projects are undertaken to help organizations innovate, while others are taken to boost profits or improve operations. And then, there are the client projects that you are hired to do. In this chapter, I'll primarily focus on internal projects. Those are the projects that you will typically be prioritizing and selecting. External projects, done for paying clients, are more typically profit driven. And most businesses are happy to add client projects anytime they can do so profitably. Occasionally, you may have to creatively juggle resources, and your client load may impact your selection of internal projects. But the project selection considerations on external projects are not as numerous.

Over the years, I've met with more than one executive to discuss project investments and discovered that companies are often spreading themselves too thinly. The thinking is that when sales are booming, projects are needed to support growth. As a result, more and more projects are assigned to teams, which means teams are simply overloaded. Given that visions are often unclear or unstated, life in these organizations can be difficult, even if the revenues support growing salaries every year.

What is the problem with this scenario? Up to a point, being busy increases focus. Yet, at some point, people hit a wall and the work overload reduces focus. Exhaustion sets in and people get distracted by the amount of work on their lists and can no longer prioritize work effectively. This was true before COVID-19, but the pandemic exacerbated the problem.

Additionally, when the workload gets too high, existing work slows or stops in favor of the new. When internal projects are routinely cancelled midway through and replaced by something else, it is demoralizing for teams. When software code enhancements are written but not deployed, the programmers scratch their heads. And, when procedure manuals are rewritten but never effectively introduced to the team, people are inconsistent in their processes. It can be tempting to think that you can do it all, but you can't.

You may also have more project ideas than you can effectively implement. What do you do with them? I used to keep a record of my creative ideas, and that list grew so long that it was intimidating to think about reviewing it periodically. And so, what good was it if I didn't even want to look at it?

Six Strategies for Selecting Projects

Businesses need a strategy to ensure that the projects that will produce the most value for the organization are selected. With innovation projects, this will be unclear. You need an effective way to regularly close the door on low-value projects. I'll begin with six suggestions that will improve your project selection process and then discuss how organizations can tie their process into a regular reexamination of their projects so that teams are consistently working on the projects that will bring the highest value to the organization.

1. Create and document your process for selecting projects.

I'm astounded at the number of companies that have no process, an inconsistent process, or an undocumented or unknown process for selecting projects. Everything depends on the whim of the owner or the boss. I would never want to underestimate the importance of gut instinct, but we all need a process that tests our instincts when money is being spent. Even if you have a small company with an owner who calls all the shots, create and document your process for selecting projects, especially if the owner is inclined to be fickle or easily lose focus. (I'm not suggesting this will be easy, or that you circumvent the owner.)

2. Consider using a project selection committee.

Using a well-respected project selection committee gives the process some sense of independence and validity. Your organization may or may not need a formal committee, but having a process that is independent of one person can boost your company's overall performance.

I remember working with a small company that was considering a major IT project that the owner believed would help them continue a relationship with one of their strongest customers. The owner had a golfing buddy who had highly recommended a software solution and the business owner got more and more excited about it, thinking that it would help this valued customer. Unfortunately, he didn't discuss this project with anyone on his team, and after investing about $500K (a large sum for this company), he learned that this customer had no interest in this software. To add insult to injury, the work had simply delayed other projects that were more important.

The challenge of selecting the highest-value projects doesn't necessarily end if you are talking about client-driven projects. Think about a law firm and how lawyers get called to take on new client matters. The temptation is to say yes, but has someone evaluated the request to ensure that there are no conflicts and that the matter can be appropriately staffed? Can the matter be priced so that it is profitable for the firm? Don't forget the hidden costs – of difficult clients, time spent resolving firm conflicts, or bad publicity from taking on a hot issue. Has someone, other than the lawyer who got the request, evaluated all of this?

Try to build a diverse project selection committee and include someone who understands the mechanics of your operations. Suppose you are a research hospital doing clinical trials. A pharmaceutical company or the National Institutes of Health may approach one of your doctors about a trial. Academic medicine rewards doctors who get grants. And so, when a doctor gets that call, everyone starts getting excited. If you don't have someone on your project selection committee who understands the mechanics of executing trials, you may commit to a trial that is simply not feasible without major operational adjustments that come with a price tag you had not considered.

3. Align projects with your corporate (or entity) strategy.

   There are quantifiable ways to do this, which I will

get to, but first you need a strategy to ensure that projects are aligned with your organizational strategy. I will keep this simple and limited since the subject is so broad.

Projects are an investment that companies make in their future. It's not too different from the stock, bond, or real estate portfolios that individuals have. Most larger companies invest in multiple projects at the same time and seek to diversify their portfolios to manage risk. The collection of all their projects can be referred to as a portfolio of project investments, though some larger companies will segregate their collection of project investments into multiple portfolios.

As smart companies seek to diversify their portfolios, they may look at the portfolio in different ways. For example, they may analyze projects on a spectrum from those that are highly innovative and explorative to those that are designed to keep operations flourishing. A simple strategy might be to split the investments 50/50 - with half going to maintenance projects, and half going towards innovation projects. Or the company might seek a 75/25 split with a larger investment in innovation.

You might want to balance allocations between specific product lines or divisions. Or the company might want to measure the benefits that will be derived from each project proposal and choose those projects that have the highest benefits. The point here is simply to get you to think about what your strategy is so that you can engage your teams in the challenge of maintaining alignment between active projects and organizational strategy. It will be unique for every company.

4. Have a selection strategy that increases project focus.

Project focus is rarely improved by throwing projects at teams every time a new idea is proposed. You can use a

Kanban-like approach where you limit the number of projects that any team is working on to a reasonable number. I talk about singular focus later in this book, but for now, hold onto this simple notion: people who are focused on too many things are not as effective as they could be.

Some groups allow employees to vote on projects by posting project ideas on a dashboard, and letting available teams, or perhaps people, choose which projects they want to work on. The disadvantage of this approach is that some projects will not be as compelling as others, even though they may be required by regulators or critical to sustaining company operations. The advantage is that teams and people are more excited about working on the projects they have selected themselves. Be aware that you may have trouble drumming up general enthusiasm for projects that are required by regulatory bodies, although there are folks who seem to prefer such projects.

5. Focus on the people in your organization.

It's great when an organization puts a strong emphasis on selecting the right projects, but that's not enough. You need to consider people in your project selection process — and that focus doesn't stop once the projects are selected. Here are some questions to ask when you are considering internal projects:

- How will this project impact your clients, customers, and your employees? What are those groups saying?
- Do you have a strong project team that is excited about this project?
- How committed is senior leadership to this project?

Be careful about simply looking at the raw scoring data. People are critical to your success. You need strong executive buy-in and an excited project team, and you will need to build enthusiastic support from key stakeholders.

This is particularly true when you are thinking about projects that may impact people outside of your organization.

Suppose you are working on a project to relocate your offices to a new location. That decision may impact other businesses in another neighborhood, or it may have traffic implications. And consider the human factors on controversial projects that affect whole communities. There can often be human factors that you need to consider when you are selecting projects.

6. Opt for the simple and achievable, when possible.

This is particularly true when we are talking about massive technology projects. Large IT projects have an exceptionally high failure rate. For just two examples, consider the largely disastrous rollout of the US Affordable Care website, which ran well over $600 million.[22] Also, the UK Electronic Health Records Project, which the UK government scrapped in 2011 after a 9-year effort, cost $16 billion.[23] In 2019, the Standish Group reported that "83.9% of IT projects partially or completely fail."[24]

There is a "bigger is better" mindset that can overtake all leaders. I understand that. But you will be more successful if you accomplish many, many smaller goals that deliver value than you will be when you fail to accomplish anything because you invested everything in a huge pipe dream. As you think about your projects, take a lean approach, and ask yourself what it is that you can do that will generate the most value in the short term, for the lowest cost. Begin there. Accomplish that. Reevaluate. And then, repeat.

In strong organizations, the project approval process involves some type of analysis of the value that the project brings to an organization. Will it reduce costs or increase revenues, and if so, by how much? How does the ROI, net present value, or payback period compare with other project opportunities? Is the project a high-impact/high-effort, a high-impact/low-effort, a low-impact/high-effort, or a low-impact/low-effort project? Where does it fit in your project portfolio?

How to Maintain Alignment Between Projects and Strategy

Now that you have created a strategy for selecting projects, how will you go about maintaining alignment between the strategy and your active projects? This is where your project teams can be valuable, provided you properly train them and communicate with them. Teams need to understand where to focus their efforts. Leaders need to be clear about strategy and careful not to send mixed signals.

In a world of rapid change, the challenge in the business world is to fairly assess the business case for internal projects on an ongoing basis. When the business case for a project drops or completely vanishes, it may be time to cancel the project in midstream. Never let sunk costs drive future decisions.

The need to periodically reassess the business value of a project represents a challenge for project teams and project managers. Change is hard for people. When people are faced with the uncertainty of whether their project might be cancelled, it can cause stress. That stress can become pervasive in the organization. There can be a conflict of interest in having teams measure the business case. Let's face it, if they are concerned that their project will be eliminated, they may be inclined to overstate the case for the project. Egos and reputations can get in the way. Can we get teams to objectively analyze the business case?

The answer is: it depends. But there are four steps you can take to help.

1. Make business case analysis a regular, periodic event.

   When we only do it on an occasional basis, it will scare the team. When business case analysis is done regularly and not associated with management discussions about project cancellations, it's easier to expect the team to do this.

2. Develop a simple process.

   It should involve questions that are objective and concrete, rather than a process that involves too much subjective analysis. Create quantitative metrics. Admittedly, not all aspects of a project are quantifiable, but you can create a list of questions with multiple-choice answers, and that will serve you better than completely subjective questions. I've provided an example of a business case questionnaire in Appendix 2.

3. Be clear with project teams.

   Projects must continue to add value to a company's line of work. When projects fail to do that, the employee's time is being misused. Future salary increases are typically higher for those who bring value to a company. When you can help employees understand that their projects are no longer bringing value to the company, they will be more tolerant of plans to redirect work.

4. Reuse project teams.

   When you finally develop a project team that bonds and is working effectively, consider using the same team on future projects. Why spend mega dollars building a great resource and then wasting it? When teams understand that the company has a backlog of projects waiting and that the whole team can stay together and be moved to a different project, they are less inclined to overstate the case for a project that is no longer needed.

What Business Case Questions Deserve a Periodic Examination?

When creating a strategy for examining the business case on projects, I like to think of the questions in three categories. I'll introduce those categories here and in Appendix 2, I'll offer a detailed sample method for assessing the business case.

1. Strategy alignment questions

Is the project still strategically aligned to your mission and/or the objectives of your organization? Has the mission recently changed or is it expected to change soon? In most cases, projects should align with the corporate strategy or the mission of the organization. What happens to projects that are in midstream when a major strategy change is orchestrated? It depends. Hopefully, the question of whether to cancel the project has already been discussed in any strategic planning process.

2. Financial questions

The second group of questions centers on financial considerations. How much increase in revenues (net of project costs) can we anticipate? How much decrease in costs (net of project costs) can we forecast? What is the payback period or net present value on the project? In many cases, projects are undertaken that will improve the bottom line, but as project costs can change from original estimates, and new technologies are constantly evolving, financial impacts should periodically be reexamined. These metrics may well change as new information comes to light.

3. Portfolio strategy questions

While the first set of questions is about aligning your project portfolio with the organization's strategy or mission, the third set of questions zeroes in on how your project portfolio strategy is crafted. Said differently, these questions are more about how projects are selected. They include such questions as:

- Is the project objective legally mandated?
- How widespread are the social benefits from completing this project?
- What are the environmental benefits of completing this project?
- How will this effort improve company culture or team effectiveness?

More and more, organizations and nonprofits are factoring in environmental improvements and social benefits to project portfolio decision-making. And since innovation and improving organizational management are clearly pressing concerns today, we should consider how your projects might impact the team culture, the corporate (or entity) culture, and the larger community.

How Will the Project Realize the Planned Benefits?

The subject of benefits realization management could be a chapter or a book unto itself. Simply put, benefits realization management is the process of identifying the benefits that a project is expected to realize *after* it has been completed, and then, when the project is finished, continuing to measure those benefits to ensure that the project realizes its purpose. (Sometimes project benefits are not immediately realized but instead materialize over time. And sometimes they can begin to materialize during the project.) Benefits realization management is different from business case analysis, which considers whether your projects continue to be valuable portfolio investments during the life of the project.

It is unfair to punish a project team because management failed in its decision-making process. Take, for example, the decision to open a new retail location for a clothing store. Assume that the project team delivers the project on time, on budget, according to the specifications outlined, and everyone was happy at project closure. If the store then fails to achieve projected sales goals, it is not the fault of the project team that was simply tasked with opening the new location, as that team wasn't responsible for the original strategic analysis and decision to choose that location.

Depending on the size of the organization, the responsibility for benefits realization management can rest with a single individual or an entire department, but I don't recommend assigning it to the project team.

Organizations lose their effectiveness when they fail to select and execute effectively on projects that will deliver the highest value to their organizations and their clients.

Now that we've covered project profitability, cost and risk management, and project selection, how will you continue to improve what you are doing and the decisions you are making? That's what we cover in the next chapter.

Chapter 7

Are You Continuously Improving?

Continuous improvement is both a mindset and an analytics-driven way of constantly striving to improve efforts. It involves looking at efficiency and effectiveness. I'll discuss those topics, along with Six Sigma, Lean thinking, Kaizen, and several concerns that I have about applying these principles too tightly. It's important to keep in mind that some companies will be more interested in focusing on their own effectiveness and efficiency, while other companies will get paid to help their clients focus on those factors.

What are Six Sigma, Kanban, Lean Thinking, and Kaizen?

Six Sigma is a methodology that measures defects, to get them as close to zero as possible, and thereby reduce waste. Six Sigma is a set of tools developed by Motorola in the late 1980s to cut waste, and thus improve efficiencies. These tools and techniques are well suited for manufacturing, but also used to reduce waste in business processes. Perhaps one of Six Sigma's greatest benefits is the data-driven focus on the bottom line and a disciplined approach that provides quantification of the cost savings.

Lean thinking, while similar in its overall objective, takes a different approach. Developed by Toyota, its focus is on removing tasks that don't add value to the process and introducing a system for managing the flow of work from point to point. The goal is to reduce the number of steps and the time it takes to do those steps.

Kanban is a visual scheduling approach that is frequently used in Lean thinking organizations where the goal is to limit work in progress. You may also hear the term "just-in-time planning" or "just-in-time manufacturing" to refer to an approach that reduces inventory, supplies, or work in progress to what is needed. Again, the goal is to reduce waste. Yet, when transportation systems and businesses shut down for an extended period during the COVID-19 pandemic, it threw a major monkey wrench into just-in-time thinking, particularly regarding supply chain management. Perhaps there are lessons on just-in-time manufacturing that need to be learned. Perhaps there is a gap between just-in-time and just-in-case thinking that we need to address. Occasionally, as a project team member over the years, I have gone the extra step to address a concern, just in case. Are those efforts always needed?

Kaizen is a Japanese term that means continuous improvement. To be more exact, "Kai" means "change" and "zen" means "for the better." There can be some crossover between Kaizen and design thinking, an approach to innovation projects. In practicing Kaizen, when something goes wrong, teams ask "why," over and over, until they understand the root of the problem. The same process can be followed when things go well to help replicate success.

Some of you may be familiar with the term "Total Quality Management," or TQM and see it as a fad that has come and gone. You may remember countless meetings that distracted you from what you wanted to be doing and wonder if the rest of these are passing fads. I will speculate that businesses that don't make an ongoing effort to improve the way they operate may find that their competitors outsmart them.

Should We Focus on Efficiency or Effectiveness?

Six Sigma, Kanban, Lean thinking, and Kaizen are all terms that describe an approach to improving efficiency and/or effectiveness. While a thesaurus may say "efficiency" and "effectiveness" are synonyms, business writers have coined different definitions. "Effective" means doing the right things and "efficiency" means doing them well. Said differently, effective is about the what, and efficient is about the how. I'm not sure it matters whether we get bogged down in the semantics. I'm looking for sensible ways to continuously improve.

As a project manager, I often catch myself spending too much time planning a project – and I ask myself if the extent to which I'm thinking about the project adds value. Sometimes you won't know, until something goes wrong. And then, you might be glad you did that planning. Or you may decide it was a waste of time.

Sometimes it has been clear to me that creating detailed weekly client reports was not adding value – particularly when the client wasn't opening them. Unfortunately, when I have seen that happen, it's often been on government projects where the reports were mandated under the contract. Software developers can find that time spent writing code on a new software feature is not time well spent when they recognize that the client has changed her mind on the design.

Increasingly, businesses are asking project teams to do more with less. We can do that through continuous improvement projects, which are specifically designed to improve a process. In these projects, the team first reduces waste by carefully identifying and analyzing all the steps in an existing process, and then eliminates any unnecessary steps. After that process, the team can find ways to do the remaining work in a more efficient manner.

To reduce project waste, you first need to understand what is needed on each activity so that you aren't overworking it. Do you need a 20-page, carefully edited document, or a 1-page emailed summary? If you are working on a construction project, do you want a basic bath design with a shower, toilet, and pedestal sink, or do you want a bath with a Jacuzzi and double vanities? Who needs to approve the final product or the bath design? Time to finish is inversely proportionate to the number of approvals needed.

Isolate workflows. By focusing on identifiable workflows, organizations can automate repeatable processes. That said, be careful about spending too much time or money trying to automate something that is knowledge dependent, requires substantial curiosity, or has considerable variation.

After you eliminate the unnecessary work, focus on the second piece of continuous improvement by looking for ways to do the remaining work in a more efficient manner. To improve efficiency, we could consider any number of ideas, such as: partially staffing your project team with people who reside in areas with a lower cost of living or outsourcing work that can be done by others more efficiently. For example, suppose you are planning to engage in extensive litigation in New York City, Los Angeles, or Washington, DC – expensive areas from which to staff a project.

Can you partially staff the project with people in a smaller office located in some less expensive area? We no longer work in a world where everyone *must* be co-located, and while I often think it improves performance for everyone to be together, sometimes it makes more sense to go with remote teams. Get creative about finding ways to be more efficient.

Concerns about Six Sigma

As discussed, many of the tools and techniques that have been developed over the years to help businesses improve their efficiency and effectiveness were developed in manufacturing companies. And yet, some service businesses, including law firms, have borrowed these concepts, and applied them to their business projects. Some of this can be valuable. My concern about strictly applying principles developed in a manufacturing environment to a non-manufacturing environment is that we risk getting so consumed by misleading data that we miss the mark. The unavoidable and salient fact is that humans are not machines. I remember reading a major bank's annual report back in the early 2000s. There was too much talk about their Six Sigma improvements and no discussion of their customers and their needs. It totally explained why I, and other customers, thought this bank didn't care about us.

W. Edwards Deming, the twentieth-century statistician and leadership thinker, was a pioneer in the field of continuous improvement processes. He is often credited with the following statement: "If you can't describe what you are doing as a process, you don't know what you are doing." It is important to focus on the fact that Deming's methods were developed in a machine world. Many of the projects being done today, both in businesses and professional organizations, are being done by humans and they often involve tasks which have never been done before.

The nature of work has simply evolved over time. To be sure, there are still manufacturing and real estate projects done today. But there are also IT projects, innovation efforts, and change initiatives. These projects share the common element that they are being done by smart people, using their brains. And these people are not punching a time clock when they report to work. They want increasing autonomy and to work on flexible schedules; and they often work on multiple projects at the same time.

Work has simply evolved quickly in the twenty-first century, in part because of increasing global competition and rapid technological changes. I believe we should be careful about strictly applying the tools and techniques that were developed for a manufacturing world to a different type of work being done by people, for the following reasons:

- **Intellectual capacity.** The intellectual capacity that humans bring to a task varies considerably from person to person.
- **Instruction processing.** Humans don't always process instructions the same way. Consider this instruction: "Will you pick up a gallon of milk at the store?" Was the person receiving this instruction supposed to buy the milk? Get whole milk, low-fat, fat-free, or lactose-free milk? Buy a particular brand of milk, and are substitutes allowed? Substitute two half-gallon containers if there aren't any gallon containers? You get the point.
- **Curiosity.** Humans have differing levels of curiosity. This can slow the completion of repetitive tasks, but people who are more curious can offer great insights into things that other people haven't considered. Take

for example, document reviews. I spend much longer on a document review than others because my insatiable curiosity will cause me to raise ten questions that others haven't thought about. Remember that some clients may not want to pay for curiosity.

- **Energy and focus.** Humans work with varying levels of energy, simply wear out, or get distracted. Putting aside mechanical disturbances, typically machines work as well in March as they do in February, while human productivity (at least among fans of college basketball in the US) goes way down during March Madness.
- **Speed.** Not all humans work at the same speed. One person may spend twice as much time developing the same instruction manual as another. The quality of the instruction manual may or may not reflect the larger time investment.

Humans are not like machines. We should exercise some caution in applying Six Sigma or lean data analytics to tasks performed by people. Two machines with the same specs will perform similarly. On the other hand, humans vary considerably, from day to day, and from each other, in many ways, including their intellectual capacity, instruction-processing ability, distractibility, curiosity, energy, focus, and processing speed.

Do You Have a Repeatable Process or a Complex Project?

There may be repeatable processes involved within any project. Yet, it's important to understand the difference between a repeatable process and a project. A process is a step-by-step set of actions taken to achieve a result. If you are regularly repeating that process, you may stand to gain from some form of automation. Continuous improvement projects often involve an effort to streamline a repeatable process to reduce the defects (or mistakes) and therefore, improve efficiencies.

Before you decide to use the standard process mapping tools typically used in a continuous improvement project, make sure you are talking about a repeatable process. When you can use automation to improve a repeatable process, you can achieve cost savings. That said, to find efficiencies, you must be repeating that process often enough to recoup the cost of your effort, as Clifford Chance, one of the largest law firms in the world reported it did in a 2014 white paper on its continuous improvement experiences.

In that paper, the firm notes that one of its first projects was to streamline the process of producing bound volumes of documents. At the end of large corporate matters, law firms typically bind the important transactional documents from the matter and distribute a copy of the book to the key players. Or at least, they *used* to do this. The law firm reported that its London office alone produced 1,500 bound documents each year, so the area was ripe for improvement. As a result of the continuous innovation project, Clifford Chance now begins to identify which documents will ultimately get bound much earlier in the process and relies on technology to a greater extent. According to the firm, the "new process has reduced the cost of producing a bound volume by approximately 60% and has reduced the time taken to dispatch a bound volume following the end of a transaction by up to 80%."[25]

Do the Data Add Value for Your Client?

Some firms, seeking to improve both efficiency and effectiveness, will initiate a continuous improvement project, often after hearing from a client. Sometimes they undertake such a project on behalf of clients, perhaps to improve the client relationship. Sometimes they are done to improve efficiencies and effectiveness with the hope of cutting costs within their organization.

Proponents of Six Sigma often have "math minds" and tend to get excited about statistical data. Sometimes clients like the sound of the project but aren't as excited by data. You may need to translate the Six Sigma technical details into nontechnical reports or stories that have more value for your client.

I have already expressed my concerns about the validity of applying a concept originally developed for measuring machine defects to the work done by humans. Perhaps we could improve the process without spending as much time on the Six Sigma part.

Despite my concerns about the analytics piece, Six Sigma, Kanban, Lean thinking, and Kaizen offer valuable lessons for businesses today. Focusing on these lessons will improve the way you do business and the way you manage your projects. It makes sense to pursue continual improvement. Maybe we shouldn't get so bogged down doing the work that we forget to find ways to improve *how* we do the work.

Are You Automating Tasks for Your Clients?

In your efforts to show continual improvement to your clients, you may embark on a project to automate a process. Before considering task automation for clients, ask if the task requires a level of curiosity or industry knowledge.

In the Clifford Chance white paper referenced above, the author notes: "Almost any task that has a beginning, a middle and an end can be construed as a process, including the practice of law."[26] And yet, if the process requires significant curiosity or knowledge, I question the benefit of automation, at least right now.

That wraps up Part 1, with its focus on executives and the project analytics that drive effective decision-making. It is essential that we begin to understand that the approach we have been using can be flawed when the analytics are not reliable. And until we reinvent project management and abandon a century-old technique that simply doesn't work well in rapidly changing times, we will continue to see too much waste. If you'd like more reading on analytics, check out this webpage: https://smartprojex.com/category/analysis/.

In Part 2, I switch the focus to leadership and what we need from our leaders as we continue this journey to reimagine project management for a new era.

Part 2
Leadership

"Human resources are like natural resources. They're often buried deep. You have to go looking for them. They're not just lying around on the surface. You have to create the circumstances where they show themselves."[27]

— *Sir Ken Robinson*

Chapter 8

People, Not Computers, Do Projects!

As important as reliable analytics, efficient methodologies, and modern technologies are, your people are the key to getting your projects done. And people require effective leadership. Part 2 focuses on building the leadership competencies that will help your organization thrive. In this chapter, I discuss the leadership gifts that some personality types offer, what evolving scientific research tells us about people and project leadership, and how acting with love changes the way that people behave.

After all, despite our significant technological advances, we still depend on people to do the hard work of making change happen and delivering benefits to the organization. And regardless of the project methodology that we use, project leadership in a world of chaos and change is much more dependent on your ability to manage relationships than on your ability to manage tasks.

As I watch humans looking for a bit more fairness, equality, respect, and dignity in the workforce, I am struck by the aptness of the herding smart cats metaphor. People want to be successful and accomplish great things. I see very few innovative and dynamic people looking for a dictatorial work environment.

I believe we make a serious mistake if we underestimate the importance of relationship management in the business world, including the government arena. And yet, for many organizations, the project approach continues to be more about assigning tasks, controlling the schedule, and punishing people.

Gurpreet Dhillon, who holds the G. Brint Ryan Endowed Chair of Artificial Intelligence and Cybersecurity at the University of North Texas, wrote about the impact of power structures on IT projects in a 2003 case study in which he analyzed a project at the Nevada Department of Motor Vehicles and Public Safety (DMV). Briefly, the goal was to reduce the complexity of systems used by employees at the DMV and improve customer satisfaction. While in some ways the project succeeded and the technology appears to still be in use, the implementation was fraught with problems, frustrations, and disappointments.[28]

While the technical problems were great, the human problems were greater, and Dhillon notes that employees were poorly trained and often unable to use the system. Offices were routinely understaffed, resulting in horrid wait times. Assumptions about what consumers wanted, as well as the ease of use of the developed system, were flawed. In conclusion, Dhillon writes, "Good project management goes far beyond the technical development of a system. Indeed, it is far more important to understand the human behavioral aspects of analysis, design and management of systems."[29] Undeniably, project management goes beyond whatever technologies and systems we use to manage our projects. We need project systems that focus on people and their diverse ways of working and leading.

Different Personality Types Produce Different Varieties of Leaders

Project leadership is one area where quieter, more introverted leaders can shine. The work of leading a project requires a lot more listening and documenting than talking. The project manager may not necessarily be that leader who seems to have all of the answers on how to best do some task at hand. In fact, on any project team, there can be multiple leaders, exercising different skills to move the project forward.

People often have various combinations of innate leadership qualities. Some are great listeners and others are better decision-makers. Some seem to have certain visionary abilities, while others naturally talk or write more persuasively. We need to find a way to appreciate the skills in these people for the value they add, direct people into the appropriate positions, and communicate with them to minimize the risk that their leadership skills could become divisive.

Experts debate whether leadership can be taught or is inborn. People who are highly motivational often seem to have been born that way. And highly motivational people seem to be natural leaders. In project management, that type may not be the best person for the project manager spot. Those charismatic, extroverted, inspirational, and motivational leaders are sometimes terrible at detail work, and project management – by anyone's definition – requires an attention to detail. If such leaders have a senior status in the organization, they may make great project sponsors (or project champions) with the right managers. If they are selected to lead a project, they need to delegate as much detail work as possible.

How does effective project leadership differ from traditional management? Simply put, projects can be effectively completed by teams of leaders, all leading in different, but compatible ways. The best project sponsors and project managers encourage this leadership. And on these high-functioning project teams, you will observe a different chemistry than you find in a small company where there is a boss, and everyone follows the boss, hoping that he or she can quickly develop better leadership skills.

What are the different kinds of natural leaders we find in project work, and how can they best be utilized effectively?

The Pied Piper

The pied piper is the seemingly extroverted individual who naturally has a line of people who are following him or her. They are often lively, smiling, fun people. Pied pipers have no idea why people follow them and often do not seek out this role. They are naturals.

Life on your project will be great when your pied pipers are committed to the project and performing a strong function that you need. When one of your pied pipers becomes dissatisfied with the direction that the project is taking, he or she can quickly lead others into a place of tension and destruction.

I believe pied pipers are in the group of individuals that Professors Kim and Mauborgne refer to when they talk about turning your focus to the people with an undue influence on your organization in their classic book, *Blue Ocean Strategy*.[30] When you focus your efforts on the 20% of the people, places, and behaviors that exercise disproportionate influence, it greatly reduces the time it takes to make change. It's akin to the Pareto principle, a management technique named for the economist who developed it, Vilfredo Pareto. According to the Pareto principle, we should focus on the 20% of activities that will generate 80% of the results.

The Inspirational Motivator

Another category of folks who perhaps have disproportionate influence are your inspirational motivators. They can fall into several different camps, depending on their level of extroversion or introversion. More introverted leaders can inspire through great ideas or communication skills, and often seem to listen well.

Some well-known sports coaches often appear to be extroverted inspirational motivators, and we can watch them shouting at their teams from the sidelines. The good ones know when to stop talking and listen.

To reinvent project management for the business world, we can study the best coaches and take some lessons on how to motivate teams. Admittedly, some of them seem to be breaking all the rules – they yell and scream, and they don't empower teams to chart their own course. I'm not suggesting that we begin to emulate those behaviors in the corporate world, or anywhere else for that matter. But the good coaches love their teams and seem to find a way to build up that love among team members. The good coaches have learned how to groom players who can regularly pass the ball to others and sacrifice their own need for achievement in favor of team performance. These are the skills that we need to build in our project leaders.

How can project managers adopt a coaching spirit that empowers a team? By allowing teams to self-manage and by not getting in the way, an effective project manager can build a team of leaders who all enjoy working with one another. The project manager can serve as a sounding board, reflecting what he or she sees and hears back to the team – and then allowing the team to process that feedback and find their own way.

The Detail Documenter

There are some people who are always writing down details, thinking about something that everyone else has forgotten, planning without knowing it, or making lists. These people can make excellent project managers, provided they have sufficient social skills to lead a team.

A "sous chef" type of approach can be effective when your project manager is a detail documenter. In this approach, the goal is to build a team with a strong project sponsor and utilize other folks on the team as activity leaders, and risk or money managers, terms that are exactly what they sound like, and which I discuss more fully in Part 3 (on methodology). Sous chef types, who are happy to share the glory and don't require a lot of hands-on management, can be effective, and other team members often enjoy working with a leader who shares credit for success.

The Delegator

Some people can delegate effectively, while others are terrified of losing control. It's even harder to delegate in new groups where folks have not yet proven themselves. Some of the best project managers seem to be able to delegate in a way that allows the team to fail, learn, and grow. So, look for people who can delegate effectively for project management positions.

If you have someone who enjoys control and has a hard time letting others take over, it may be better to use them as an activity leader, rather than a project manager. People who enjoy controlling things are often highly dependable and accountable for results. They may not want to be responsible for someone else's mistakes, but that doesn't mean that they can't add value to your project team. Their high personal expectations, work ethic, and lack of tolerance for their own mistakes can be inspirational to others.

The Boss

Bosses, or those people who have been officially put in charge of a project, a division, or an organization, seem to come in all shapes and sizes, with varying leadership competencies, unlimited variations in temperaments, and differing needs for personal glory. Finding the perfect boss – that person whom folks want to spend half of their waking life trying to please – is the elusive dream for many. Salary and benefits help, but many employees leave bosses, not jobs.

Choosing the right project manager and a strong group of initial project team members can mean the difference between finding the right resources for your project or not. Some organizations allow people to choose their own projects. Guess what? No one wants to work for a jerk. Be smart and avoid selecting jerks to manage your projects.

When there is no way around that option, the challenge for the team is to learn how to manage upwards; in other words, how to quietly manage the boss. It's about giving management what it needs to do its job, protecting management from surprises, and communicating so that it's easy for management to identify the important and the urgent. Transparent systems can be helpful here, though there are some people who reject transparency out of fear.

Documenting understandings and progress is essential, and if the boss can reasonably access that documentation, the team may find that the boss is less intrusive.

There are other valid ways that different personality types impact your project work and help you develop your leaders. Trained and experienced project managers will have seen many of them.

Leadership is about managing both up and down. It means understanding your responsibility to provide those above you and below you with what they need to do their jobs. Managing up and down requires us to look in the mirror when things aren't going well.

Having everyone committed to a well-defined vision on a project that is clearly bringing value to the organization is essential. And having a system where "hot button" issues can be flagged helps ensure that the boss is in the loop on the important matters.

How Does Modern Science Inform Project Management?

Solid leadership principles have been informed by emerging brain science over the last fifty years or so, and this impacts project leadership as well. We have learned much about the brain since the advent of brain imaging technologies and more research. Much of this research centers around bias and how it shapes our decision-making. I'll discuss a few of these biases and how they impact project work, though I will defer the discussion on race and gender biases to Chapter 9, where I talk about hiring policies.

We need to begin to recognize bias for what it is. In a 2014 PMI conference paper, authors Panos Chatzipanos and Theofanis Giotis wrote that some cognitive biases "manifest automatically and unconsciously over a wide range of human reasoning and frequently result in seeing things that are not really there, in being nonsensical, in just being wrong, and in unintelligently refusing to see the facts. When cognitive biases influence individuals, real—or problematic—complexity may arise. When these biases impact a group, an organization, or a business, the problems can be dramatically worse."[31]

Clearly, we have this problem on some project teams. And advancing brain science is making it increasingly clear that humans come wired with some biases. I'll discuss bias in two categories: first, how bias impacts how we manage project details, and second, how it impacts how we manage people.

What Does Modern Science Show Us About How We Should Manage Project Details?

The "planning fallacy" was first proposed by Daniel Kahneman and Amos Tversky in 1979 to explain the problem of failed projects. In general, we live in a world of optimists, and that's probably a good thing. But it does mean that time and money estimates are often optimistic. And if the estimates are optimistic, our project will likely not meet the forecast; thus, by some definitions, we have a failed project.[32]

In further studies done in 1994 by Roger Buehler, Dale Griffin, and Michael Ross, the authors tested three hypotheses "concerning people's predictions of task completion times: (a) People underestimate their own but not others' completion times, (b) people focus on plan-based scenarios rather than on relevant past experiences while generating their predictions, and (c) people's attributions diminish the relevance of past experiences. Results supported each hypothesis."[33] Seasoned project managers are well acquainted with horror stories about optimistic predictions on both cost and schedule and this study explains some of that optimism and alerts us all to be cognizant of this bias.

Confirmation bias is that tendency to hear what we want to hear – to hear data that supports or confirms what we previously thought. We have a bias tendency to ignore findings that conflict with what we *want* to believe.

In a 2006 confirmation bias study done at MIT, researchers used functional magnetic resonance imaging (fMRI) technology to study the brains of committed partisans who were asked questions about information that threatened their preferred presidential candidate in the 2004 Bush versus Kerry election. For the first time, researchers watched the neural activity when participants were asked to make judgments when they were presented with data that confirmed or rejected previously held beliefs about their candidates. It was clear from the imaging studies that participants resisted making judgments that would adversely impact their previously held beliefs about their preferred candidate.[34] In short, they saw what they wanted to see. This represents a problem that we should recognize on our project teams, particularly when passions on the project are high.

In his book *The Undoing Project*, Michael Lewis writes about the groundbreaking work of Amos Tversky (the self-confident extrovert) and Daniel Kahnemann (the introvert who struggled with self-doubt). Lewis describes the confirmation bias problem in the hiring of Jeremy Lin, who simply didn't "look like" a professional basketball player.[35] While Lin was tall, many early observers did not see him as particularly athletic. Experts could not quite envision Chinese players as National Basketball Association stars. There is a difficulty in seeing things that we don't expect to see and the tendency to see what we want to see. It is hard to identify when it is happening, and it's a big problem when hiring and staffing projects.

What Does Science Show Us About How We Should Manage People?

In his book, *Drive: The Surprising Truth About What Motivates Us*, Dan Pink writes about the science of motivation, and the need to rethink management, considering what science has taught us. We need to hire people with strong intrinsic motivation. He describes the period we are in today as motivation 3.0 and says that the carrot-and-stick approaches that we've used for years don't work. People are more motivated by purpose, autonomy, and mastery.[36] We should ask people what is motivating them instead of assuming we know. We should let team members pick the activities that are the most appealing to them, whenever possible.

As bias studies have shown, it is easy to see that when emotions are high, people struggle with analytical tasks and decision-making. As most parents eventually learn, it's better to stop trying to negotiate with children who are in the middle of a temper tantrum. What works better than negotiating or arguing is listening, learning, and showing empathy. And this is what we need to do on our projects, particularly when passions run high.

According to a 2017 article by Michael O'Brochta in PM *World Journal*, many IT projects are kept alive long after they should have been cancelled. Among the contributing factors were groupthink, sunk costs, and a natural inclination to feel accountable and responsible. O'Brochta noted that research done by T. Liang & N. Yen (2016) "suggests that these behaviors are rooted deep within the neural science of our brains."[37]

Additionally, we have learned that the way we frame a problem, task, or challenge can significantly impact our decisions and results. It's like the difference between asking someone on your team when it might be reasonable to expect a response to an email and asking that person to please respond by an arbitrary and unimportant date.

The purpose of Liang and Yen's work was to study two theories – the framing effect and self-responsibility – and determine if there is a neurological basis that explains how these biases impact decisions that ultimately result in an inability to shut down a bad project. Their findings "support that both theories at least partially explain the escalation of commitment in software project management."[38]

In the previously referenced academic paper by Panos Chatzipanos and Theofanis Giotis, the authors discuss status quo bias as a major factor explaining why change is so hard to achieve. Combined with a bias against losses (aversion bias) and the sunk cost fallacy, people are inclined to continue their path, rather than changing course even in the face of overwhelming pressure to do so.[39]

Recognize the neurological basis of these tendencies and then manage your people with a greater awareness of the propensity for groupthink, and a tendency to feel responsible and want to save a troubled project.

There is also emerging research on the use of sociometers to study the effectiveness of small group work in face-to-face settings. These devices, worn around the necks of everyone in the group, measure factors such as speech timing and volume, movement, and spatial orientation. While these studies are in the infancy stage, the speculation is that team creativity is enhanced when people work face-to-face, though research was primarily focused on how creativity and social signals are connected.

One study using sociometers, for example, suggested that a high level of successful interruptions suggested higher individual creativity and enjoyment, while longer uninterrupted speech segments suggested a lower level of creativity and enjoyment.[40] Generally, to improve team creativity and personal enjoyment, find a conversational balance where ideas from everyone are well integrated and people are actively listening.

This ties into work that Robert D. Putnam, Harvard professor of public policy, is doing. He is researching how the loss of community in America has resulted in a movement from a highly collaborative "we" society, to a much more narcissistic "I" society.[41] If we build an increased sense of community on our teams, will that improve collaboration?

Tony Hsieh successfully opted for that route at Zappos by heavily investing in team building, developing and promoting values, and creating fun in the organization. Hsieh felt so strongly about the importance of colleagues knowing one another that he built an extra step, called the Face Game, into their system sign-on routine. A photo of a colleague appeared, and the user had to select the correct name from a multiple-choice listing.[42]

When we finally emerge from the current COVID-19 pandemic, it will be interesting to watch how businesses balance these trade-offs. The debates on remote work continue, but sooner or later we'll have to come to grips with how to work together in the face of viruses. From my perspective, technology can help, particularly as it improves. But there are benefits to working together, face-to-face, when teams are doing the creative work of innovation. We are humans and we need other people to help us retain our sense of humanity, creativity, and drive.

The pandemic has been a wake-up call on work-life balance. People don't want to work excessive hours every week, endure long daily commutes, spend hours a day in unnecessary video meetings, or feel that they are on call 24/7.

For those who believe that 70-hour work weeks are essential, I would caution that there is growing body of evidence about the impact of sleep on people's brains and productivity. In a study entitled "Circadian Rhythms, Sleep Deprivation, and Human Performance," the authors found that sophisticated and detailed imaging studies consistently report "significant reductions in metabolic rates in the thalamic, parietal, and prefrontal regions after sleep loss, which correlated with declines of cognitive performance and alertness."[43] The study included a discussion about the types of cognitive behavior, critical to business performance, and their direct correlation to circadian rhythms. Furthermore, it discussed how certain lifestyle habits, such as diet, caffeine intake, posture, lighting, and boredom can mask the circadian rhythms.

The implications are significant. Project managers need to find sustainable patterns in how they divide up project activities over the course of a project. We can't keep pushing people to perform without sleeping. We need to recognize that periodic breaks are a good thing. To the extent possible, we are probably better off if we allow people to work in sync with their natural body clocks. While most of us function better during the day, there are true night owls who perform better in the evening. We need to focus on healthy eating when we provide snacks for team meetings.

These findings, and other ongoing scientific research, which grows by the day, should have a major impact on how we hire and manage in the future, how we coach our project teams, and how we assign and monitor work.

Spread the Love

When we act with love, which means recognizing everyone's individual humanity and treating them with respect, it changes our mindset. Three ways that organizations can embrace this new mindset are: to develop our talent, build multipliers, and create joyful organizations. This helps us create environments characterized by open communications, high standards, accountability, and camaraderie. While I don't want to underestimate the value of analytics and left-brain thinking, our future success depends increasingly on our ability to nurture relationships and lead effectively.

Brené Brown, researcher and author, claims as a fact in her book *The Gifts of Imperfection* that "A deep sense of love and belonging is an irreducible need of all women, men, and children. We are biologically, cognitively, physically, and spiritually wired to love, to be loved, and to belong."[44]

Different approaches to project management often result in different ways of treating people. In my experience with those using a more traditional Waterfall methodology approach, the project manager functions more like a manager, assigning responsibilities and deadlines to those on the team. He or she also negotiates with functional managers for resources. Team members are expected to provide schedules of availability to the project manager. That is not to say that there is no love on the team or for the project manager. But the focus is on driving the previously planned schedule.

In a more Agile environment, teams are formed to address problems and are often allowed to stay together as an increasingly better-functioning group – thus improving the execution speed and profitability of a project. There is a large focus on relationship management and improving the team's commitment to delivering value regularly and rapidly. Agility is key.

Is there a way to achieve the agility that Scrum offers and the insights that Waterfall offers? That's what I have worked on for years, and what you can think about doing in your own approach to project management.

To begin to develop such an environment, ask the people on your project team what it is they would like to accomplish from working on this project. People will work harder when they are achieving their own goals while they help you achieve yours. Said differently, it is important for people to reap abundantly from their project work. When you know what professional goals people on your teams have, other than drawing a paycheck, it may help determine how you divide up the activities.

For example, the team member who wants to build new skills may want activities that are entirely new – with an understanding that progress may be slower. The team member who is more interested in fun may be assigned activities that they perceive to be fun. And the team member who is interested in climbing the corporate ladder may want to work on activities with more visibility. It varies from person to person. When your people are interested in what they are doing, they will perform at a higher level. Don't assume that everyone wants the same thing.

Businesspeople are often working on several different projects at the same time, with work varying weekly depending on project needs. Increasingly, I notice that smart people want to manage their own schedules and wish for more flexibility. They are often happy to commit to results but have more trouble committing to a schedule.

What happens when the project manager moves from managing to coaching, and encourages teams to self-manage? If we can learn anything from the Scrum movement, it suggests that team effectiveness and work output will improve. I'm not walking away from the need to manage the project. I'm suggesting that coaching and allowing teams to self-manage reaps benefits.

Hard things are hard because no one has a road map. And no one wants to show weakness by asking for help. As technology entrepreneur, author, and investor Ben Horowitz writes in *The Hard Thing About Hard Things: Building a Business When There Are No Easy Answers*, "They are hard because your emotions are at odds with your logic."[45] When the team culture encourages honesty and helpfulness, small issues are addressed before they become big problems. Asking for help and asking how you can help becomes part of the culture. It's about collaborating effectively to get the work done.

Relationships are more important than tasks and schedules. When a team gets behind a vision, when regular meetings keep team members focused and accountable, and when objectives are clear, teams have fun turning dreams into reality.

During a Navy SEAL team Hell Week program, commanding officers noticed that one boat crew was consistently winning while another was consistently losing. The instructors reversed the boat crew leaders. The results were striking. The boat which had lost consistently went on to win, demonstrating the critical importance of leadership. This story was recounted in *Extreme Ownership: How U.S. Navy SEALs Lead and Win*, written by two former SEAL officers, Jocko Willink and Leif Babin.[46] Leadership matters.

And while I'm talking about spreading some love, it's important to understand that while there are many things we can change, and change quickly, people do not fall into that category. Hearts and minds can be rigid in the best of souls. We're better off focusing on changing ourselves and how we react to situations than to overtly try to change others. Don't waste time trying to change the core personalities of others on the team if they are not interested in changing. If someone on the team is never going to be a good fit, perhaps they need to be deployed elsewhere. In Chapter 9, I talk about the need for diverse organizations and teams; it's important to remember that building these relationships takes time. Give others some space and grace.

Growing Talent

We read regularly about the problems that organizations have in finding and retaining top talent. Project managers can rarely demand the perfect resources for their projects. We must hunt for the right people, and we must develop them.

Author Daniel Coyle has spent a fair amount of time searching the globe for pockets of unusual talent. He has investigated how and why these places, often run-down and underfunded, are able to successfully groom "normal" people – those without extraordinary talent. In his book *The Talent Code*, Coyle explores the connection between myelin, an insulation layer that covers the nerve fibers in the body, and skill development.[47]

Coyle digs deeply into the research of University of California Los Angeles neurology professor George Bartzokis, who described myelin as "the key to talking, reading, learning skills, being human."[48]

Building skill is required for developing talent, and that includes the talent on your project teams. To build myelin, Coyle recommends deep practice, that type of work that we do when we are "in the zone." It involves practicing at a deep level where you are forced to slow down; you will make mistakes, you fix them, and then you repeat the process over and over. Progress is made when the people on your team aim towards goals that allow them to reach somewhat beyond their current level. Too much blind struggling does not help. "Deep practice is assisted by the attainment of a primal state, one where we are attentive, hungry, and focused, even desperate."[49]

The challenge is for leaders to help their people reach what Coyle calls "ignition," which he describes as the spark that drives individuals to continue practicing. Those who successfully create that spark do so through primal cues that create a huge amount of energy. Examples of primal cues include a sense of belonging to something great, a feeling that things are not safe, or a feeling of being behind and needing to catch up. Many Americans saw that spark in the student-organized March for Our Lives demonstration that occurred in March 2018, following the Marjory Stoneman Douglas High School shooting.

This spark or ignition that Coyle discusses is one of the reasons that I continue to advocate that project leaders spend time creating an inspirational vision statement that will motivate their teams. Keeping that energy alive long after a project has launched pays dividends but requires work.

According to Coyle, Kaizen (discussed in Chapter 7) is a type of deep practice. It's about continuously seeking to improve, about identifying small problems, and fixing them.[50] This approach of looking for small problems, fixing them, and improving can be incorporated into your project work through a focus on lessons learned, as well as how you execute the project, both of which I discuss in Part 3 on methodology. Another similar approach is the one that Tony Hsieh discusses in his book, *Delivering Happiness: A Path to Profits, Passion, and Purpose*. He always encouraged employees to look for one small improvement each week and noted that if everyone at Zappos did that, they would see 50,000 improvements in a year.[51]

Developing Multipliers

When it comes to grooming talent, another approach is to find your multipliers. Liz Wiseman, a former Oracle executive, best-selling author, executive advisor, and thrice ranked in the top 50 management thinkers, discusses this in her book, *Multipliers: How the Best Leaders Make Everyone Smarter.*

According to Wiseman, some people have a knack for making others look like geniuses, building intelligence on their teams, and magnifying the impact of the work that people are doing.[52] We cannot keep adding people when we need more results. Instead, we need to magnify the results of those around us.

Multipliers engage their teams by putting people on projects that stretch them. It's not just about doing more with less; it's about making people smarter. Wiseman notes that multipliers ask their teams to tell them when they are behaving in a way that is causing others to shut down. They have a growth mindset for themselves and others. Rather than seeing the intelligence of others as fixed or limited, they believe that the people around them can achieve greatness.[53]

If you are the leader, try identifying your ideas as soft opinions or hard opinions. Soft opinions are those that you are offering for consideration. Save your hard opinions for important matters; in other words, pick your battles wisely. By identifying your opinions as soft or hard, you give your teams space to comfortably and openly disagree or wrestle with different options without fear of being shut down. If you are not the leader, ask the leader if the opinion expressed is a soft opinion and explain the concept.[54]

Wiseman believes that we diminish others when we talk too much, even when our thoughts are brilliant. One suggestion that I loved was to allow yourself only five "poker chips" when you go into a meeting – with each chip being worth a certain amount of time. Once you have spent your chips, you can't say anything else.[55] Keep this mind when you are leading a project meeting.

Joyful Organizations

Douglas Abrams, an editor, author, and founder of Idea Architects, a book and media agency for visionaries, spearheaded a collaborative effort to bring His Holiness the Dalai Lama and Archbishop Desmond Tutu together. He documented the results in *The Book of Joy: Lasting Happiness in a Changing World.*

In this book, the Dalai Lama talks about how we control our suffering and that applies to us as individuals, project teams, and organizations. Our ability to bring joy to a project depends on "the attitudes, the perspectives, and the reactions we bring" to the project and the people associated with the project.[56] According to the Dalai Lama, "If you really feel a sense of concern for the well-being of others, then trust will come. That's the basis of friendship."[57] To build trust on your teams and in your organizations, help people create a stronger sense of compassion for each other.

Smiling and humor go a long way in the working world. "Research has shown that the simple act of smiling for as little as twenty seconds can trigger positive emotions, jump-starting joy and happiness. Smiling stimulates the release of neuropeptides that work toward fighting off stress and unleashes a feel-good cocktail of the neurotransmitters serotonin, dopamine, and endorphins."[58] These two men teased each other throughout the five days and consider it a "sign of intimacy and friendship." Their jokes were never attempts to put the other down, but rather a constant reinforcement of their friendship.[59] According to Archbishop Tutu, the teasing is a "statement of trust in the relationship."[60]

We all have mirror neurons, those smart brain cells that respond to emotions or behaviors in others. They help us interpret and relate to the actions and feelings of others. Leaders with stronger mirror neurons will be more empathetic. Abrams describes the sensation as a "tingling in my forehead and then a sharpening of focus as various parts of my brain started to quiet and calm...."[61] We do need to understand that we might unknowingly mirror the actions or emotions of others and, depending on the kind of behavior that we are "mirroring," we can act without thinking. Meditation can help lengthen the time between the stimulus and our response.

When leaders can build teams and organizations that find joy in their work and with each other, everyone benefits.

It is impossible to overstate the importance of effective leadership. According to Paul C. Light, a Brookings Institute researcher who has been researching US government failures for years, the problems most often involve improper oversight, confusing missions, and poor leadership.[62] From my experience, this is true whether we are talking about projects, operations, or outsourced work done by contractors.

Before I move to the next chapter, I want to reiterate that people do projects. And leadership is about people. It's about increasing that sense of belonging. It's about inspiring them to achieve greater results, for the team, the client, and themselves.

Ask yourself this question: Is your organization worried about beating the competition, or focused on winning metrics that drive bad behaviors? This focus on winning metrics or beating the competition results when we use finite thinking, rather than infinite thinking, as discussed by Simon Sinek in his book, *The Infinite Game*. The thesis of his book is that there are finite games, such as football, backgammon, or bridge. The games have an ending, and someone wins the game.

Business is an infinite game. The goal is to continue playing, not to win. When we play finite games, we know who the players are, and they don't change once the game has started. There are established rules. And everyone understands what must happen for someone to win.[63] None of that is true in infinite games. Much of what is behind the Smart Projex methodology that I discuss in Part 3 involves moving leaders to an infinite games mindset.

While project work has historically been defined as finite work, since there is a deadline, the world has gotten increasingly chaotic, and more agility is needed. We can apply many of the best principles related to project management, such as risk management, issue tracking, stakeholder management, and procurement contract management to all work in the business. What is stopping us?

In the next chapter, I focus on how great leaders set direction. That begins with having a clear and compelling vision. And while I largely focus on project work, these same principles can be applied throughout the organization.

Chapter 9

How Great Leaders Shape Direction

According to *In Search of Excellence* authors Thomas Peters and Robert Waterman, "complaints against American management" seem to fall into several categories. These include "managers don't personally identify with what their companies do," "managers don't take enough interest in their people," and "top managers and their staff have become isolated in their analytic ivory towers."[64] Leaders shape direction in many ways. This chapter focuses on three of these: a strong vision, hiring policies, and an appropriately aligned compensation structure. While the direction over these topics begins at the top, and impacts operational work also, I primarily discuss how these factors impact projects.

Your Vision Is Your Guiding Star

Leaders begin by having clear visions and communicating them effectively. Every leader needs a clear vision of where he/she wants to take the organization. Simon Sinek talks about the "Just Cause" – or the vision behind why a company or product exists.[65] He talks about beginning with your "why." This gives meaning to the work and the people. To the extent that your clients and vendors know and believe in your "why," they will become more loyal clients who pass on the cheaper alternatives because they believe in your why.[66] By keeping this powerful vision in the foreground, executives are less likely to fall into finite thinking (discussed in Chapter 8).

This same technique can be applied to projects, which are finite undertakings. Every project needs a clear and compelling vision that will sustain teams when troubles arise. When developing your project "why," resist the urge to be so heavenly that you are no earthly good. Remember to take a lean approach and focus on an achievable project that has value, rather than a pipe dream. And when that project vision doesn't seem inspiring or clear, try a little harder. It's worth the effort to make sure that you have a crystal-clear vision that everyone embraces.

In *Start with Why*, Simon Sinek tells a great story that illustrates the need to ensure alignment between our what, why, and how. A Little League coach was trying to tell his losing team of youngsters that it didn't matter. He explained that he wanted them to play fair and enjoy the game, to which one child responded by asking why they kept score.[67] The child understood the importance of winning, a basic human desire in some cultures and people. But who judges what is a win?

It is critical to understand the importance of aligning your organization's vision with the policies, pronouncements, and actions throughout your company. I don't know about your mother, but mine was famous for reminding me that actions speak louder than words. Think about the number of times that large, well-known companies have taken actions that didn't align with their stated vision and have been called to task for it, particularly in this socially connected world. Pay attention to what your actions say about who you are.

In Chapter 14, I talk about the importance of understanding project success criteria. And I do think that understanding what constitutes success and how to measure it are important. Yet Sinek points out that, "Problems arise, however, when the metric becomes the only measure of success, when what you achieve is no longer tied to WHY you set out to achieve it in the first place."[68] Some commonsense judgment is needed.

Sinek also discusses the neurology of the brain and notes that the part of the brain that understands why, on a gut level, is not the same part of the brain that is responsible for language.[69] This makes it hard to explain why you love a product or an idea. It explains why it is so essential for leaders to communicate their visions at a gut level. It's not about getting the intellect committed. It's about getting the heart committed.

Colin Powell, in his book It *Worked for Me: In Life and Leadership*, says, "Purpose is the destination of a vision. It energizes that vision, gives it force and drive. It should be positive and powerful, and serve the better angels of an organization.... Good leaders set vision, missions, and goals. Great leaders inspire every follower at every level to internalize their purpose, and to understand that their purpose goes far beyond the mere details of their job."[70]

If you review the most successful projects, you quickly understand that a compelling vision drives the project's success. As Steve Jobs reportedly said, "If you are working on something exciting that you really care about, you don't have to be pushed. The vision pulls you." Knowing that, how can we ensure that all our projects have a compelling vision behind them?

In Powell's book, he tells a story, as recounted in a television documentary about the Empire State Building.

"Towards the end of the show, the interviewer talked with several guys in a huge basement trash room filled with the daily waste. One of the guys proudly declared: 'Our job is to make sure that tomorrow morning when people from all over the world come to this wonderful building, it shines, it is clean, and it looks great.' His job was to drag bags, but he knew his purpose. He didn't feel he was just a trash hauler. His work was vital, and his purpose blended into the purpose of the building's most senior management eighty floors above."[71]

Would the people on your teams have a response so clear and compelling? Have you explained, for example, that your company has chosen to move its offices to provide safer employee parking, or that you are moving the offices to provide larger executive suites or enhanced technologies? Putting in a new inventory control system when the objective is to reduce inventory is different from a system that ensures that inventory is always available to service customer needs. And the scope of a nonprofit event to increase public awareness with the millennial crowd will differ considerably from the same event being held to raise millions from older wealthy patrons.

As your organization begins any new project, consider the impact that change can have on people. Some organizations and people handle change better than others. If your client (or your firm or your team) is a change-resistant organization, avoid having a meeting to introduce a major change to a group of decision-makers until you know that they are all on board. Yes, it takes time for the project sponsor to have individual face-to-face meetings to get buy-in from all stakeholders. But a vocal dissenter can quickly silence your supporters and stop you in your tracks. Explain the increase in business value or improvements to efficiency that will result.

Getting a team committed to a project is much easier when everyone understands *why* the project is being undertaken. Additionally, in some projects, you might need to create a sense of urgency for the project within the larger organization, especially if you need widespread support from a large group of stakeholders. That vision can help you there too. Spend the time that it takes to develop that compelling vision statement and keep that statement front and center, like a guiding star, during the entire course of the project. If you lose that focus, don't be surprised when things start falling apart.

There is another factor, though. Organizations don't change. People do, or they don't. And they probably won't change just because the boss orders it, or because you create a vision that they aren't particularly interested in. People change because of what is in it for them. Let's face it. Change is messy. And for an organization to move to a radically different (hopefully, better) place, all the people in the organization will have to change. That kind of change is often more the result of unintended consequences and almost accidental happenings than managed change. And yet, building highly effective teams that are devoted to your important vision, which I discuss more fully in Chapter 11, is key.

Hiring Policies

Hiring is one of the most critical aspects of leadership throughout the organization. Leaders at the top control the process. If your process is flawed, you cannot expect to hire the brightest and best. After you have hired the best candidates you can find, there are other policies that can impact your culture and the retention of those people you hired. For example, a slow onboarding process will cause the brightest people to quickly become bored and disengaged.

Since project teams are often composed of employees in an organization, the strength of the hiring process can directly influence the success of your projects. In this section, I focus on three areas that have a huge impact on culture, and thus, on the culture of your project teams. They are the value of diversity, gender and sex discrimination, and racial and ethnic discrimination.

Diversity – Discrimination, Bias, and Prejudice

There is an ancient legend about blind men and an elephant that has been used to illustrate various truths through the years. In a version of this story, the blind men struggle with what the elephant is, and depending on their perspective, they describe the elephant as a rope, spear, snake, fan, rug, cave, high mountain, water hose, wall, or tree. When a sighted man comes along and describes the beast, the sightless men realize how blind they are.

Leaders have an obligation to focus on diversity in their hiring process, and on their project teams, since diversity strengthens results and improves the culture. The more perspectives we include on our project teams, the more varied our ideas will be. Diversity not only includes ethnic, race, age, and gender diversity, but work type diversity. Resist the urge to take the easy route and staff your team with people who think and work alike. Take your time in hiring the right people. Build a diverse team to get the best results. And make sure your project team has at least one person who will challenge assumptions and approaches.

You may need to take time to understand cultural

differences and/or develop a code of conduct or team charter that governs how teams work together, but in the end, a diverse team can develop more creative products.

The word "discrimination" has taken on a pejorative tone in recent years, and when we talk about sex, gender, racial, or ethnic discrimination, we must agree that those are wrong. But the ability to make good judgments, to discriminate if you will, is a key skill for leaders. And I believe we should view the word "discrimination" from a more neutral perspective.

It seems to me that "bias" has gone from being a more negative word to a more neutral word as brain research has begun to support the fact that we all have biases – and it's important for us to begin to understand them. Prejudice, defined as actions or judgements that injure or harm others, is always wrong.

Next, I want to intentionally address two specific types of discrimination that we continue to wrestle with, particularly in the United States. I suspect that other countries have similar issues.

Gender and Sex Discrimination

In Joanne Lipman's book, *That's What She Said: What Men Need to Know (and Women Need to Tell Them) About Working Together*, she advocates for men to become involved in the fight to close the gender gap, because businesses simply perform better when their leadership is diverse.[72]

The research on gender diversity is mixed. In a 2019 *Harvard Business Review* article, the authors discussed their research into how gender diversity may be related to country or industry culture. The study concluded that gender diversity, in organizations that value gender diversity, results in better performance, as measured by revenue and market value. But in cultures where gender diversity was not valued, such as the patriarchal culture in Japan, that was not the case.[73] And yet, we must note that gender issues are evolving quickly, as the public saw when Momoko Nojo, a 22-year-old Japanese student, launched an online campaign against Yoshiro Mori, the head of the Tokyo Olympics, and quickly brought about his resignation after he tweeted about women "talking too much."[74]

The authors of that *Harvard Business Review* study noted three reasons why the actual value that diversity brings is less significant than the belief that diversity matters. First, in pro-diversity cultures, job seekers and employees simply prefer to work for organizations that value gender diversity. And a cycle is created. The brightest and best prefer gender-diverse organizations, and those organizations then perform better. Second, gender diversity simply produces more innovative ideas. Women working in organizations that do not promote diversity are reluctant to speak up, and the organization suffers for that. From my perspective, this factor is particularly significant for project teams, as they innovate, create, and produce value for their clients or organization. Third, investors, particularly those in more gender-diverse communities, associate gender diversity with better leadership and are more inclined to invest in those companies.[75]

Lipman discusses the 3D brain imagery work done by Dr. Ragini Verma, who observed that the connections in women's brains cross from one hemisphere to the other more frequently, suggesting that they are predisposed to multitasking. Men's brain scans show fewer connections between the left and right hemispheres.[76] Does that observation explain why some believe that men and women often have very different approaches to solving the same problem?

Google has invested considerable time and energy trying to understand why women have such a hard time getting hired there. Google says it tries hard to hire the right people, because hiring the wrong person can do such damage to the company. Yet Google's hiring process screens out women at a significantly higher rate than it screens out men.[77] To improve gender diversity in our organizations, we need to ensure that our hiring process fairly evaluates male and female candidates without structural biases.

And then, to increase the percentage of women in the C-suite, we must keep them in the pipeline. When women decide to stay home to raise their children, as many women have done, it can be exceedingly difficult to reenter the workforce in influential positions. And the COVID-19 world has been particularly hard for working mothers.

In a study done at Yale University, 127 scientists were asked to evaluate candidates for a lab assistant position. "The résumés were identical—except for the applicant's sex. The scientists, like Google executives, were certain that they were making evidence-based decisions. Yet they judged the 'male' applicants to be more competent, and offered them salaries that averaged $4,000 more than the women's. The scientists were biased against women in ways they weren't even aware of."[78]

And Lipman points out that women, more than men, will take negative feedback so personally that it undermines their confidence. Seeing this phenomenon, some men have stopped providing negative feedback to women, even though such feedback might help them improve their performance.[79] And in this #MeToo era, some men have taken it a step further and refused to travel or dine with women.

I understand the need to be smart, but we must find

a way to work together successfully, and managers need to manage. If you are taking the men on your teams to lunch for one-on-ones, it's hard to justify not doing the same with the women on your teams.

Racial and Ethnic Discrimination

I would argue that, similarly, leaders need to become involved in the corporate fight to close the racial and ethnic gap. We are living through difficult times in the United States, as protestors demand that we focus on the inequities that people of color have lived with for centuries. All leaders, regardless of race or color, need to dig within themselves and examine their feelings when they interview candidates who don't look like them – and begin to understand where racism and biases, perhaps unconscious or unadmitted, may be influencing their hiring decisions.

Licensed and independent clinical social worker Resmaa Menakem writes in his 2017 book, *My Grandmother's Hands: Racialized Trauma and the Pathway to Mending Our Hearts and Bodies*, about the physical and neurological impact on the body from long-term racism and abuse, dating back to the Middle Ages. He writes that this trauma is passed on for generations and lies deep within our bodies. It informs how our "lizard brains," not our thinking brains, react to stress. We can only make progress on healing this trauma when we pay attention to how our bodies react when we read news reports or hear information that makes us uncomfortable.[80]

As leaders, we have a duty to pay attention to the reactions of those around as well. This is why, in Chapter 13 when I talk about meetings, I note my strong preference for in-person meetings (when possible). They allow us to observe body language, in addition to facial indicators.

Can hiring managers offer candidates a chance to tell their personal story when they interview? It depends on the organization. Legally, there are questions that we can't ask in job interviews. But we all have stories to tell, and we all profit from hearing the stories of others.

In a 1999 *New York Times* article, "When Fear of Firing Deters Hiring," Jeffrey Seglin writes about a concern that has emerged in today's litigious society. Some companies are simply not as interested in hiring candidates who are in protected classes under antidiscrimination laws, because the risk of a lawsuit if the relationship sours is simply greater than the perceived benefit to the organization.[81] What a shame! I wonder if that tide has turned since the article was published.

Put aside the reasons or logic behind unconscious biases; sex, gender, racial, or ethnic discrimination; or judgmental attitudes that might factor into hiring decisions. You need a diverse team to get the best results. Yet, it's important to keep in mind that diversity on your teams has the objective of improving performance. Let's not get too excited and pat ourselves on the back because we've made some diverse hires and then forget to manage them. You must hold them accountable for their performance. And regardless of race, gender, etc., you need to document difficulties, should they arise. Great managers make a difference.

According to Adrian Gostick and Chester Elton, authors of The Best Team Wins, researchers at Gallup found that "manager behaviors explain 70 percent of the variance in employees' daily work engagement, and academics from Stanford University and the University of Utah have discovered that nine-person teams led by engaging bosses are as productive as ten-person teams led by average or poor bosses."[82] You must continue to guide, inspire, and motivate your employees and your project teams.

Compensation System

Project managers rarely have any control over their organization's compensation system. But they will suffer when the compensation system is set up for failure.

If bonuses are tied to the success of operational goals, don't be surprised if team members shortcut some project work. And when people are clearly being rewarded to produce new clients, they won't be as interested in spending time on needed documentation or process improvements. If you ask a commission-only salesperson to work on a side project, be prepared to compensate for that work. While input from salespeople may be needed on a new design project, they won't be highly motivated to contribute if they aren't being paid for that work.

If you are paying contractors to work on your project on an hourly basis, this rewards inefficiency. Have you considered fixed-price engagements or incentives for coming in under budget or early? Clearly the popularity of freelance sites (such as Fiver) that allow you to hire contractors on a fixed-price basis suggests some interest in that approach. Everything I read suggests the gig economy is expanding, though recent legal decisions may impact how we treat gig workers.

Have you set up a compensation structure that rewards individual performance when aiming to improve team performance? Ensure that your compensation structure is aligned with your goals and objectives so that you are financially rewarding the behaviors you want to encourage.

Setting direction is one of the key responsibilities of leaders. Can you imagine going on a flight or a cruise if the pilot or captain wasn't clear on the destination? First, CEOs must know what direction they want to take, and then they must be able to communicate that direction effectively. The vision, as espoused by top leaders, together with HR policies and compensation structures, must all align. It doesn't work when everyone isn't on the same page.

And this applies at the project level as well as the organization level. In the next chapter, I discuss some ways to build better leaders in your organization.

Chapter 10

Can Effective Leaders Be Groomed?

Effective leaders, both at the project and the organization level, often share a handful of characteristics that can be developed. People must *want* to improve, but perhaps they need a little encouragement from more senior leaders. In this chapter, I examine emotional intelligence, perspective, and communication skills, and offer suggestions for how to improve them. Strong organizations and project teams depend on the ability of leaders to inspire, energize, and motivate others.

Albert Schweitzer reportedly remarked, "In everyone's life, at some time, our inner fire goes out. It is then burst into flame by an encounter with another human being. We should all be thankful for those people who rekindle the inner spirit."

Emotional Intelligence

High emotional intelligence (EI) is essential for effective leadership. Daniel Goleman notes in *Leadership: The Power of Emotional Intelligence* that we see EI in four areas: self-awareness, social awareness, relationship management, and self-management.[83] Let's look briefly at each of these.

Self-Awareness

To be self-aware, we must understand ourselves. We must be able to recognize what is driving us – our minds or our emotions. This awareness helps us to provide constructive feedback when needed. And people who are self-aware can comfortably discuss their own strengths and weaknesses.[84]

Self-awareness means that we can take a good long look in the mirror and be honest about whether our ego is interfering. Strong leaders, with self-awareness, can make tough decisions and execute them. These leaders ask a lot of questions and learn from their key team members. Pay attention to situations in which you intellectually know how you should behave, but you aren't behaving that way. It may indicate that your ego is interfering. It may come in the form of procrastination, argumentativeness, defensiveness, conflict avoidance, people pleasing, or a host of other knee-jerk reactions.

Social Awareness

People with high levels of social awareness typically show great empathy, are organizationally astute, and often have a service mindset. They know when to offer constructive feedback. They get along well with others, listen attentively, and can spot power imbalances.

Empathy is increasingly important for several reasons. Globalization and the resulting diversity of teams and organizations requires teams to make greater efforts to understand cultural differences and give people the benefit of the doubt. Work is growing increasingly complex as rapidly changing technologies offer us greater options. This comes with pressures to retain, grow, and inspire talent and it's hard to do that in a culture that doesn't reflect any empathy. And yet, it's important to understand that empathy can be used for unethical reasons, for example, in some police interrogations, military operations, and/or political posturing.

Servant leadership is a term coined by Robert Greenleaf in the 1970s, though some would argue that Jesus Christ introduced the idea. The basic concept is that leaders serve the people, including employees, clients, vendors, members, or the public. Leadership is less about power and more about service. The subject has become increasingly popular with the business community as peer-reviewed studies and new books are published that suggest its effectiveness.

Relationship Management

Relationship management requires that we ask ourselves if we need to be right, or if we need a resolution. Take the high road. Find agreement. Ask the other person to share their perspective. Avoid a rebuttal. Share your side too, but avoid sharing examples that are an effort to outdo the other person. Pursue forward movement. Eliminate sarcasm from your relationship management approach (or better yet, from your workplace, entirely). Sarcasm usually masks conflict instead of addressing it effectively.

Self-Management

Self-management can be seen in one's ability to control impulsivity. People who are good at regulating their behavior typically spend time on reflection and are more comfortable with change and ambiguity. They usually have a high level of integrity. To be effective, leaders (including project leaders) must have the motivation to channel their positive emotions into results. The best leaders can use multiple styles of leadership and evaluate when to use each, for the best results.

Figure 2 illustrates the four areas of emotional intelligence that Goleman discusses.

Figure 2: Emotional Intelligence

Self-Awareness

How aware are you of your strengths and weaknesses?

Social Awareness

How aware are you of the impact you have on others?

What are you doing to improve on your weaknesses?

Self-Management

How can you use your strengths to improve your relationships?

Relationship Management

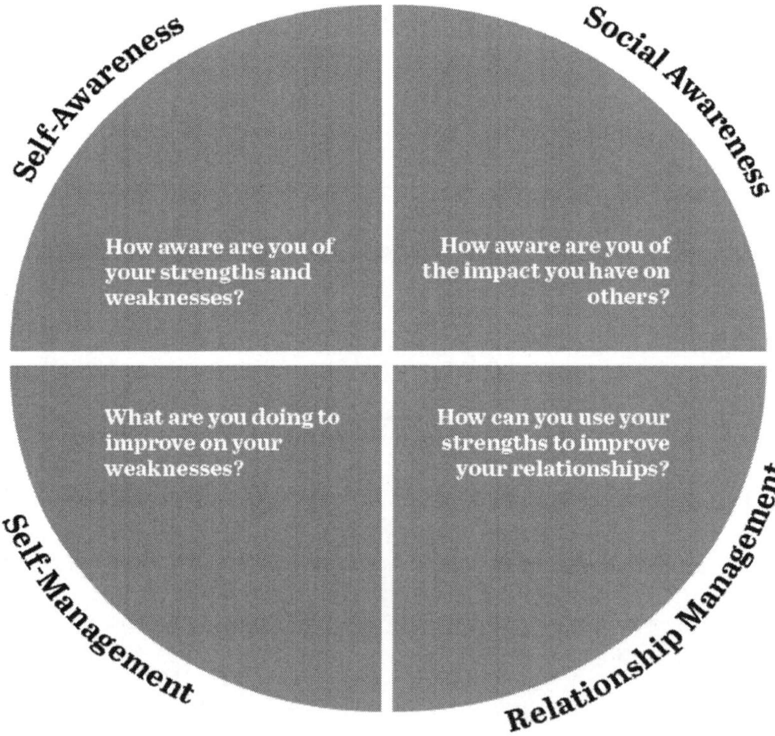

Identifying Emotions

Drs. Travis Bradberry and Jean Greaves, in their 2009 book *Emotional Intelligence* 2.0, recommend that we accept that we will feel events and conversations on an emotional level before we process them on a rational level. That's the way the brain is physically structured. The authors report that all emotions stem from five basic feelings – shame, fear, anger, sadness, and happiness.[85]

We need to encourage people on our project teams, and throughout our organizations, to name their emotions without judging them. Feelings are not "good" or "bad." People are entitled to feel whatever they feel. They can name that feeling but they still need to show up and go to work the next day. It is okay to feel angry, for example. It is not okay to sabotage your project, withhold valuable information, or act with malice or disrespect to the people around you because you are angry. As leaders, we need to remember that behavior can be a little bit like a volcano; there can be a lot of rumbling under the surface, before the lava spews out.[86]

Perspective

Closely tied to emotional intelligence is the ability to capitalize on perspectives, to understand your own perspective, and those of others. Where are you standing?

I remember one of the first high-profile projects that I managed. I was young and inexperienced and running the commercial credit services department for a major bank. It was a project to completely redecorate some offices that included a large room containing many, many paper files, stored on shelving from floor to ceiling. There were files on all the bank's customers – past and present, local, national, and international. There were no backup files online. This was it. Nothing could get lost or misplaced. No exceptions.

The major activity for the coming weekend was to replace the carpeting, which looked about 100 years old.

The project came and went, rather successfully – as best I remember. But what I vividly remember was a conversation when it was all over, with an older and wiser man who worked in one of the offices that we renovated.

He called me in, allegedly to thank me for my hard work, but, in our conversation, he asked me if I had ever watched any old Westerns on television. He asked me if I knew where the Indian chief was during a battle. I said no. The Indian chief, he proceeded to tell me, was on top of the mountain. That way, he could see everything unfolding.

He noted that I had spent much of my time in the trenches with the team, ensuring that everything was happening according to the plan. To this day, I'm not sure what he thought I missed by being in the trenches. Perhaps he thought one of the carpet installers took too many breaks or that a lending officer had snuck into the space and stolen a few files. Nevertheless, his point was still valid. Perspective matters. Where are you standing?

For example, traditional project management often looks at resources from a perspective of scarcity. Project managers bargain with functional managers for the "best" resources (in this case, people) and may complain that they can't get the people they need when they need them. It can be considered a badge of honor to be wanted by these feisty project managers who fight on behalf of their projects.

There is another perspective. When we change our mindset, we can view our projects and organizations with a sense of gratitude and abundance. Even in the most cash-strapped and resource-lacking organizations, viewing resources from the perspective of abundance refocuses the conversation from frustration to gratitude, from lemons to lemonade, from resource availability to available resources. Managing resources becomes a question of how creatively you can think, and how you value or treat your resources.

Think about how hardship forces companies to get creative. Businesses undergo complete pivots, often changing processes, procedures, and resource structuring. The less creative companies have often been forced out of business.

Start-ups frequently think about resources more creatively than long-established companies, which often regard free parking as a major employee perk. Over the years, we have seen pool and ping-pong tables, meditation rooms, and office happy hours on the list of touted offerings thought to attract people. Now, we are likely to view a work from home option as a desirable perk when the COVID-19 virus concerns wane and we begin a real return to "normal" (whatever that may be). Any creatively thinking project team will have a list of things that it considers resources; that list could include intangible items, such as meditation breaks, recreation opportunities, or even a neighborhood park where it likes to meet. How can you use your resources more creatively?

David Whyte, the English poet, and business consultant, helps businesses "harness the insights and metaphors that poetry can offer to broaden their language, improve interaction within the workplace and stir imaginations."[87]

According to Whyte, we look at things differently when we are tired or stressed. Until I started reading about Whyte, I viewed that as a bad thing – and rarely pushed myself to use those times of exhaustion to question what is happening. But perhaps our teams can use poetry, among other tools, to better reflect on next steps during challenging or exhausting times. The *London Times* reported that Whyte likes to use the images and metaphors often found in poetry to explore the problems and conversations that arise in work. He finds that, "A lot of the images will have to do with being lost, with not having the usual bearings, and therefore looking at the world in a different way."[88]

Our perspective, whether it is based on exhaustion from meeting too many deadlines, joy following a family vacation, extra rest stemming from imposed solitude, or years of diverse project experience, can be a valuable resource – as are the perspectives of your varied team members.

One of my favorite stories that speaks to the importance of how our perspective can guide our communication comes from a book on Abraham Lincoln. According to author Donald T. Phillips, Lincoln believed in people, in individual rights, and in the need to stay close to his people. He reportedly said: "Gentlemen, suppose all the property you were worth was in gold and this you had placed in the hands of one man to carry across the Niagara River on a rope. Would you shake the cable and keep shouting at him: 'Stand up a little straighter; stoop a little more, go a little faster, go a little slower, lean a little more to the south?' No, you would hold your breath, as well as your tongue, and keep your hands off until he got safely over. The Government is carrying an enormous weight. Untold treasure is in their hands. Don't badger them. Keep silence and we will get you safely across."[89]

When you organize your project using the methodology that I discuss in Part 3, you need to start by trusting the team to deliver the results that they promised. Only when they begin to fail to do that should you begin interfering with what they are doing or attempting to micromanage the work. You need to focus your efforts on building a culture characterized by trust, respect, and acceptance to innovate, create, and quickly deliver results that matter.

Strong Communication Skills

Communication has always been considered a critical part of project leadership, but in recent years, people increasingly understand that it's not just about well-written emails or memos. Effective project communications are needed to inform people about project events, industry trends, and stakeholder conflicts. We need to properly communicate changes effectively, understand the constant barrage of decisions that are routinely made as projects unfold, and reduce deliverable acceptance problems. Sometimes our communications must be persuasive and thorough, while other times they must simply alert people to changes that are underway.

The Smart Projex methodology (discussed in Part 3) involves meetings with face-to-face communications, because much can get lost in the clutter of emails, texts, faxes, mailings, and phone messages. Here are some ways to improve communication skills.

Increase Transparency in Communications

One way that leaders protect their people is to explain their decisions, rather than keeping people in the dark. Think about how it feels to arrive at a campsite after dark and how scary the darkness can be. That's the way employees feel when they are not kept informed. Your teams are not mushrooms. Don't keep them in the dark and feed them fertilizer.

Use Meeting Time Effectively

I discuss meetings more fully in Chapter 13. Here, I offer some suggestions to help you use your meetings to improve your communications. Insist that participants arrive at meetings on time and put away their phones. You want everyone's full attention. Start on time. End on time. Respect people's schedules and other commitments.

Some firms love to have company-wide presentations with mandatory attendance. Typically, participants hate them – unless there is a huge and exciting announcement, and everyone needs to hear the message together.

For most of your meetings, I recommend that you engage with your participants. To encourage dialogue, use open-ended questions. Ask questions that will help differentiate opinions from facts. Ask for disagreement or collaboration. Use questions wisely to get people to think. Don't treat the meeting as a listening session, except perhaps for yourself, if you are in charge. Encourage participants to practice active listening. And listen for what is not being said. Don't be afraid of silence.

Consider using a talking stick if your in-person meetings tend to be on the rowdy side. The person who is holding the stick is the only one who can talk. And, when people finish talking, they need to return the talking stick to a central location. This time while the speaker is returning the talking stick is a valuable time for people to process the comments that have just been made.

Plan Your Meetings in Advance

Understand the purpose of each meeting conversation. Think through want you want to accomplish so that you can appropriately direct the conversations. Know what decisions need to be made or what actions need to be taken. Rambling chitchat with no focus doesn't advance your project. Eliminate side chatter and ensure that all dialogue on the topic is directed to the whole group. Don't be afraid to call out people who are having side banter and politely ask them if there is a matter that needs the group's attention. Or request that they postpone their private discussion until after the meeting.

Some experts recommend real-time meeting agendas for some meetings. This means that the first few minutes of the meeting are spent outlining what needs to be covered. The idea is that meetings will be used to address what is most important to the participants, based on what is happening on the ground. While there may be times when this is an appropriate strategy, I usually think that a little forethought about the objectives for the meeting will produce better results.

If things are changing so fast that a meeting agenda becomes obsolete before you convene the meeting, I'd start by creating a real-time agenda, but then I'd get clarity on what outcomes are needed from the topics at hand. Avoid endless talk that doesn't get you anywhere. Brainstorming is great but it can quickly become a time suck. Stick to your agenda, or to your objectives. Don't let "shiny object syndrome" take over. Agree to set aside some items for further attention, document them in a list, defer them until another meeting, and continue with your agenda.

While you should put out an advance agenda and perhaps supplementary materials, avoid handing out wordy PowerPoint slides immediately before a meeting. According to author and communications professional Eric Bergman, "cognitive science tells us that humans cannot read and listen at the same time. In fact, trying to do both is absolutely the least effective option and a virtual waste of time—terrible news for the 'average' slide-driven presentation delivered in boardrooms, meeting rooms, training rooms and conference halls."[90]

People remember the best meetings as those during which participants solved some pressing problems, made specific decisions, and accomplished important objectives. Before you adjourn, review the accomplishments and action items to ensure that everyone is on the same page.

Develop Consensus About the Messaging Before the Meeting Adjourns

Very importantly, ensure that there is agreement on the message that is to be communicated after the meeting. When people leave a meeting and pass along different ideas to their subordinates, it sabotages your efforts to build alignment among your teams. People need to hear consistent messages from all the leaders.

Learn How to Handle Difficult People Effectively

In a perfect world, we would always hire the best people, and never have difficult colleagues, clients, or vendors. But we don't live in a perfect world. And so, we do need some ability to work with difficult people.

And to innovate, sometimes it's essential that we spark healthy conflicts. People will have different opinions. Teams need to engage in vigorous debate. It may well get tense. That's okay.

According Kerry Patterson and Joseph Grenny, authors of *Crucial Conversations: Tools for Talking When Stakes Are High*, "close to 80 percent of the projects that require cross-functional cooperation cost far more than expected, produce less than hoped for, and run significantly over budget."[91] The authors provided no citation on this statistic. The 80 percent may be high, but the point is valid. The authors believe the root problem is people's inability to have difficult conversations.[92]

It's best to begin with the assumption that folks are doing the best they can. If that assumption fails you, here are eight tips:

1. Avoid acting in anger.

Reasoned conversations require rationality, which evaporates in the presence of anger. Don't try to reason with anyone who is angry or emotionally charged for any reason. Find a way to manage your own anger and wait to work out problems when you are more rational. That means not tweeting or sending emails when you are angry.

2. Get to know your people.

It's harder to hate the people you know well. We need to show up and embrace others when they are experiencing pain or joy. Times of collective emotion remind us of what is possible and the goodness of humanity.

3. Show empathy as you seek solutions.

Empathize with the other person by understanding what strategy might be most important to him or her. And then strive for commonalities, working towards a win-win solution. Keep the focus away from personalities and on finding good solutions.

4. Focus on the big goals.

Keep your overall goal in mind when you are talking with difficult people. Begin with the right motives. What do you want out of this relationship in the longer term and what does the difficult person want or need? Can you help this person get where they want to go? Can this person help you get where you want to go? Can there be a win-win result? Considering those answers, how should you behave?

5. Don't waste time trying to change others.

The only person you can change is yourself. Don't waste your time trying to change others. Be aware that dialogue is harder with people who have a strong need to win. Ask yourself if you need a resolution that works, or if you need to win.

6. Ask for feedback.

Try using open-ended questions and actively listen. Don't expect people to read your mind. When you are in group meetings, make it safe for everyone to contribute. When groups engage in dialogue about difficult subjects, it's easier to get commitment to the final decision. Don't avoid the messy middle part of conversations. That's where the magic often emerges.

7. Use face-to-face meetings to resolve conflicts.

It's hard to resolve serious conflicts over Zoom. But conflicts must be resolved. And once you have done that, consider recapping what transpired in a follow-up email. But be careful about what you document and how you disseminate that communication. It's best to get advice from your HR team, particularly if someone is likely to be terminated.

8. Turn on your better self.

Use your charming personality when dealing with difficult people; be kind and share any credit that they rightfully deserve. Remember that they want to feel important too. Thank them for their hard work, if appropriate. Great managers take all the blame when problems arise and share the credit when success is achieved.

Project and organizational leaders should be finding ways to improve their leadership abilities – by focusing on their emotional intelligence, perspectives, and communication skills. And as they do that, they can begin to build more effective teams, which I cover in the next chapter.

Chapter 11

Build Strong Teams to Improve Project Results

One important job of leaders is to build stronger teams and thereby improve project results. Nineteenth-century steel magnate and noted philanthropist Andrew Carnegie reportedly said: "Teamwork is the ability to work together toward a common vision. The ability to direct individual accomplishments toward organizational objectives. It is the fuel that allows common people to attain uncommon results." In this chapter, I discuss three important ways that leaders can do that. They create a healthy culture characterized by trust and kindness, focus on delivering work to and communicating with the client more frequently, and build accountable and self-managing teams.

Create a Healthy Culture

Culture is everything. And if you aren't sure of the truth of that statement, consider the colossal failure of the Boeing 737 project. In 2019, 346 people died because a Boeing plane crashed. The investigation pointed to major design flaws exacerbated by a culture characterized by deception and massive cost-cutting efforts. And that's just one Boeing story.

Culture begins at the organizational level but cascades down into the ranks. Project teams develop their own cultures, but they should align with the values of the organization. Strong companies are characterized by cohesive leadership teams that are united in their focus and know how to communicate it effectively. Values aren't just public statements but are part of the DNA of the organization. When your organization and projects are led by people who are individually focused on departmental goals, silos can develop, and organizational health can deteriorate.

In this socially connected world, we frequently read of companies that have been called out for disconnects between what the company says and how it acts. Be careful about the values that you espouse. Make sure they aren't just feel-good ideas, but instead, values that you fully support. For example, transparency sounds great until your mistakes are exposed to the entire world. And will actions that align with the values that your company espouses deprive employees of their personal freedoms? It's more complicated than it looks on the surface.

And it's going to get increasingly more complicated as artificial intelligence, bioengineering, and emerging technologies that I can't fathom present us with choices that will test the limits of our society. For example, when autonomous vehicles become the norm, how will decisions be made about whose life is more valuable in the nanoseconds before a car crash? Which passenger or pedestrian is spared? Should humans be able to marry robots and what rights do robots have? Just because we can turn a person into a robot, should we? And aren't some of these consequential decisions much larger than any one organization, or even any one country?

If these questions seem too far removed from the reality that you imagine, consider that CNN reported that "thousands of people in Sweden have inserted microchips in their hands that could one day replace keys and cards. Elon Musk recently showed off a working brain implant in pigs made by Neuralink, his brain-computer interface company."[93] And Greg Yanke, a securities lawyer and academic, published an article on robot marriage in *AI & Society* in 2021. In it, he says "Technological progress may eventually produce sophisticated robots with human-like traits that result in humans forming meaningful relationships with them. Such relationships would likely lead to a demand for human–artificial intelligence (AI) matrimony."[94] He discusses what will need to happen, legally and technologically, before this happens but clearly thinks it is on the horizon.

Use Thematic Goals to Align the Culture

Patrick Lencioni, in his book *The Advantage*, advocates the use of a thematic goal to serve as the organization's single focus. A thematic goal is achievable in a defined time frame and shared across the entire organization. Clarity and full executive support are key.[95]

This is what Paul O'Neill did to turn Alcoa around when he took over in 1987. He focused exclusively on worker safety. Even though Alcoa's safety record was strong, O'Neill baffled investors by choosing worker safety as the focus. He understood that the people in the trenches would rally around worker safety, more than improving financial results. And he understood that to eliminate worker accidents, you must dissect every process, thus ultimately improving financial results.

According to Lencioni, leadership teams need to be able to outline the company's focus on one page. It might consist of one thematic goal, several defining objectives, and several standard operating objectives. Defining objectives are the projects that need to occur to accomplish the thematic goal. Standard operating objectives are the operational activities that must occur for a company to stay in business. They are not tied to the calendar and are often ongoing objectives.[96, 97]

It is essential that the thematic goal and the defining and operational objectives are supported by the entire executive team, and not simply divided up among functional heads, which can lead to division in your organization.[98, 99]

In another book, *Silos, Politics and Turf Wars: A Leadership Fable About Destroying the Barriers That Turn Colleagues into Competitors*, Lencioni urges caution in assigning metrics to objectives. Dates are good. Some metrics are appropriate. But even executives can lose interest in meeting revenue goals every month. It's more powerful to drive the energy into time-bound thematic goals that will result in improved revenues or reduced expenditures.[100]

Perhaps I should mention that a singular focus, as Lencioni describes it, can become a keystone habit, as Charles Duhigg terms it. Keystone habits, which are patterns or habits that seem to promote a chain reaction, can transform organizations. Changing them opens the door to changing other things. When businesses can identify a keystone habit and change that, it often results in improvements down the line.[101] And the kinds of regular meetings that I discuss in Chapter 13 can become keystone habits, and ultimately transform your organization.

Increase Safety in the Organization

A healthy organizational culture is also characterized by a sense of safety, where people aren't afraid and they feel supported. However, that sense of safety can be hard to maintain in times of chaos. One suggestion for creating a sense of safety is to model a tone of voice that de-escalates conversations during times of tension. We've all worked with folks who have an annoying habit of quickly becoming agitated or who seem angry much of the time, perhaps for good reason. But this angry tone tends to escalate the tension. If we can train ourselves to step back, think, take a few breaths, and respond in a soothing or comforting tone of voice, we can be the calming influence that our teams need. Great times of productivity don't have to emerge from a place of anger. They can come from a place of love, caring, investment, and desire. Those emotions can be about the future, but anger, by definition, is about the past. Projects should be about the future.

In *Leaders Eat Last: Why Some Teams Pull Together and Others Don't*, Simon Sinek talks about the "Circle of Safety" and retells an Aesop fable from the sixth century BC. "A lion used to prowl about a field in which Four Oxen used to dwell. Many a time he tried to attack them; but whenever he came near they turned their tails to one another, so that whichever way he approached them he was met by the horns of one of them. At last, however, they fell a-quarrelling among themselves, and each went off to pasture alone in a separate corner of the field. Then the Lion attacked them one by one and soon made an end of all four."[102]

Sinek focuses extensively on our natural biological state and how stress, chaos, lack of trust, and ruthless behaviors impact teams. Dopamine and endorphins are the chemicals that drive us to achieve, whether that means finding food, building things, or accomplishing goals. Oxytocin and serotonin are the chemicals that help with sociability. Serotonin is responsible for that sense of pride that we take in the people who work for us, while oxytocin inspires loyalty, trust, and kindness. Leaders need to develop cultures that work with the natural biological state.[103]

Putting aside the question of whether there is any scientific basis for what Sinek argues, what would it look like if leaders were able to capitalize on what nature gives humanity in how they develop their team culture?

Teams are better able to manage themselves and the challenges of the project when they don't have to cope with dangers inside of the organization. Leaders need to build a safe environment in their organizations. A short-term-oriented, numbers-driven culture harms the people in our organizations, and our society at large.

Even Jack Welch, who was famous for ruthlessly rearranging teams to improve results, understood the need for protecting employees. Author Robert Slater was given great access to Welch and his team when he wrote *Jack Welch & The G.E. Way*. And in Slater's book, *29 Leadership Secrets from Jack Welch*, Slater credited Welch with this thought: "The way to get faster, more productive, and more competitive is to unleash the energy and intelligence and raw, ornery self-confidence of the American worker, who is still by far the most productive and innovative in the world.... The way to harness the power of these people is to protect them, not to sit on them, but to turn them loose, let them go—get the management layers off their backs, the bureaucratic shackles off their feet, and the function barriers out of their way."[104]

Can We Build Kindness in Our Teams?

As my grandmother said, we get more flies with honey than vinegar. Can we treat people like they want to be treated? Can we be a little kinder? Can we focus on helping our teams work together a little better?

In their book *The Best Team Wins*, Adrian Gostick and Chester Elton recount the experience of Chris Hadfield, who served as commander of the International Space Station for five months. He attributes the success of their mission to one rule that he enforced with his team. Each day, every person on the team had to perform at least one kind act for someone else on the team. Hadfield reports that he spent an enormous amount of time making sure that everyone on the team knew each other well.[105]

Focus on Delivering Work to the Client More Frequently

The second way leaders can build stronger teams for better project results is to have a client focus. If you have never been through a serious business downturn, you may not understand the importance of your paying clients. Treat them with appreciation and respect. In traditional Scrum methodology, teams work in "sprints" (short, specific, recurring periods of time) on a set of activities (often, software features) that are supposed to be delivered by the end of the sprint. Teams get no credit, so to speak, for unfinished features. This is a different mindset from what I frequently see in business projects where teams keep working away (and perhaps, billing time), but don't ever seem to deliver anything to the client.

Take for example, an advertising agency that is hired to design a campaign for a new retail store opening. The team is formed after the contract is signed. There are meetings, discussions, and emails, and two days before the deadline, the team locks itself in a room until the first project phase is finished. I understand the need for ideas to percolate, but what happens if the client hates the work?

Client relationships can be hard to dissect, particularly when your client is a large company. Who is authorized to make routine project decisions? Who is to be involved in periodic meetings with the team? Who authorizes bill payments? Who approves major changes? Who approves quality? What escalation process is there to ensure that major project news is communicated to the appropriate people?

Focus on understanding your client's needs, preferences, desires, and business model. Continue to engage the client throughout the project so that changing needs are identified promptly. And provide more value with each succeeding encounter.

And if your client has another client who is the ultimate user and paying for the work, don't leave them out of your client planning process.

I should add that I'm specifically referring to relationships where you are creating a product or service to meet the needs of a single client(s) or in-house projects. When you are creating products that are then sold to many customers, such as software or razors, there is the notion of paying too much attention to the customer. That is different. I'm specifically talking about projects being completed for a single client (though it may well be a large entity) or projects being completed in-house, where your management team functions as the project team's client. Can we focus more on delighting the clients who are paying us for our work?

Build Accountable, Self-Managing Teams

In addition to building a healthy culture and focusing on delivering value to their clients, the most effective leaders build accountable teams and allow them some autonomy. Here are three ways leaders can do that.

Expect the Team to Struggle and Grow

Understand that if you want to build team effectiveness, the team needs to go through a development process, sometimes affectionately referred to as forming, storming, norming, and performing. Let this happen. It is completely normal, and the team will gain much as it struggles to find its own way.

A team charter can help; it allows the team to document the behavioral and work expectations. Different cultures will have different rules, and these need to be discussed and documented.

In her book *Braving the Wilderness*, Brené Brown puts forth the acronym BRAVING to remind us of what it means to brave the wilderness. This acronym, depicted in Figure 3, is a great way to think about your project team culture.

Figure 3: BRAVING

Boundaries: And the need to respect them;
Reliability: Do what you promised;
Accountability: Own your mistakes;
Vault: Are there secrets that shouldn't be shared outside the team?
Integrity: Choose what is right;
Needs: Are people free to request help and get it without judgment?
Generosity: Be generous in how you interpret words and deeds.[106]

If your project manager has insufficient coaching experience, consider hiring a professional coach to work with your team and your project manager.

When we can help everyone in the organization to focus on their own growth, it can help reduce system-wide cultural dysfunctions.

According to Slater, the previously mentioned authority on Jack Welch, managing less can mean managing better. Rarely does it improve performance when managers hover or over-manage the people under them. "Emphasize vision, not supervision," says Slater.[107]

Build Accountability to Each Other and the Client

Assign a person on the team to oversee each activity or let team members pick the activities they are most interested in leading. Allow these leaders to manage their activities. When I built Smart Projex 1.0 (the software), I recommended having a backup activity leader as well. While teams must be accountable to clients and management for performance, this is only possible if everyone on the team has clear expectations about what each participant is expected to accomplish. By helping people be accountable to each other, we enable teams to be accountable to the client.

Leah Weiss is a leading researcher, author, and consultant who teaches at the Stanford Graduate School of Business and is an expert on leadership, compassion, and mindfulness. According to her book, *How We Work: Live Your Purpose, Reclaim Your Sanity, and Embrace the Daily Grind*, work is one place where we can train our minds to be more compassionate and to engage others to hold us accountable for being better people. Compassion and empathy aren't the same. According to Weiss, compassion drives us to action while empathy simply allows us to relate to another's feelings.[108]

Let Go and Allow the Team to Self-Manage

When you can empower a team to self-manage, everyone benefits. If you have the good fortune to work for multiple clients, your teams will need to frequently reprioritize their work. This depends on the industry, of course. Information technology (IT) is particularly fraught with prioritization problems, where building construction work is less so. But from your client's perspective, anything can happen.

If a subcontractor fails to show up with the required materials on one of your job sites, this can immediately throw everything up in the air. You may have to cancel some scheduled work, but will you seize any opportunity to adjust other work in some beneficial way? Someone needs to be at the 10,000-foot level watching everything and preparing to pivot.

In the IT world, not only can anything happen – it often does. One of your websites can go down. A hacker can wreak havoc. A software deployment can unleash undiscovered bugs. Every piece of software that you use produces frequent updates that impact everything else.

This is when it pays to work with great people whom you trust. Shopping for the lowest-cost provider will often result in problems down the road when things don't go well.

Understanding what your client is going through every day helps immensely. Recognize that salespeople typically overpromise because they aren't the ones called on to deliver – and they get paid to *sell*. As a result, we sometimes keep our clients and customers happy by loading up the product development folks with project activities that aren't aligned with other aspects of our strategic objectives.

For most organizations, retaining good customers is paramount. Depending on your product mix and your business model, client or customer acquisition can be expensive. Good clients can be hard to find. But when you are spending a disproportionate amount of time and money to retain clients, you may need to reevaluate whether specific clients are worth the investment. Yes, you can fire a client. I don't recommend doing it willy-nilly. But sometimes, the client relationship is unhealthy, unprofitable, and unsalvageable.

Do you have good metrics on what your client acquisition and retention work is costing you and the profit margin for your high-dollar clients? This is particularly important in high-dollar service-oriented businesses, such as law firms, luxury custom furniture makers, and highly customized enterprise level software products.

So much depends on your industry and your organization, but having a culture that is team-oriented and encourages open dialogue where problems are discussed honestly and frequently works far better than expecting people to just solve their own problems and work in silos. While you seek to improve your culture, build more effective teams, and improve your client responsiveness, it's important to be clear about the various roles that people are fulfilling on your projects. In the next chapter, I outline some strategies for improving role clarity.

Chapter 12

Clarify Project Roles to Reduce the Cats' Confusion

When a new project is launched, executives will typically introduce the project manager and the project sponsor, but these key people may have different titles. There are other players, some more key than others, who can impact your projects, and I outline some of them in this chapter. While trained project managers certainly understand the importance of role clarity, I discuss this here because the Smart Projex methodology is so much more focused on relationship management than schedule or task management.

But first, I need to talk about the importance of having an effective project manager and strong capabilities on the implementation team, including any hired contractors. There is no substitute for skill knowledge. Consider the FBI's 2000 effort to develop a case management system, in a major technology upgrade, referred to as the Trilogy project. Five years later, the project was abandoned after a loss of $170 million. After the 9/11 attacks, Robert Mueller pushed the three-year schedule forward because of public pressure. The Office of the Inspector General noted in its audit report that: "Despite the use of two contractors to provide three major project components, the FBI did not hire a professional project integrator to manage contractor interfaces and take responsibility for the overall integrity of the final product until the end of 2003. According to FBI IT managers, FBI officials performed the project integrator function even though they had no experience performing such a role."[109]

It's critical that you take some time to find the right people, particularly for your leadership roles, because these people will make or break your project. Build alliances with the people around you, along with clients, customers, and competitors. Alliances can build strength, while divisiveness can create weakness. Create energy in those around you by clearly communicating your powerful vision.

Many of your key players will have important roles and responsibilities, which you should document. Here are some insights on the key players who will influence your project.

Stakeholders

Stakeholder is a collective word that refers to anyone who has the ability or potential to impact your project positively or negatively. The list can be huge, particularly in school and government projects. I've seen it many times. We start a project and get halfway through before anyone realizes that some person or group, in another building, city, state, or country, will be hugely impacted. In some organizations and projects, identifying the impacted stakeholders is often an afterthought. Don't make this mistake.

Identify and understand your stakeholders at the project's start so that you can ensure effective communications with everyone. As you consider how to do this work, you may, for pragmatic reasons, need to consider groups of stakeholders and make some assumptions. And, as you get to know your stakeholders, don't stop with the troublemakers or the loudest voices. The fans of your project are an important base too. It's important to remember that the word "stakeholder," which sounds rather clinical, refers to real people with feelings, emotions, and differing interests and skills.

Ben Horowitz cautions in *The Hard Thing About Hard Things* that teams need to pay attention to stakeholder management. Know the identity of that one "person who can delay the entire project."[110] If only there was just one person who could potentially delay your project.

There will be many stakeholders who are only peripherally involved. However, they too have opinions that matter, and you need to discover what their hot buttons and sweet spots are. You need to know what communication styles work for each stakeholder or stakeholder group. Not everyone does email well. Sometimes a text, phone call, or letter in the mail might be the only way to get a particular person's attention. As you plan the project, you will want to document the communication needs for each stakeholder or group.

Different projects may have special concerns in tracking stakeholder needs, opinions, and communication preferences. Government projects are notorious for having many "interested stakeholders," including the public. International aid projects can have foreign government stakeholders, often in politically unstable and/or less developed countries. Nonprofit projects can have lots of volunteers, making communications a headache. Schools can have student stakeholders and parent stakeholders where interests can diverge.

Have you spent time identifying all the groups that will be impacted by your projects? Have you sat down and talked with representatives from those groups to uncover unknown implications? Have you documented the hot buttons and sweet spots for each group or person? Have you identified how those stakeholders want you to communicate with them? The idea here is to do all you can to prevent the cries of "Nobody asked us/me!"

On large, high-profile projects, you may need a communications professional, supported by a public relations department, to organize this effort. But it's better to understand it from the outset than to wait until you are in the middle of a crisis.

Project Manager

The role of a project manager can vary considerably from firm to firm, and project to project. And the title of a project manager can vary as well. I have adopted this term in this book and define the role as a hybrid between the traditional project manager and a Scrum Master. The project manager sometimes wears a management hat, assigning responsibilities to other team members. Or, the project manager can wear a coaching hat, motivating the team to greatness. The challenge is to know which hat to wear and when. When a project manager, as coach, can successfully empower a team to self-manage, everyone benefits.

Look for leaders with good relationship management skills, as discussed in Chapter 10. They are inspirational and influential. They know how to manage conflict, build teams, lead change initiatives, and develop others.

In some organizations, this role will be called the project leader, and if you are in a Scrum-oriented organization, you will be familiar with Scrum Masters. Most professionals are familiar with the term "project manager" even if they aren't sure exactly what project managers do.

Frequently, the people assigned to your project will officially report to others, and often are paid out of other budgets. Leading a project team of folks without any real management authority is like herding cats. Much depends on the organizational structure, but many organizations operate in functional silos and people are assigned to projects that cross silos. The people working on your project often report up through the silo chain of command and, like cats, they don't have to pay too much attention to you if they are being fed by someone else.

There is a temptation to think that the only thing that project managers do is to manage the flow of work. While that is a big piece of what projects are all about, don't underestimate the importance of relationship building. Not only do project leaders need to manage activities and people, but there are a host of other details that I discuss in Part 3 (methodology).

Project Sponsor

Perhaps one of the most important roles is the project sponsor, though the title can vary by the nature of the project, organization, and industry. In the 2021 PMI *Pulse of the Profession* report, the effectiveness of the project sponsor was deemed the most important success driver, globally.[111] The project sponsor is typically a member of senior management who is the champion for the project. There probably isn't a project sponsor on projects being done for clients; instead, there is more likely a client relationship manager.

A project manager's amount of expertise will often govern the level of oversight that a sponsor needs to exercise over the project manager. In general, the project manager should always act in a way that ensures that the project sponsor will not be caught off guard by his or her management team – whether that is the CEO, an EVP, the board, or the client. It's also a good idea to make sure that no one is caught off guard by the press. Bad surprises are rarely received well.

Regardless of what names you give these various roles, figure out where the relationships are and iron out your communication plan carefully.

If your company is currently operating in a Scrum world, you may be using the term "product owner." And you may have people in your organization who perform the role of product manager – which does seem to be a growing role these days. Later in this chapter, I discuss product managers separately, as they are easily confused.

Regardless of the title, at a minimum, someone on your project must perform these functions to ensure project success:

- Approve the project plan
- Acquire resources
- Prioritize work
- Ensure continued funding (whether it comes from management or a client)
- Approve scope, budget, and schedule changes
- Cancel the project in the event it loses its business value or funding.

Client

One of the most critical players on some projects is the client. During the early phase of a project, it helps to quickly understand the client, its people, its budget range, and its hot-button issues.

Sometimes it's harder than it seems to know your client. With mergers and acquisitions, your client can change. While you may be working with a client representative, there are others in the client's organization, or your own, who can directly impact the project. It is important to identify those players, pinpoint their concerns and perspectives, and document them for future reference. It may be hard to drag this information out of your client in the early days, but continue trying.

When other cultures or languages will impact your project, you need to recognize that fact. You may need to brush up on your knowledge of Ukrainian culture if your software project team includes programmers who are based there, for example.

I have worked on many projects where someone from the client's organization popped up on the radar screen months after the project started and threw monkey wrenches into the product design. I've worked with people in companies where a couple owned the business, and they weren't always aligned on key matters. I've worked with companies where investors played a generally silent role but could intervene in big decisions. The key is to know who these people are and to plan for any potential involvement.

Consider also that your client may have its own customer(s) and perhaps that customer is the ultimate user of whatever you have been hired to build or create. The client's customer may also be funding the work. If you know nothing about that ultimate customer or user, you may be caught unprepared if your client goes too far without checking in with them. You should ask questions of your client that force it to stay in regular contact about the needs of its customer(s) and the ultimate user(s.) Remember, you need periodic feedback from the ultimate user.

Some clients don't like to think about budgets, but that doesn't necessarily mean that they have a blank check or don't care about money. I discuss some money management strategies in later chapters.

Keeping the client engaged on project work is often challenging when company leaders have a gazillion things on their plate and there can be lots of different pieces of technology at play (some of them more effective than others). If you are using Zendesk or some similar ticket-type system to engage with clients, you may find that some of your clients don't like engaging with it, and prefer to email, call, or text you. The same is true of Slack and many project management tools. Keeping the documentation in any one software tool can be tough. But try. It is hugely wasteful to constantly be looking for documentation and customer communications.

If the work you are doing is in-house work, then management functions similarly to your client. Stay connected to your management. Yes, some people are a little harder to work with than others. Deal with it.

As a parent, I always chuckled at other parents who quickly complained to their school administrators when their child's teacher, or a fellow student, was "being difficult." Having "difficult" people in your life can be excellent training for the real world.

Project Team

Complex projects don't go from start to finish without a concerted team effort. It takes different people providing different kinds of assistance to successfully develop and execute complex projects.

Business teams are often made up of diverse groups of people who work with varying levels of time commitment to the project. Subject matter experts can be engaged on a periodic basis to supplement the core team.

And swarm teams, or a group of people who are brought in rapidly and temporarily to focus intently and solve a specific problem, are growing in popularity.

Team effectiveness can be increased when a core

group of team members, who together have the necessary skill sets to execute the project, has a solid commitment to the outcome.

Some people on your team may not be shy about voicing their opinions or concerns and a lot of energy can be spent navigating the differing opinions on how to best accomplish specific activities. Multiple perspectives can help push new ideas to the top, but too many perspectives can paralyze a team. Sooner or later, we must do something and accept the risk that not all stakeholders will be happy.

While not a solution to this challenge, it does help to have software that allows you to document differing perspectives. An Excel spreadsheet will work in a pinch. The key is to make it usable. Sometimes, it is sufficient for everyone to be heard. Most people understand that not everyone gets their way on every issue. Understanding that the team has considered multiple perspectives and after careful thought, has chosen the option that it considered best, will sometimes help.

In the beginning of a project, leaders will need to wrestle with who they want on the project team. This is a critical step and it's important to remember several things:

- you may have to hunt for the right people;
- if your project is compelling, people will want to work on it; and
- reuse your best project teams for greater efficiency.

In the IT world, organizations build highly effective teams and then continue to use them from project to project. It makes the time spent on team building worth the money when a team stays together for years.

Yet elsewhere in the business world, teams frequently come together for a specific project and are then disbanded at the end. What a shame. A highly functioning team is a golden resource – in and of itself. A team that knows how to work well together is more valuable than the sum of its parts. The team members bring out the best in each other.

Build a work distribution approach that allows you to reuse your effective teams. And then occasionally tweak things – to keep your teams energized.

We also need to understand the role those nonconformists play on our teams. Teams benefit from creative thinking, but some people may not react well to new and different ideas. Adam Grant writes about this in his book, *Originals: How Non-Conformists Move the World*. While originals, nonconformists, or people who think differently can be an asset on your project teams, they may come with challenges. According to research conducted by Alison Fragile of the University of North Carolina, organizations can punish employees for making suggestions or trying to exert influence before they have developed status.[112]

Building a culture that welcomes nonconformists can take time. As employees develop status in an organization, they build "idiosyncrasy credits" which they can then use when they have a creative (or wacky) idea that they want to suggest. People simply pay more attention to wacky ideas expressed by people with power.[113] Teach your nonconformists who are new that when they want to propose a new idea, to lead with the weaknesses of the idea. It can make you look smart, since you've already figured out the negatives. It builds trust and can win over the audience.[114] Also, according to Grant, "To form alliances, originals can temper their radicalism by smuggling their real vision inside a Trojan horse."[115]

✓ Leslie

✓ Betsy dorothy

Jinx thompson

new contract 3492894

✓ finish June bday

derm epapers

	3	1.0
... - BOX	25	8.3
...ugh Swirl - BOX	23	7.7
... and Pomegranate Flavoured Bar - BOX	10	3.3
~~...Vanilla Oatmeal - PACKET~~	1	0.3
...armesan Mushroom Pasta - BOX	2	0.7
...eal - BOX	4	1.3
...olate Pudding Mix - PACKET	1	0.3
...Zippers - BOX	6	2.0
...ocolate Brownie - BOX	27	9.0
...and Cheese Omelet Mix - BOX	4	1.3
...cake Mix - BOX	5	1.7
...sing - Bottle	2	0.7
...fers - BOX	6	2.0
...ored Oatmeal - BOX	22	7.3
...ored Syrup - Individual	2	0.7
...late Crisp - BOX	6	2.0
... Bottle	8	2.7

Product Manager

The roles of project manager and product manager are often confused. Let's begin by distinguishing between the *product* that is being created and the *project* to create the product. Products have life cycles, while projects have phases, as Figures 4A and 4B depict. Different people and organizations might use different terminologies.

Figure 4A Product Cycle

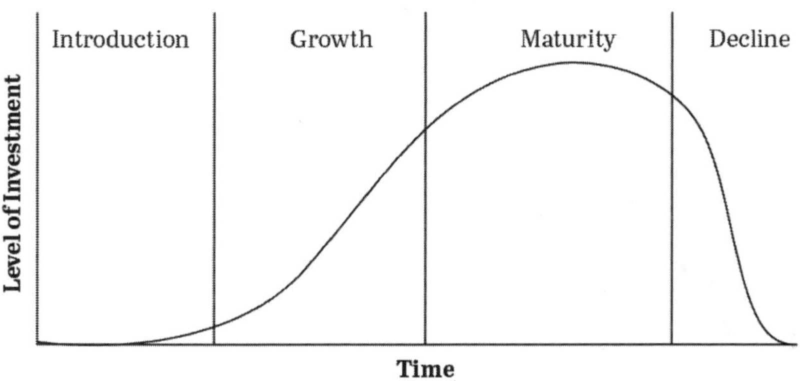

Figure 4B: Project Phases

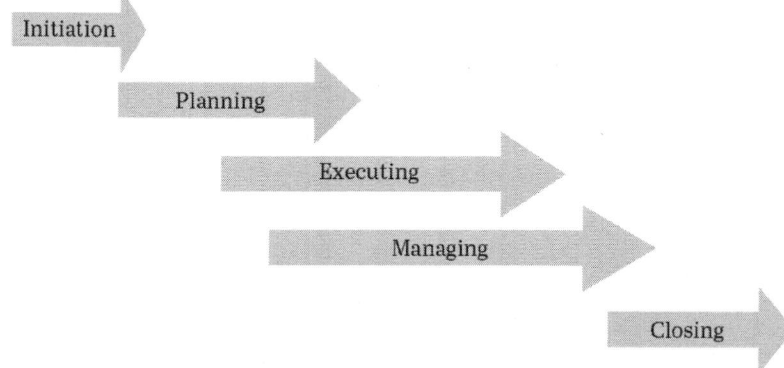

Products begin in the introductory stage, or cycle, progress through the growth cycle, peak in the maturity stage, and finally enter the decline stage. Most companies will not invest project money in a product that has entered the decline cycle but will choose instead to invest in newer products.

Projects begin with an initiation phase, and progress through the planning, executing, managing, and closing phases.

Product managers often remain with their products, in a management role, for years – through many projects. In smaller companies, one person may wear both hats at the same time, but to be successful, it requires role clarity.

In a *product manager* role, the relevant questions might include:

- Is the product meeting or exceeding the ultimate customer's expectations?
- Does the product give us a key competitive advantage?
- What product improvements would boost the company's bottom line?

The *project manager* is focused on a different set of questions, such as:

- How can the team accomplish the project objectives most effectively?
- Which project activities will bring the most value *now*?
- What risks and issues need consideration?
- Do I have the right resources deployed at the right time?
- Is project execution moving according to our plan?

The product manager will be heavily involved in decisions about whether to do a project and what the scope should be. The project manager will be more involved in the logistics of project planning, execution, and management.

For example, consider a project to design and build a new stroller for a company that manufactures baby equipment. The company likely has someone who manages that line of baby equipment. That person is analyzing what customers want, what the competitors are doing, which strollers in their line might be approaching the point of termination, and which strollers are still growing in popularity. This person will be involved in marketing decisions.

The project manager will be trying to get the project (designing and building the new stroller) done as cost-effectively and as efficiently as possible. The project manager will be managing costs, assessing and deploying resources, and evaluating risks and issues that arise. They will hopefully be working with the product manager on any questions that come up. One issue that might surface is the need to test out possible designs with potential customers. Typically, the product manager will be heavily focused on the needs of customers – in this case, the ultimate users. And project managers will be more focused on client needs – that is, the client who is paying for the project.

Another issue that may come up, particularly if the deadline is tight and/or money is limited, is the prioritization of features. There is a technique that I occasionally recommend that helps with this. It's called the MoSCoW prioritization model. In a nutshell, the name is an acronym for Must haves, Should haves, Could haves, and Won't haves. Try dividing your features into those groups and see if that helps. Another option is for the project sponsor or product owner to rank the features, though you can expect, and should encourage, changes in the rankings as time goes on.

Roles and Responsibilities

There are often overlaps on the many functions that people in your organization provide; on complex projects, it can get overwhelming. Get to know people well, so you can predict how they will behave in various situations, and particularly when they are under stress. Listen carefully to what they say and don't say, especially to those who are closest to your client.

One suggestion for organizing and clarifying the roles that people play on your project is to develop a responsibility matrix, often called a RACI. A responsibility matrix, as portrayed in Figure 5 documents who has final Responsibility, some Accountability, should be Consulted, or simply Informed about each activity. Hence, the acronym RACI.

Figure 5: Responsibility Matrix (RACI)

R: Responsibile, A: Accountable, C: Consulted, I: Informed

Activity	Alice	Ben	Chandra	Dimitri	Evelyn
1.1	R	A	I	A	I
1.2	R	A	C	A	I
2.1	A	C	R	C	I
2.2	A	C	R	C	C
2.3	A	C	C	R	I
3.1	I	R	A	I	A
4.1	I	I	A	I	R

This minimizes confusion and ensures that everyone understands their many important functions on the project. It's easier to enjoy your project work when everyone understands their function. Get clear about roles and responsibilities from the beginning.

In some organizations, including law firms, leaders have changed the acronym to LACI – to indicate that someone is going to lead the activity, but not necessarily be responsible for it. From my reading, this seems to apply more when a client is involved, perhaps on the belief that the client is ultimately responsible.

And Brené Brown discusses using a TASC in her book *Dare to Lead*. She describes it as a series of questions that you should ask the team about every activity.

- T - Do you know who owns the task?
- A - Does the owner have sufficient authority since they need to be held accountable?
- S - Is the team well positioned for success?
- C - And do you have a checklist of what is needed?[116]

I recommend that teams take it further than a traditional RACI. When you get into questions about contracts, money, risks, issues, and other aspects of the project (which I discuss in Part 3), you will need to know who, for example, can approve a budget change for every activity, who will sign off on quality approvals, or who can approve a scope change. You should keep it simple, but you need to think about those things, and document expectations. Once you have the roles clearly delineated, it's time to be sure people working on the project can communicate well.

As I have said, I believe strongly in the value of people talking about problems and solutions, risks and issues, needs and decisions. Sometimes written communications are vitally important – particularly to document understandings. But it's hard to argue effectively over email or chat, particularly if tensions are high. And all projects have problems. They need to be discussed. In the next chapter, I offer some strategies for how to have these discussions, since endless and undirected conversations do not move your project forward.

Chapter 13

Stop the Chatter! Make Meetings Matter!

Meetings are a fact of project management life in most organizations. But when meetings consist of poorly directed chatter, nothing gets done. Let's explore how different kinds of structured meetings can be used to effectively execute and manage a project, how to make the most of your meeting time and communications, and how having a common project language could improve both your meetings and overall communications.

Use Structured Meetings Effectively

Getting projects completed involves a lot of doing. And all the essential activities that you define in the planning phase, and that I discuss more fully in Part 3, will have lots of steps, many of which won't unfold until you gain more clarity on the "how."

Sometimes, depending on the project, these steps can be taken without fanfare. Other times, you will decide that it is important to document all the little tasks, perhaps assign them to others, and possibly document copious amounts of notes. It depends on the size of the project, the size of the team, the people you are working with, and the complexity of the activities. It's like flower gardens, where some gardens require more attention than others. The advantage to documenting individual tasks is that someone can take over more easily in the event of a problem.

Projects may turn strategy into reality, but teams make it happen. As surgeon, health researcher, and writer for *The New Yorker* Atul Gawande argues, "we yearn for frictionless, technological solutions... But people talking to people is still the way that norms and standards change."[117] Different teams will have different tolerances for meetings, but all teams will agree that ineffective, wasteful meetings are unacceptable.

Later in this chapter, I outline the different kinds of meetings that teams use in the Smart Projex world. The goal, in this world, is to find a rhythm to your meeting schedule that results in the highest level of productivity and effectiveness. If your teams are spending so much time meeting that they don't have time to do the actual work that needs to get done between meetings, that's a problem. While some groups seem to manage well without meeting at all, I find that some level of meetings builds energy, commitment, and accountability, particularly when innovation and creativity are needed.

When you have a meeting, look around at who is there, and mentally estimate the aggregate amount of income (including benefits) the participants are receiving. That's the cost of that meeting time, plus organization time, closure time, and any materials or space costs. Meetings are expensive. But sometimes they are the most effective way to move a project forward.

As wonderful as videoconferencing technology may be for meetings, it is still not the same as in-person meetings. Face it, we've all been in those online meetings and felt the awkwardness. It's hard to know who has the floor, and it can be easy to misread visual clues about intent. Then there are the technology failures, lost calls, and the difficulty of understanding people when there is static on the line. We've come a long way, but I'll lean in the direction of in-person meetings, when possible, especially in three scenarios: first, the early days of team formation; second, when trying to create something new; and third, in difficult situations.

When you are starting out as a team, or as a company, or on a new complex mega-project, plan some retreats so that people can get to know each other, and learn to collaborate effectively. And if you are trying to develop something new, know that research on using sociometers on team projects supports the notion that people are simply more creative when they meet face-to-face (as discussed in Chapter 8). Finally, video calls are a hard place to duke it out, so to speak.

Richard Branson, in *Business Stripped Bare: Adventures of a Global Entrepreneur*, says that face-to-face conversations over a "shared pot of tea" are still more effective than the alternatives.[118] When your team needs some time to build relationships, plan offsites where people can relax together, break bread, play, and generally have fun. Teams that enjoy working together simply perform better and it takes time to build those teams. When you can reuse those teams or when a lot is at stake, it makes sense to make that investment.

National Geographic has reported that the brain drain from teleconference meetings is real and mounting. According to Andrew Franklin at Virginia's Norfolk State, "Gallery view—where all meeting participants appear Brady Bunch-style—challenges the brain's central vision, forcing it to decode so many people at once that no one comes through meaningfully, not even the speaker."[119] So, limit your time in those meetings. If you have the option of choosing which meetings to attend, opt for the smaller ones. Switch from gallery style to active speaker mode and accept that some people in the meeting are multitasking. Turn off the camera or video feed if you need to. We all need to protect our own brain functioning first. As the airlines say, put on your own oxygen mask first before helping others.

If you don't have a reason to meet, don't meet. Your participants are giving up valuable time that could be used to create client deliverables or get internal project work done. Don't waste that time and money. Try to think ahead about your upcoming scheduled meetings; if there is no reason to meet, give your teams the courtesy of some advance notice if you decide to cancel a meeting. And if you are scheduled to attend a meeting and haven't received an agenda, ask the organizer for one, so that you can be better prepared for the conversations. If there is no documented objective for the meeting and you are not required to attend, send your regrets and don't attend.

When meeting attendance is a problem, try setting up a process so that *everyone* can confirm attendance or regret by a certain date. And then, cancel the meeting if you haven't gotten the responses you are seeking. The objective is to put some peer pressure on slow or nonresponders to encourage a respect for people's time. This suggestion may not work all the time, but you need to develop a culture of respect for time and energy.

Types of Meetings

In the Smart Projex methodology, which I outline more fully in Part 3, there are two specific kinds of meetings, standing meetings and Checkpoint meetings, for which agendas are pre-defined. Then, there are other kinds of meetings that you will need to have. Most fall in the categories of planning, brainstorming, or problem resolution.

1. Standing meetings

Standing meetings are short meetings, where members of the team each answer three questions while standing (not sitting):

- What have you accomplished since the last meeting?
- What do you plan to accomplish next? Note the focus is on what people have accomplished, not what they have worked on.
- What problems have arisen?

Keep these meetings short (5 to 10 minutes or so, depending on the number of participants) so that the team believes that the time was well spent. Standing up, instead of sitting down in a comfortable chair at a conference table, will help keep meetings shorter.

Standing meetings are not a time for discussing how to solve the problems that have arisen. That's not to say that teams can't make exceptions when the problem involves the entire team, but you run the risk that the meetings will soon grow longer, and people will begin to resist them.

Depending on the project and the speed with which you need to move, you may choose to do a standing meeting every day or once, twice, or three times a week.

One of the keys to effective standing meetings is building a culture where problems are disclosed early. Paul Light of the Brookings Institute noted in his research on government project failures that "most of the failures involved errors of omission, not commission."[120]

2. Checkpoint meetings

I used this term in my Smart Projex software and discuss these meetings more fully in Part 3. Checkpoint meetings are a time when teams gather to review the compelling vision that they created, assess accomplishments, plan the next batch of work, and then review the project schedule, risks, issues, money, and lessons learned.

I typically recommend that teams start working in two-week sprints, which is a block of time during which your team commits to work on and ideally finish specific activities. Checkpoint meetings bookmark these sprints. Two weeks is usually sufficient time to accomplish some level of meaningful work, but you can opt for something shorter or longer, depending on how active your project is.

Depending on your situation, you may choose to invite your client to these meetings, or perhaps invite your client to one a month. If not, I would encourage you to send a client update with your monthly billings, or on a regular basis, particularly if your invoices are short on details.

3. Planning meetings or brainstorming meetings of any kind

Planning meetings are what they sound like, typically decision-making meetings. There can be brainstorming meetings, or special meetings called throughout a project for solving specific problems. They are all different and so each one needs a clearly defined objective(s), an agenda, and a written post-meeting follow-up of some sort. I even find that the quick, two-person meetings to solve a particular problem, or catch up on where things stand, are well-served by thinking ahead about what you want to accomplish and how. And when decisions need to be made in the meeting, document and disseminate in advance the questions that need to be answered, and then document the decisions that were made, at the end of the meeting.

Use Meeting Time and Communications Effectively

Time Blocking

This is helpful when you begin scheduling project work. To achieve maximum execution flexibility, use time blocking and designate the activities that the team can realistically achieve in a single time block. Work relentlessly on that group of activities. Finish as many as you can, and then bite off another chunk for the next time block. You will be surprised at how much your team can accomplish when they are committed and focused.

Meeting Agendas

Use meeting agendas with defined timeframes and objectives. While it is a standard practice to communicate the length of meetings, it is even more helpful to participants to indicate the length of time estimated for each item on the agenda, as well as a few helpful details about what you want to accomplish (for example, what decisions need to be made?).

Meeting Minutes

Document the decisions and outcomes of the meeting. These should be documented in some type of easily referenced system. Make it easy on your team. If you aren't using a tool that helps you with this and you are writing meeting minutes *and* your team reads them, congratulations. A document or system that helps team members remember what decisions were made and what assignments are coming up is helpful, but only if it is usable. Bullet points and short declarative sentences are your friends in meeting summaries! So are clear lists of who's responsible for what, and by when. No one has the time to read or create pages and pages of minutes.

Use Relationship Building and Peer Pressure Effectively

I encourage you to think carefully about how you build your teams, get to know them, and use peer pressure to your advantage.

In his book *The Tipping Point: How Little Things Can Make a Big Difference*, Malcolm Gladwell says that relationships and peer pressure are more important to execution than edicts from management. The Rule of 150, developed by Robin Dunbar, a British anthropologist, says that organizations larger than about 150 people lose the power of effective social relationships. This explains why W. L. Gore and Associates, the company that makes Gore-Tex fabric, builds plants that are almost next door to each other. A plant with 150 employees or less functions most effectively, with stable relationships between workers who drive performance.[121]

When Looking to the Past to Plan for the Future, Reflect. Don't Ruminate.

According to Leah Weiss in *How We Work*, reflection means to thoughtfully review something that has happened, without judgment. Rumination focuses on what went wrong and placing blame. Reflecting and learning from an experience helps us grow. Rumination simply leads to unproductive periods of being stuck.[122]

During your meetings, focus on observations, not judgments. Observations are akin to what a camera would record. Judgments are fixed – and are often threatening, which can cause others to shut down. So, stay focused on observing and reflecting, rather than judging and blaming.

Suggestions for Online Team Meetings

Sometimes, teams are distributed geographically and cannot meet face-to-face, or are forced to choose between online and phone meetings. Here are some suggestions:

1. For international teams, vary your meeting time.

This is important when the members of your project teams are in significantly different time zones. No one person or group should ever be forced to wake at 3 a.m. for a project meeting every week.

2. Take advantage of video technology.

Use webcams and video conferencing software, rather than audio-only phones, when possible. Facial language is important. But be aware that video meetings can drain the brain, as mentioned earlier. So, do what you can to reduce the time spent in large video meetings where you are trying to juggle a screen full of faces.

3. Play.

Turn your project work into a game if that makes sense. It can be as simple as creating a race to the finish when you want to inspire the folks on your team to push a little harder. The internet is loaded with game suggestions.

4. Use check-ins.

When you don't see your team every day, it can be hard to know how your key people, as well as the "extras" who aren't working on this every day, are feeling. Begin meetings with a brief check-in where everyone describes their personal situation in one word, or one short phrase – i.e., exhausted from sick child, joyful, frustrated, confused, isolated, etc.

5. Be positive.

To keep your teams motivated, start a chat thread to disseminate positive and encouraging news. This thread is not for reminding people about deadlines or asking questions about project details. It's simply about pumping people up – and sharing exciting news.

6. Use humor.

Begin meetings with a joke or a funny story. Laughter goes a long way towards getting teams to relax and intellectually engage. An article in the spring 2010 *Harvard Mahoney Neuroscience Institute Letter* discusses the nuanced distinction in the way the body processes humor and laughter: "Humor is an evoked response to storytelling and shifting expectations. Laughter is a social signal among humans. It's like a punctuation mark."[123] Scientists have only recently begun exploring the veracity of the old maxim that laughter is good for the soul.

Standardize Your Project Language

Project work is full of confusing words, and with each new methodology comes a new lingo. Perhaps one of the first words that you need to agree on is "project." Put aside official definitions. The question here is: what kinds of projects do you need or want to monitor? Are executives trying to monitor all the projects in the organization, or a subset of more important projects? Are client engagements being monitored in the same way that in-house projects are being overseen? For technology companies, are bug fix requests managed the same way as large projects?

I frequently see people in HR, marketing, compliance departments, or the office of general counsel working on projects that no one else knows a thing about. Salaried employees are doing the work and making no effort to track labor costs. You need to know what your long-term oversight goal is first. Are you trying to track all the project investments, or some of them? Which ones, and why? What factors determine whether a project falls into the category that warrants management oversight?

In my work with organizations, I've observed that projects rarely fail in a vacuum. They fail in the context of the gazillion other things that are being done in the organization. This makes risk management incredibly important. You will encounter risks in many areas – for example, organizational risks, environmental risks, project risks, and human risks, to name a few.

"Issues" and "risks" are two terms that need to be defined for your organization, particularly if your technology folks are using Jira, a software tool that uses "issue" to refer to an individual piece of work, rather than a problem that needs to be solved. What is the difference between an issue and an impediment? Is an issue the same as a risk? Can risks be eliminated? Does the term "risk" refer to project risks or product risks? Be sure everyone in your organization understands what you mean by these terms.

Another area where you can standardize terminology is the concept of "activities" and "tasks," which I talk about in greater detail in Chapter 15. There are lots of words that can be used to describe something that needs to get done on a project, as well as the operating processes in your company. These can include user stories, activities, tasks, work packages, tickets, action items, milestones, work streams, requirements, backlog, cards, sheets, and so forth. I'm sure I've missed some. Definitions can vary from person to person.

This concludes Part 2 and our focus on general leadership principles. If you'd like to read more on leadership, check out this link: https://smartprojex.com/category/leadership/. For more on teamwork, try this link: https://smartprojex.com/category/teamwork/.

In Part 3, I specifically focus on project leadership and the Smart Projex methodology, elaborating on many of the concepts and terms that I have introduced so far. For now, I do want executives to understand the needless confusion that arises when we don't all speak the same project language. The proliferation of acronyms doesn't help. To communicate effectively, organizations need a common project language. It is simply ineffective to have some teams using "earned value" to talk about status, some talking about too many deadlines that no one understands, and others talking about incomplete user stories. Can we agree that standardizing our project language makes sense?

Part 3
Methodology

“Blindly following the maxim that good managers should keep close to their customers can sometimes be a fatal mistake.”[124]
— *Clayton M. Christiansen*

Chapter 14

Start Smart to Boost Project Results

In the first two parts of this book, I focused on the need for properly selecting project investments, ways to analyze your investment decisions, and how to build the necessary leadership to move your projects to the finish line successfully. Now, I get to the crux of the Smart Projex methodology. By the way, the core elements of this methodology can be used with many different project software solutions, including basic Excel spreadsheets.

My methodology is a client-centered approach that works when you are herding smart cats. It focuses on project disciplines that are designed for volatility, uncertainty, complexity, and ambiguity. Yet your teams will need to make time to follow the process. As I mentioned earlier, these processes were built to help teams develop keystone habits. The methodology is heavily focused on building a culture that is relationship oriented, because as Peter Drucker famously said, "culture eats strategy for breakfast." I begin with the need to start smart.

Every Great Start Begins with a Compelling Vision

Development officers often reach out to those who have benefited from donated dollars to have them tell their story of what those gifts have done for them and how their life was changed by the gift. People rally around those kinds of stories.

It makes sense that the first step that a smart leader chooses when launching a new project is to create and communicate a vision that will inspire the team. The type of project doesn't change the need for a compelling vision. I do agree that it can be easier to craft a compelling vision for more creative, imaginative projects, but your basic regulatory project or home construction project needs one just as much, maybe even more. If you get it right, you are halfway there. And if you don't, I predict you'll be calling in a rescue team down the road.

There are at least two ways to approach developing this compelling vision if it doesn't evolve naturally. First, can you tell a story about your project? You don't have to tell a long story; in fact, you shouldn't. But all good stories involve conflict and characters. What is the problem you are solving or the need you are addressing? Who will benefit? Make your characters real. Perhaps you can include the benefits that the project is expected to achieve as the resolution to your story. Does it help to think about your beginning, middle, and end?

The second approach is to craft a pithy statement that addresses why you are doing the project. Your goal is to create an inspiring story or vision statement that will get shared, and that people (your "smart cats") will want to work on. Think of this short story or pithy statement as your guiding star; a focus that will energize, excite, and empower your team. Remind your team of that statement during regular project meetings. Quiz your team members unexpectedly. Don't expect them to remember it because they won't. Almost universally, executives think their teams and employees can restate the mission of the organization much better than they actually can when asked. The same is true of project visions.

Supercharge Your Project Charter

In traditional project management, a project begins with a discernment phase, sometimes called project initiation. During this part of the project, senior management is looking at the project idea to ensure that it offers the organization sufficient value and how best to move it forward. If no client is involved, the project officially begins when management issues a charter statement. This is typically a short document that announces the project and the project manager, asks for support, explains why the company is embarking on this endeavor, and defines the general objective(s). Note that this general objective may or may not be the compelling vision that will inspire your team.

There are different opinions about what a project charter should include. The challenge is to find that sweet spot between something that allows the project to morph appropriately and yet still provides enough structure to help teams understand what the project is all about.

If a client is involved, the project may begin with an engagement letter, a document that varies considerably depending on the project scope, the company and industry, and the nature of the relationship between the company and the client.

A word of caution about projects that come from clients: Be sure the client has approved the project before investing hours. How many times has a client or a prospect called with a request and given you just enough information to get you excited? Once the brain gets to work on an interesting idea, it can be tough to shut it off. Unnecessary time spent on a project that hasn't been authorized may never be compensated and, worse yet, distracts you from what is more important.

Following the issuance of the charter or engagement letter, one of the first things that the project manager should do, if they haven't already done so, is to create that compelling vision statement discussed earlier.

Here are several areas of consideration that will supercharge your project charter and kick your project off for success.

People

The charter should name the project manager and ask for support. It may name the project sponsor or other key people on the team. It's important to understand the people who are affiliated with your project. I discussed several key roles in Chapter 12 and discuss other leadership roles in later chapters.

What's Most Important? The Triple Constraint?

Do you understand what is most important to your client or to your management? We all know the adage: You can have it fast, cheap, or good. Pick one. Maybe two. But not all three. I've added quality and risk to the question – for those clients that are particularly risk or quality focused.

It may be a difficult question when you ask your client what is most important, and give them the choices of scope, cost, quality, risk, and schedule. They may tell you they want it all. Part of making clients happy is managing expectations, and no one can have it all. Determining early on what is most important to your client will inform the way that a project is planned, executed, and managed. High quality is neither fast nor cheap. Your client may be budget conscious, risk averse, or quality driven.

And don't assume that their needs won't change. When you are suddenly thrust into a new competitive environment or a radically changing economic situation, what's most important may well change. As a project leader, you need to keep abreast of changing times. Confirm what's most important to your client throughout the duration of the project.

Budget Factors

While I elaborate on scope, costs, quality, risks, and schedule considerations later in this book, let me throw in a few preliminary considerations now.

At this point, you will not know what this project is going to cost you. It's simply too early. But it helps to understand whether the client (or your management team) has enough money to relocate its offices to a larger location with more parking, or simply add a few more workstations to the existing offices. Getting the client to identify a budget range can quickly help you understand how to focus future conversations.

It's also important to understand how cost sensitive your client or management team is. Once the project is approved, what budget variance is acceptable to your management or your client? How much communication will they want on cost overruns? This should become increasingly clear as you get into planning the project.

Timeline

Does the client (or management) have a completion date in mind? You will not have any schedule or timeline at this point. You haven't even figured out what you are doing. But you might discover, if you ask, that the client (or someone on your management team) has already decided when this project needs to be finished.

Don't commit to anything quite yet. But understanding that goal will help your conversations as you think about what to include in your project scope.

Success and Failure Criteria

What needs to happen for the client or management to be ecstatic? What could happen that might cause them to be devastated, or not want to pay your bill? Identify the success and failure criteria for your project and find a way to measure them. This is different from the benefits realization management that I discussed in Chapter 6. These are the success and failure measures for your project.

What gets measured gets done, so measure the right things. For example: For that event you are planning, do you want to earn $1 million, net of expenses or generate $5 million in revenues? Will the new website you are building for a client be successful if the client likes it, or if it generates $25,000 in book purchases in the first weekend? These nuanced distinctions in how you view the project can make a big difference in how you plan and execute the work.

When you and the client seek to identify the success and failure criteria, consider whether it is beyond your control. As an example, you can control how many tickets you sell to an event, but you can't control whether the ticketholders show up for the event. You don't want to be stranded in a swampland over which you have no control.

Constraints

A constraint is any limitation on the project or the team. Thankfully, most projects in the real world have budget, timeline and/or resource constraints. How will your constraints restrict your project execution or impact your timeline or budget? You will use these constraints to your advantage in planning the project. After planning, you may want to consider them risks that you manage for the project duration. There may be other constraints that you should understand to ensure that you can live with them.

For example, suppose you are the project manager on a project that is expected to take a year to complete. You are told that the owner's son will be your assistant. Suppose he is known to be difficult. How will you handle that? I don't have an easy answer to that question. But I do suggest that you understand your constraints and how you plan to handle them.

Assumptions

An assumption is anything that is taken to be true or false, which may not be so. Will your assumptions prove true or false, and how will that impact planning? As the team moves into planning the project, it will need to test or verify the assumptions. It will need to use those assumptions to clarify expectations from management.

Let's consider an example. You want to plan a training seminar for a group of professionals to help them understand the accounting changes in a new federal law. You've done these events before and they have become great networking events. You've rotated your events between the East Coast and the West Coast every year. The assumption might be that the next event will stick with that plan. And then, a pandemic hits, upending travel plans. You need to revisit that assumption about location and frequency. You need to know what assumptions you made.

There is a popular mantra in the start-up world: fail fast and fail often. I understand that logic. We need to take risks to conquer new territories. But so often, I believe these costly failures could have been avoided if the team had understood more about what was needed and not needed. I'm not suggesting that we don't move forward until we have certainty. But maybe the mantra should be "fail small and learn fast." It is not prudent to waste investors' money on failures that shouldn't have happened. And making the same mistakes repeatedly is demoralizing for teams. But teams that can experiment quickly and frequently, and learn from those experiments, will be more successful.

As a project leader, you have more human capital at the start than you will when things get tough. In the beginning, people are excited. Funding has been committed. The need for the project seems high. Over time, people will lose some interest. Use that capital to ask some tough questions in the beginning and get those answers down on paper. Ensure that people agree on the basics before you sail into uncharted territories.

I remember one renovation project for an old building. In the beginning, a highly successful capital campaign was held, and the organization raised significant funds for needed renovations. As more and more problems surfaced in the renovation, and as the community was unable to use the facility for a much longer period than predicted, people grew tired of the delays and debates, and it became harder and harder to positively engage the community. So, take advantage of this time of excitement and optimism; iron out the big issues.

How and Why Do We Focus on the Past?

Project leaders need to understand the past to plan effectively. It makes no sense to waste what we've learned in the past when we move forward. But how do we actually learn from the past?

Review the Organization's Templates, Processes, and Project Procedures

Organizations with any sort of project history have developed processes, procedures, templates, and/or guides that they have used on past projects. Find the ones that worked well. You don't always need to reinvent the wheel. Save yourself time and money by seeing if the organization already has anything that might help you. This is particularly true if you are being brought in from the outside or have little experience with projects in the organization.

Review Applicable Lessons Learned When Starting New Projects

Save your team time and money by not making the same mistakes twice. We live in a world where businesses are trying to do so much with so little. Take the time for disciplines that matter. Cataloging lessons learned is one of those disciplines that can reap rewards down the road. And once you have cataloged these lessons, folks need to review them when they begin new projects.

With everything you learn as you begin a new project, at some point, management will formally launch the project by publishing a charter. That's when the real project work begins. At this point, it might be tempting to go off like gangbusters with all the enthusiasm you can muster. I would still caution you to take it slowly and focus on some proper planning. Many dollars have been wasted because teams failed to properly plan a project. The next two chapters are about this subject because planning a project for success requires us to think about the details, of which there are many, as well as the larger view. Too often teams get stuck in the weeds and fail to see the big picture. So, I look at planning from both perspectives.

Chapter 15

Planning a Project with an Eye from the Sky

Starting and planning your project wisely is perhaps the key to your success. In this chapter, I look at the project from a 10,000-foot perspective, and outline some ways to develop scope clarity, document your scope, and set up the basics of your work breakdown structure. The goal is to begin planning without getting lost in the weeds. That said, it's important to understand that some projects need more planning than others.

Many a project has gone off the rails early because the team was so focused on moving into execution that it didn't stop and properly think through the project needs. If your project has a lot at stake, recognize that planning is even more important. When you can break a larger project into smaller projects, try to do so. It's far better to accomplish a smaller project that delivers value than to get bogged down on a huge project that is ultimately scrapped. Remember "lean" principles.

One of the first big tasks of teams is to plan the project. It may be tempting to think that this activity can be done by the project manager, either alone or in concert with one other person. However, as I noted in Part 2 on leadership, using a diverse team for project planning will improve your outcomes.

The eternal debate that faces all project teams is the extent to which planning is helpful. Too much time spent planning delays execution. Too little time planning can cause a project to fail. Recognize that some projects simply require more planning than others. It is essential that we embrace just-in-time planning when appropriate and align planning needs with project needs so that we aren't unnecessarily overplanning.

Yet, proper planning depends on the nature of the project. If you're renovating an old building in a crowded city, with limited on-site storage for supplies, detailed planning is a must. You'll need to arrange for subcontractors to show up on exactly the right day, account for potential weather issues, ensure the right materials are at the right site, at the right time, and that the necessary preliminary work has been finished.

On the other hand, if you are working on a project to create a new baby product and wondering what kind of product might become the newest fad, you don't want to get too far ahead in your planning. You want to be able to experiment and adapt. Increasingly, more and more projects, even those construction projects that need more detailed planning, seem to require agility in a world where things are changing so frequently.

Scope – Clear as Mud? Or Crystal Clear?

With a clear vision in mind, and as you begin to gain clarity on your people, especially your client or your management team, it's time to get a handle on the project scope. Scope is simply what you plan to do. But figuring that out, especially in an ever-changing or ambiguous world, is rarely simple. Don't focus on the "how" right now. Instead, ask *what* you are going to do to accomplish the project. What are the pieces of work that need to be delivered to the client, or to your management team? In the technology world, we might talk about the features you plan to build. In the legal world, we might talk about what issues need to be researched and what depositions need to be taken. In the pharmaceutical world, we might talk about what experiments need to be done or what hypotheses need to be proven. Remember, we are talking about *what* needs to be done – not *how* it's going to get done.

At this point, I like to think about scope at a high level. Right now, you don't know enough to get too granular. What you *should* know at this point is what your high-level vision is, and a budget range. You should be able to reconcile that vision with the budget range. You probably cannot have your dream house for a family of six at a budget range that doesn't exceed $100K if you live in the United States. Get real!

I'll warn you that scope planning is hard. Consider trying to plan your family vacation on a limited budget. You decide to go to Europe and make Switzerland your home base. But how do you divide up your time between Zurich, Bern, Lucerne, Geneva, or Zermatt? How will you get around? Where will you stay and what will you do? And, Germany is so close, and oh, shouldn't you just take a train up to Munich? And while you're there, your daughter, who you thought was about out of the Sleeping Beauty phase, simply must see the Neuschwanstein Castle. And then, your teenager is way more interested in jetting over to see Paris and pick up some of the latest fashions. You see the problem?

As your project team keeps its eye on its vision statement, that guiding star, it begins to determine what the project scope is. Here are several questions that might help.

What Are You NOT Going to Do?

Even when the sky is the limit, so to speak, you still need some boundaries. Knowing what you are *not* going to do will help you build clarity around what you *are* going to do. I recommend that teams document both the scope inclusions *and* exclusions.

Suppose you and your team are working on a project to create a company-wide staff training event. Can you decide that it will not be done overseas? Does it need to be done in person or can you rule that out too? As you think about what you can rule out, you can gain clarity on what needs to be part of the scope. The effort to find project scope clarity will be iterative and it will involve multiple discussions over a period of days or weeks, and sometimes longer. On innovation projects, it will evolve over the course of the project as you try some things, fail, and learn.

Time blocking those discussions will help. If you give yourself a day to talk about any subject, and especially scope, you may find that it takes a day. If you give yourself only an hour, or maybe just fifteen minutes, you may be surprised at how the extra focus can help move that conversation forward. Go into the conversation with a specific, defined objective. Remember to document, document, document.

Use the Details of Your Project Charter to Help You

In the previous chapter, we talked about constraints. Money is often a big one, but there may be others. Can they help you find some more scope clarity? Spend some time testing your assumptions. That may lead you to understand a piece of scope in a new way. This is a highly iterative process.

As you begin to understand what you are going to do, the Work Breakdown Structure approach that I discuss next can offer more guidance than pure brainstorming. And as I have recommended, time block these discussions with crystal-clear objectives. You can't do everything at the same time. But at the end of each meeting, it's important to feel a sense of forward motion.

Work Breakdown Structure

One of the first steps a team takes after initiating a project is to break it down into the essential activities that are needed to meet the project objectives. The traditional project management term for the result is a "work breakdown structure," or WBS for short.

Professionals call this "decomposing" a project, and the point is to take a disciplined approach to building an understanding of the complete scope and ensure that big pieces of the project are not forgotten. Focus on defining the meaningful deliverables that are needed to accomplish the project scope. The result, as depicted in Figure 6, can resemble an organizational chart with columns of activities, though some teams prefer mind mapping or a less visual approach that more resembles an Excel list of activities. I tend to recommend the organizational chart approach because it offers more structure than a mind map. That structure will provide benefits later.

Figure 6: Work Breakdown Structure (WBS)

Event	Donors	Social Media	Emails
Run of Events	Outreach	Design graphics	Write copy
Design materials	Emails	Schedule posts	Collate images
Invitations	Sponsorship		Create mailing list
Programs	Acquire donations		Follow up
Tech check			

The more you decompose a project, the more clarity you will have around your budget and schedule, but there are times when it is more important to get a high-level work breakdown structure done and insert placeholders for what you don't know and save that part for later. This is especially true on innovation projects, where the results of one step will determine the next steps. When costs are important, break the project down far enough to be able to estimate a cost (and revenue) for each activity or phase. If changes are needed later, that's okay, provided everyone agrees.

I also advocate that you ultimately break projects into activities that don't take longer than one (ideally) or two sprints. (As discussed earlier, in the Smart Projex world, teams work in sprints, or time blocks, often two weeks long.) First, delivering value to your clients more frequently allows everyone to better understand what is working and what is not. Second, it motivates teams when they can celebrate small wins. It is demoralizing when teams sense that no progress is being seen, week after week.

I have found that, on some business projects, it can be hard to break down certain activities into discrete and valuable chunks of work that can be finished in a week or two. For example, if you're developing a project to create a new onboarding process, what is the value that you can create for the client (or your management team) at the end of the first two weeks or so? If you are doing a project to design a new part for a car, and you simply haven't yet found a design that works, what can you give the client that has value to them?

The answer may involve changing the way you think about projects entirely. It may require you to be more client centered. And remember that if you are working on an in-house project, your management team is your client. You need to rethink how you break the project down. Are you thinking about the little steps that need to be done from your perspective or from your client's viewpoint? Do all the steps add value for the client?

Work in short sprints to remain flexible and aim to deliver something of value to the client at the end of each sprint. Your deliverable may be a small piece of working software. It may be a PowerPoint presentation to senior executives that outlines a new budgeting system for the organization. It could be five miles of completely repaved roadway. It may be executive agreement on a new compensation plan. The point is to deliver something of value at the end of every sprint, and to deliver something that allows you to test your assumptions about what the client wants and likes.

Don't Get Stuck in the Weeds

When you are breaking your project down, distinguish between essential activities and necessary small tasks. To be clear, in the Smart Projex methodology there is a distinction between "activities," which are the larger packages of work that need to be completed in order to accomplish the scope, and "tasks," which are the smaller items such as document reviews, bug fixes, or even the design of a part for a product you are developing.

There is no bold line between activities and tasks. What seems like an activity on one day may seem like a task on another day. The ambiguity is by design. But at this point, focus on your activities.

Let's take a mundane example that most people will understand. Suppose the activity is to clean the office supply closet or your closet at home. That seems like a task on some days, and on other days, it's an activity. Will you empty the closet, wipe the insides down, and put everything back as it was, but tidier? Will you remove all the items, rethink their importance, or ascertain if more quantity is needed? Or will you dust around the items and straighten the closet? See what I mean? Thinking through the scope of the activity will help you decide if it is an activity or a task. Activities are clearly defined and generally take a day or more to accomplish, while tasks can typically be done in minutes or several hours. We need a way to track tasks quickly and simply. And we need a way to get real clarity on activities, which take more time, to ensure that we're not wasting time by going in the wrong direction.

So often, people list the many activities and tasks that they plan to do on a new project without thinking through what is needed. I understand wanting to capture ideas before you forget them. But one of the big advantages to developing a work breakdown structure in a graphic overview format, focusing specifically on the larger essential activities, and not including every small task on that overview, is that it keeps the project team from getting stuck in the weeds. The Gantt chart that takes 50 pages to print and covers an entire wall of an office is difficult to manage when change is a constant.

Document Your Scope

Break your project into activities that will provide real value to the client or your management team.

Storytelling has always been an effective way of aligning teams behind a goal. That's why I love the concept of user stories. The concept, which evolved in the Agile community, has been around for about the last twenty years. User stories are a simple and effective way of documenting scope. Think about creating this kind of statement for each project deliverable:

> *As a __(role – the who)______, I need a _____(deliverable – the what)_____, so that _____(benefit – the why)_____.*

Here are some examples:

- As a start-up owner, I need a website, so that I can sell products, build a customer base, and provide a way for prospects to contact me.
- As a start-up owner, I need a website, so that I can build energy for a new idea in advance of the launch.
- As a start-up employee, I need a website with clear pricing, so that I don't waste time on prospects that can't afford us.

That's three different ideas - and understanding exactly what you need on each deliverable from the outset will save you money.

Document both your scope inclusions and exclusions. A clear understanding of what you plan to do and not do for your client, or for your management team, is essential.

Another approach that you can try alternatively, or in tandem, is to have the person doing the work define, in writing, their understanding of what "done" means. Confirm this understanding with the client.

How many times have we seen projects go awry because the three- or four-word activity description on the Gantt chart or Google spreadsheet was ambiguous, and team members went off on a tangent? And how many times have we seen projects go into execution without a clear understanding of what the client wanted?

Brené Brown talks about this phenomenon in her book *Dare to Lead*, and names it "paint done." For some time, Brown struggled with assistants who kept misunderstanding her instructions. To solve this problem, she empowered her team to ask for clarity by using the phrase "paint done." This forced everyone to think through what was needed on an activity.[125]

Sometimes a lack of clarity stems from the client not knowing what it wants. That is understandable, to a point. In this ever-changing world, we can think we know what we are doing, and after putting some effort into the project, realize that we are going in the wrong direction. The objective is to learn quickly and to stay in close contact with those who are setting the direction. This includes staying in touch with the ultimate user, though I'm not suggesting that you bypass the client that hired you.

As Brown found when she and her team were in search of "paint done" on an activity, the team is forced to wrestle with the requirements and ask tough questions. That is a learning process. Be sure to document the decisions from those conversations.

For example, if the activity is to develop the marketing materials for a product launch, will the activity be "done" (meaning completely finished) when the proofs have been approved or when the final materials are in hand? And if it's the former, who needs to approve the proofs? If your activity is to develop three viable candidates for the new chief information officer position, what kind of screening is the project team supposed to do before submitting the candidates? If the activity is to procure the alcohol for a big event, do you want a keg of Budweiser, locally sourced craft beers, or an open bar with signature cocktails? And does the activity include remembering to provide those pesky corkscrews?

Developing a clear understanding of what is needed will at some point include thinking about quality objectives, risks, and money; we cover those tips in later chapters.

Understand what reporting is most meaningful to your client. The columns in a work breakdown structure can be organized using functional headings, milestones, phases, work streams, or perhaps a combination that is more meaningful to the users. Which is easier for your client to understand? Ask your client how it wants to see projects broken down, and what kind of reporting and involvement it wants. Some clients don't care that much or won't know how to answer the question. In that case, I might organize it by the budget categories that you plan to use. This way, it will at least align with your bills.

Every client is different. Some clients may wish to be more involved than others. Most want to understand their costs and what they will get for that cost. Some clients may even want to share some of the work to better control costs.

To plan a project well enough to create a reliable budget and finish date, all essential activities must be clearly defined. It is impossible to estimate the cost of an activity if you don't understand it. Only you can decide how much planning is smart. Try to stay lean when you can and focus on your client needs. In the next chapter, we look at planning the details of the project to estimate the cost and finish date.

Chapter 16

Before Cats Transgress, Plan for Success

Traditional project managers often refer to the project plan, a document that outlines how the project manager intends to manage the schedule, costs, procurement contracts, quality, risks, issues, resources, and communications. But the process of getting to that point is iterative. You simply continue to learn things that will change what you thought you knew. In this chapter I offer guidance on these concepts and discuss factors that might suggest the need to cancel a project early. I also discuss program management, which is an effort to manage related projects in a coordinated way.

Project Plan Components

In the previous chapter, I spent a fair amount of time talking about breaking your project into the essential activities. You may or may not know much in the early days of scoping a project, but one goal may be to estimate the cost of the project and determine when it can be finished. To do that, I consider the various factors that will become the components of your project plan. These include resources, schedule, quality, issues, risks, money, lessons learned, and communications. All these factors, as well as procurement, which I discuss in the next chapter, need to be thought through.

Plan Your Resources

I begin with resources. In some projects, people will be your most expensive resource, though in construction projects, your costs will be in the materials that are needed. Nevertheless, I begin here because the Smart Projex methodology is a relationship-centric approach. It is much less about schedules and more about people. It is critical that you understand how you will find, lead, and juggle these resources.

One of the first things you will need to decide in order to estimate the cost is who is going to oversee each activity. Who will do the work? That person(s) needs to be involved in developing the cost. Even if you use a professional estimator, the person doing the work should be consulted before an estimate is relayed to the client. Otherwise, it will be hard, maybe impossible, to expect that person (or team) to work within the constraints of a budget. As the project unfolds, quickly document the necessary tasks in a meaningful way to ensure that they aren't forgotten and that someone can quickly take over in case of a staffing change.

You may also have to plan other resources, especially materials that need to be purchased. I discuss a process for planning and acquiring these other resources, including procurement contracts, in Chapter 17 (on execution). In traditional project management, the details of those procurements, some of which might be costly, are often defined in the planning process. I encourage teams to plan to the extent needed. If you are talking about a construction project, you will need to plan those purchases sooner. In a business project where you need more flexibility, it can often wait, depending on how cost conscious your client is.

Plan Your Schedule

In Part 1, I talked at length about a Smart Projex concept called Complexity. If you have read much about project failures, you know that many large projects failed because teams seriously underestimated the complexity of the project. In that context they are speaking generically. In the Smart Projex world, I am using Complexity in a specific and defined way, but the point remains. We need to understand what is needed on our project activities – and that's especially true on high-stakes projects.

In traditional project management, leaders estimate how long an activity will take, or the duration. As an alternative metric, I recommend Complexity. The key here is that Complexity, in the Smart Projex world, does not drive the schedule. Instead, it is used to draw meaningful insights about productivity and scheduling later, when you are executing the project.

Estimating Complexity is a much simpler concept than estimating durations and identifying dependencies, as is traditionally done. And Complexity considers the reality that until you get into a project, you often don't know how long the activities will take. However, none of this means that we don't manage the schedule, even if we have redefined what a schedule is.

It's important to document the Complexity of each activity in your project plan. Then, identify fixed deadlines. These are the critical deadlines that cannot be missed. Not all deadlines are equal. One of the reasons that teams miss deadlines is that they try to focus on meeting all deadlines, when only a handful of them are truly important. Deadlines can be motivational, but not when your team is paralyzed by too many unattainable deadlines. Meet the important deadlines and make your client happy.

Use target deadlines and effective team meetings to drive the schedule. Deliver something of value at the end of every sprint and continue to move forward. Even if what you delivered fails miserably, you have learned something valuable, which brings you closer to ultimate success.

Many traditional project managers will say that we need a schedule to ascertain whether the ultimate deadline is achievable or not. There is no question that the team needs to understand whether the deadline that management has requested is achievable. And teams and clients need to understand when timely project completion is threatened.

I would argue that the team can figure that out without spending a bunch of time creating a schedule that will change over and over. They can decide what is achievable and commit to accomplishing the deliverables according to the interim deadlines that they establish as a team. I recommend that you focus on creating a culture where people are accountable for results, which is not to be confused with the amount of time spent in the office or billed on an activity.

Some project managers spend a considerable amount of time identifying what is called the "critical path." It's a complicated way of understanding the soonest that a project can be finished, by reducing the project to the essential activities and figuring out the minimum time to complete them.

For example, let's return to that project to relocate your business office. This is a project that can take over three months or it could be done much more quickly. It depends on what is important, how large the office is, the amount of customer traffic, the office hours, and a host of other factors. Using the critical path method, you might consider hiring the movers and getting the move done as the essential activities. You might fast-track the customer notifications, strategy development, and preliminary packing by sandwiching them in between the more important work in the organization. Or these activities may become full-blown efforts that require considerable time. Only you can decide what's involved and how much time to devote to each task that needs completion. I would encourage you to think hard about overworking activities when the benefits of that time investment aren't there.

In traditional project management, where projects can be quite complex, those focusing on the critical path can spend considerable time paying attention to the path, even when software tools make it easier these days. Daily, they may be assessing the variances between estimates and reality on those essential activities. And then they are calculating the impact on the critical path to be sure that the ultimate deadline continues to be achievable.

Timely completion of a project is important. On some projects, it may be essential or even required by contract. But not all deadlines are equal. We can accomplish the objectives of the critical path method far more effectively by knowing what is important to the client, properly identifying the essential activities, truly understanding what "done" means for those activities, and knowing which deadlines are most critical.

Some people need deadlines more than others do. If you are working with people who need a deadline, ask them to give you their deadline. Have them commit to results by that date. But if it's not important and the deadline wasn't met because something more critical arose, let's not beat up on project teams over missing deadlines that don't matter. Set your projects up to meet the critical deadlines and be successful. Celebrate those wins. Focus on the positive, rather than the negative. And insist that critical deadlines are met.

Plan Your Quality

Planning your quality is an expansion of the concept that I discussed in the previous chapter – understanding "done." Identify the quality objective(s) for major deliverables early on. Understand what quality your management or client wants and remember that high quality often increases costs and/or the time to complete. If money is tight, know where the client is willing to pay for exceptional quality, and what that means, and know when "good enough" is sufficient. For example, if the activity is to conduct focus groups, consider specifying how many focus groups to conduct, what kind of participation is needed, and the types and quality of the materials to be distributed. By defining and testing quality in stages, the final project will better meet identified needs.

It is cheaper to build in quality than to repair quality that does not meet requirements. Experts regularly tout the recommendation to build in quality, rather than waiting until you are forced to repair quality. While some deliverables may not require attention to quality, most will benefit from some focus on what is needed and affordable. If you wait until the end to think about quality, it will be too late. Remember that project to relocate your business office? There are many ways to approach that project. How much packing will your team do, versus the moving company? How important are customer notifications? By assigning Complexity and thinking about what "done" looks like in advance, you can reduce wasted efforts.

Here it's important to understand that the type of project and the activity will dictate what is needed to understand quality. In a manufacturing project, quality can be highly specified and testable. In a business project, you may just be specifying that you want a Word document draft versus a fully approved and published document.

In an IT project, each activity could have detailed requirements about what is needed, or a selection of user stories. The client's level of cost sensitivity, the nature of the project, and the importance of the deadline will determine how detailed these requirements need to be. In a leaner project, the client may be happy with a user story, while in a government contract with millions or billions at stake, more requirements will be important. But even there, try to stay on the lean side, as circumstances change so rapidly in the IT world.

That's why I generally recommend that you do high-level planning first and wait until you are going to execute a specific activity before you dig into detailed requirements planning. When large contracts are involved, this gets harder. On a construction project, whether commercial or retail, there will be more detailed design documents that outline what kinds of products and installations are needed. Only you can decide if an allowance will suffice.

In the IT world and the legal world, there is often the assumption that quality means bug-free software and error-proof filings. But is that what the client wants? Sometimes, the client wants a quicker turnaround with the option of doing its own testing or reviews.

Once you have fully defined the quality requirements, assign someone on the team to test quality. Yes, quality is often hard to measure and test on business projects, but thinking ahead will make the process easier. Quality testing could involve anything from mere visual inspection to sophisticated defect measurements. It depends on the project and the activity.

Years ago, a retirement home opened with beautiful fluffy white carpeting installed in the grand main lobby. The decoration project went well but about a week after the grand opening, management realized that the Ladies Committee, which selected the carpet, had made a huge mistake. The lawyer was able to get the carpeting replaced for free, not because the color selection was inappropriate for the space, but because the quality inspector failed to ensure that the carpeting met the design specifications in the contract documents, which called for a different weight than what was installed. Make sure you understand who defines the quality requirements on each activity, tests that quality, and approves quality results.

Let's face it, projects are developed to take on new initiatives, and often no one is clear about what is wanted or needed. If a client is involved, be clear with the client about who can sign off on quality testing. Active client involvement should improve quality, ensure continued funding, and prevent overreaching, unaffordable efforts. In a business project, this step translates into knowing who, at the client or management level, is responsible for accepting a deliverable and agreeing that a particular activity has been finished. It may or may not be the same person for all your activities.

Finally, remember that quality is a neutral term. Just because McDonald's serves burgers and fries doesn't mean that the chain has poor quality – at least from a project management standpoint. The question is whether their burgers and fries meet the specifications that they have defined and promised their customers. It's not about the specifications that the health food industry would like them to define and meet.

Plan Your Issues and Risks

I discussed risks in detail in Chapter 5, but it's worth revisiting this concept to ensure that you consider it in your project planning.

Every project has issues and risks. First, let's learn the difference since they are easily confused. An issue is a problem that *has* occurred. Issues need to be resolved quickly. At a minimum, a simple issue log with instructions needs to be part of your project plan. The key is to have a process for ensuring that issues are identified and resolved quickly.

A risk is a problem or an uncertainty that *might* occur. Risks can be related to the environment, organization, project, people, or activities, and need to be managed throughout the life of your project. During the planning process, you need to create a plan for how you will identify and manage your issues and risks.

Plan Your Money

The need to track the money on a project will vary from firm to firm, and project to project. In some cases, executives may conclude that the end benefit is not worth the cost-tracking effort on some projects. We live and work in a knowledge economy and need to understand that time is money. Smart people often command large salaries, and we may be undervaluing the people on our projects when executives choose to track hard costs — from consulting fees, to supplies, materials, and office expenses — but don't track internal labor costs. And on projects that are done to generate revenue, you may decide to record project income.

Executives cannot expect to manage cash flows successfully without reliable project budgets and effective change control processes, which I discuss in the next two chapters. If costs are important to your client, it is essential to spend time thinking through which activities are required to accomplish your objectives, and what they will cost. I covered several methods of estimating costs in Chapter 4 (on project profitability).

There may be times when it is more appropriate to complete a project in phases, and therefore only a subset of the total activities will be identified, and the project budget will be for a single phase(s). The project plan will represent only that phase(s), and subsequent phases will be identified through the change control process or, perhaps, through a new engagement with the client. This approach will provide more flexibility when there are more unknowns. I discuss budget creation and money in more detail in Chapter 18 on management.

Plan How to Track Lessons Learned

There is huge value in temporarily setting aside computer reports and gathering to reflect on what happened. This is an often neglected but extraordinarily valuable activity and I talk more about it in Chapter 18.

Plan Your Communications

One important aspect of project planning that is often forgotten is to plan how you will communicate. Have you identified what is important to each key stakeholder, as discussed in Chapter 12?

Document the communication needs for every key player. Be sure you understand other perspectives and document them in a usable format. What are the hot buttons and sweet spots? How often does the client expect an update and what form should those updates take? You might consider updates via an emailed status report, inclusion in team meetings, or access to project dashboards. You don't have to give the client an unlimited choice of options, some of which you aren't financially or technologically prepared to offer, but you do need to confirm that the communication plan that you are thinking about will suffice.

What updates are needed for your firm's management? Are there triggers that might dictate a closer involvement from someone in senior management? More often, open communications will improve team functionality in the long term, because accountability is enhanced.

Weak communications will doom your efforts. Everyone on your team needs to be able to exhibit empathy and understanding in their communications. People with strong egos who are operating in command-and-control mode often cause problems when working with clients. Highly functioning teams can develop client bonds that will boost your key competitive advantage.

The hardest aspect of communication for some companies is deciding how to talk with one another. That problem is exacerbated when companies have a silo organizational structure. Here's a story that illustrates the problem with managing programs — that is, collections of related projects — across the organization.

A company celebrated the signing of three large work contracts. These new contracts had dramatically improved the company's revenue forecast; that meant additional work and several radical changes to the company's operating approach.

One of those changes was adding significant space to the warehouse. The company hired a contracting team. As the company planned the necessary changes to the warehouse, it had to procure customized equipment, make technology enhancements, and hire and onboard the new employees. Respective departments worked on these tasks, but it didn't happen as planned.

When the customized equipment arrived, it didn't work as specified. This major issue resulted in arguments and finger-pointing between the different manufacturing companies used as vendors and the technology team. All the while, the company completed the hiring, but couldn't successfully train the new employees. Tensions were high, complaints were increasingly vocal, and the new employees felt inefficient and unable to help. The organizational structure didn't lend itself to open and easy communications. People weren't talking with one other in a meaningful way.

Part of the problem was that colleagues were using different languages for their projects. The technology team was complaining about poorly defined user stories. The manufacturing companies were clueless when the technology team started talking about user stories. The contractors claimed to be on schedule, but had missed several deadlines. The people in human resources were being incredibly agile (i.e., flexible), but had no timeline for when new hires would be trained.

Standardizing your project language, as I suggested in Chapter 13, may not solve all your problems, but it's something that you can control and that can help minimize confusion.

Figure 7 summarizes the critical planning needs on any project. How you think about these items, and the extent to which you think about them, may vary from project to project, but you can't simply ignore them.

Figure 7: Project Planning Needs

Program Planning and Management

Many times, organizations find that a group of projects needs to be managed collaboratively. There are true dependencies between activities in the different projects, and the larger the group of projects, the more complicated it can become. The previous story is a great illustration of this. But I'll offer others.

One example is a collection of projects tied to a construction project. You may have, for example, a school that has a building project that is tied to the decorating project and the capital campaign. You may not want to send out a capital campaign communication to potential donors announcing tours before you have finished the hard-hat-required stage of construction. And your decorating team needs to decide what colors to paint the spaces before the painters arrive. In addition, the finish timing may be associated with a grand opening project or an academic planning effort that impacts space usage.

Another example is a law firm that is working on multiple matters for the same client. This may pose communication questions about who needs what, or potential financial questions that may cause you to put some work on hold. That's not a program in the traditional sense, but many of the same concerns can arise.

The key challenge is to be aware of these connections between projects. If you are using a more sophisticated system, you can manage the projects as a program. If not, you may want to record risks in your different project files. That will at least ensure that your teams are regularly checking in with one another to assess the status of the individual projects.

As I've said before, project success in times of uncertainty, change, and chaos depends largely on the relationships that we form and nourish.

Depending on the level of planning that is needed on your project, you will, at some point, begin project execution. Perhaps I should offer a caveat here. Many dollars have been lost on projects that should never have gone past the planning stage because too much complexity was discovered, or too little information was known to execute successfully.

Take for example, the legendary Denver Airport project to build an integrated baggage-handling system for the brand-new airport. This project, launched in 1989, was fraught with problems from the beginning. It was a complex project – and that complexity was known but seriously understated for years. In fact, initial reports indicated the complexity was too great for success; many have asked why the project was not cancelled then, or after several other red flags were raised.[126]

In the planning of this mega project, which was likely run as a program of related projects, there were multiple problems that the project team didn't handle well. Here are just a few:

- A highly specialized consulting group, Breier Neidle Patrone Associates, was hired about three years before the projected airport opening to do a feasibility analysis on building an integrated baggage system. As experts in this field, they said that the system could not be successfully built. Yet, leadership ignored the experts and continued.[127]
- Historically, baggage systems had been developed by individual airlines and the project management team assumed that would continue. Several airlines began building their own systems long before this project was up and running, and it took almost two years for the project team to recognize that this assumption was flawed.[128] As I said in Chapter 14, project teams need to document assumptions and test them. And part of the problem here is that, like risks, understanding assumptions requires that people think deeply.
- With two years remaining before the airport was scheduled to open, leadership contracted with BAE to build the integrated system, despite the knowledge that a much simpler system took workers in Munich two and a half years to build and test, and multiple warnings that this system could not be developed. Again, now two

years into the project, the team is still ignoring expert advice.[129]

- One of the biggest problems in building an integrated baggage system was related to how to predict customer usage so that luggage carts were where they were most needed when they were needed. Understanding complexity in the planning process is essential and this problem combined the difficulty of analyzing the structural build process with predicting human behavior. The team ignored expert advice that this challenge was too complex.[130]
- It took the project team for the baggage-handling system so long to develop a plan that the airport construction was well underway with no understanding of the space or power requirements needed for the baggage system. The result was a system that had to be slowed to a crawl to accommodate tight turns that were not forecast, eliminating the efficiency gains. Furthermore, power supply issues resulted in more delays.[131]

Like most project disciplines, the quest for perfect project planning is unattainable. There is no perfect plan. The idea that we can create an immutable plan, including a schedule, seems misguided to me and I argue that much of the money spent in trying to put together that perfect plan is wasted. And yet, the planning process, on some level, is invaluable and a smart investment. The challenge is to know when you are ready to launch into execution and accept that change will be needed. If the planning phase has revealed the probability that you will not be successful and you need to cancel the project, have the courage to pull the plug.

Indications That You Should Cancel a Project

Our success, as individuals and organizations, is driven by how we spend our time. Perhaps as importantly, it's driven by what we choose not to do. There are times when it simply makes sense to cancel a project early. It may be that the organization's priorities have changed, or the project has become unfeasible. Or it could be that the project is no longer contributing any business value to the organization's project portfolio. Many dollars have been lost on projects that should never have been initiated, have not gone well in the planning stage, or performed so poorly that canceling early would have been less costly. The Denver Airport project clearly points to four lessons that you need to remember once you begin executing a project.

1. Seriously consider cancelling or making major scope modifications when the experts are repeatedly telling you that it can't be done.

Executives with strong emotional commitments to a project can often be biased. Those around them, including the project team, may need to make compelling arguments in favor of cancellation or major changes. There were at least three significant times during the Denver project when the team or the sponsor ignored experts. Don't underestimate the impact of the biases that I discussed in Part 2.

2. When significant strategy changes are made by executives well into a project, consider whether you should move forward.

The original goal of the Denver Airport project was to build one of the most efficient airports in the world. Under this overarching goal, the question was always how to build an efficient baggage-handling system. But from the outset, the team failed to properly address the question of who was going to own the baggage handling system. Was it the airport or the airlines? Throughout the project, there were communication snafus and strategy flip-flops. Efforts to build an integrated system were fraught with problems. Finally, too much time passed to perfect any integrated system and the airport opened. Ten years later, the automated system, such as it was, was scrapped for a manual baggage system after maintenance costs hit $1 million a month.[132]

3. Consider cancelling when you realize well into a project that you missed a major assumption which turned out to be flawed, or when the timeline is clearly impossible.

Between the flawed assumption on human behavior as well as the impossibility of the timeline, which became increasingly clear during planning, there was simply no chance of achieving real success in Denver.

4. Be cautious when massively expensive executive decisions are made unilaterally.

In the Denver Airport case, one of the biggest decisions was made by Walter Slinger, the airport's chief engineer. He was also in charge of all airport operations and so was not devoted to this project full-time. Slinger was highly experienced in airport engineering. According to reports, he was a hands-on manager who liked to solve his own problems. But he had no experience with an integrated baggage system. No one did. It was the first one of its kind. And when complexities surfaced, no one was able to fully grasp the impact.

Slinger was the point man for all discussions with BAE. But important stakeholders, such as the airlines, were often left out of these discussions. Slinger's contact at BAE was selfishly interested in selling this system and then being able to sell it to other major airports. And Slinger badly wanted to successfully launch the first-ever integrated baggage-handling system. That had been his baby from the beginning. So, when BAE built a prototype, Slinger's confidence grew, and he ignored the clearly impossible timeline.

Nearly three years after work started on this project, Slinger died. His replacement didn't have his depth of knowledge. Soon, electrical supply issues and resulting part insufficiencies caused testing delays. Finally, an impromptu and disastrous media demonstration brought the mayor of Denver into the equation and an outside consultant was hired. But this was six months after the airport was to have initially opened – too little and too late.[133]

On a project of this size, independent reviews should be completed throughout the project. Certainly, an outside team should have reviewed the proposal and prototype before Slinger unilaterally decided to move forward.

So, why is it so hard to cancel a project early? There is no question that once a contract has been signed, other legal complications arise that make it more difficult to cancel a project. But some of these lessons were evident before the BAE contract was signed. So why did it go forward? In Chapter 8, I talked about Michael O'Brochta's research on why IT projects can be hard to kill. I suspect the same biases apply here. As project managers, sponsors, and teams, we need to understand these natural biases and call out these behaviors.

In the next two chapters, I cover project execution and management, which are done simultaneously. I offer thoughts on how to get the work done most efficiently and how to manage change so that chaos doesn't overtake you.

Before I move on, let me reiterate the importance of starting smart. If you'd like more information on that, check out this site: https://smartprojex.com/category/starting/.

Chapter 17

Smart Cats Deliver Results That Matter!

Project execution and project management (which is covered in the next chapter) are done simultaneously. Hopefully, you have started and planned wisely, and your execution will fall into place. That said, expect conflict. You cannot and should not even try to innovate without disagreement. Note that in the Smart Projex world, you will probably be continuing traditional project planning efforts as part of the execution phase. Here, I discuss three key parts of project execution: getting the work done, procuring necessary resources, and future planning, including a change management process.

Getting Work Done

This is the key to execution and one of the reasons that the Waterfall approach maddens me so much. When people are spending days calculating the critical path or assessing earned value metrics or adjusting schedules, they aren't getting the work that matters done.

Work in Time Blocks or Sprints

When teams work in time blocks (or sprints) and focus on delivering some defined result to the client at the end of each time block, it builds some urgency in the short term. It also allows for early feedback before tons of money is spent moving in the wrong direction.

When you create your work breakdown structure, it is critical that you think ahead about defining your essential activities so that you can regularly deliver results to your client. For this reason, I suggest that you not define activities that will take months to finish. At the beginning of each sprint, decide which activities you plan to focus on, and select a group of activities that you can deliver. Confirm what "done" looks like on each of those activities and focus on finishing that work. This can be harder on some types of projects, particularly when the activities seem large. Think in terms of delivering real value to your client – so that you are getting feedback early and often. It may be an executive summary of the work that has been accomplished. It may be a meeting with a leadership team, where you discuss what has been learned and gain consensus on a particular course of action. Whatever you choose to provide, there is simply no substitute for early feedback from your client. It is invaluable. Yet, the client must have something to review to offer you any feedback of value.

Use the aggregate and individual Complexity to select a group of activities that the team can realistically achieve in a single time block. Work relentlessly on that group of activities. Finish as many as you can, and then bite off another chunk for the next time block. You will be surprised at how much your team can accomplish when they are focused. But one key is to remove distractions. This can be hard when your teams are not singularly focused.

Sometimes, teams work on many projects and activities simultaneously. Use your daily standing meetings to identify and hopefully remove distractions and build focus. And understand that a crisis for one of your clients can throw a monkey wrench into the best-laid plans. That's one reason why I prefer to see organizations managing all their work, such as products, projects, operations, sales, and strategy development, in one tool.

Use Play

Our success in prior decades might have been tied to how well we executed a carefully constructed plan. Our success in the future will depend on our creativity. Play can be a way for businesspeople to bring creativity to the fore, especially when teams are stuck. It's about changing perspective. It can be as simple as a game break, starting meetings with a game of charades, temporarily moving to a different location for a few hours, or playing games with the activities that we are working on.

The Agile community has developed many games that you can try. Whether you play games, turn your team's quest to produce more value for the client into a competition, or bring some playfulness into your meetings or work time, the goal is to build a creative spirit that improves results and delights your client. If you want to be successful, build teams that experiment, learn, repeat, and communicate effectively.

Use Standing Meetings Effectively

Standing meetings (described in Chapter 13) can promote accountability, and provide the opportunity to celebrate little successes. They build energy and commitment, and often result in a speedier execution of project activities. These meetings also provide a safe place to disclose problems early, while they are easier to resolve, since that is a stated purpose of the meeting. Everyone wants to work on projects that are going well, where problems are addressed quickly and constructively, and where a culture of honesty, fun, and progress is apparent.

Every team and every project is different. And times change. You will need to find a rhythm that works for you. Distributed teams often need a different approach than co-located teams, or those teams that are all working from the same place. And as the work ebbs and flows on your project (and it might do that for legitimate reasons), you may find the need to adjust your approach. Some teams may decide that the standing meeting needs to include "how-to" discussions, while other teams stick with the three traditional standing meeting questions that I outlined in Chapter 13. Some teams prefer to use emailed status reports. I would encourage you to start with the traditional approach that I described and try to improve on it if you can. The goal is to increase everyone's accountability to each other and the work you are doing. In a rapidly changing, chaotic world, we should all be looking for better ways of working.

Stay Focused on What's Important Now

In Greg McKeown's book, *Essentialism*, he recounts a story from Larry Gelwix, the coach of the Highland High School (Salt Lake City) rugby team, which won 418 games in 36 years, with only 10 losses. When asked how he did that, the coach talked about an acronym, WIN, which means "What's Important Now?"[134]

I first began to understand the concept of "what's important now" in my early parenting days. When I had four children under the age of four, every morning became a test of reevaluating what's important. If everyone woke up in the morning healthy and happy, I counted my blessings.

And as often as not, the item that I had selected the previous night as most important seemed less important when a child needed me. It didn't get that much better as they got older. Snow days. Sick days. Playdate cancellations. Technology problems. Girlfriend or boyfriend twists. You name it. I'm pretty sure that moms and dads understand this.

It's not that different with our clients and employees. Anything can happen overnight, or even over lunch. I always admire these folks who can prioritize their day the night before. I understand the value of waking up to a plan – but more often, I wake up to revising the plan.

Coach Gelwix's point is to stay focused on the moment. It's great advice. The past is over. The future is not yet here. What we must work with is the present. I'm not ready to abandon the concept of planning for the future, but I do think focusing on the present is important. And when I'm in the middle of a meeting and watching others focusing on their cell phones, I'm more convinced than ever that being fully present is essential. Ask the question: what's important now? WIN!

Celebrate Success

Everyone needs to see that active projects are achieving goals. Even when everything is falling apart, surely there are some good things happening. It is important to focus on those successes, in part because constantly focusing on the negative is depressing.

And if you aren't celebrating some periodic successes, you may not have planned your project wisely. Remember that when you plan a project - the goal is to set it up for success. You should be delivering real value to your client every few weeks or so. If you are missing a few deadlines but still delivering value regularly and rapidly, don't beat up the team over deadlines that don't matter. Things change frequently. Focus on the accomplishment, instead of the fact that one activity was done two months or three weeks later than originally projected. Your team will be inspired.

And don't just celebrate the number of activities that have been completed. This is a time when that Complexity number I talked about earlier in this book is helpful. Track the aggregate Complexity of the work you have completed in each sprint and aim to improve when that makes sense. Sometimes, it won't make sense to try. But you should be focusing on the quality of work completed and using accomplishments to drive momentum. Focus on finishing work and delivering results that matter. Yes, some activities do take longer than others, but avoid the situation where your team works for weeks and weeks on something with no results.

Take advantage of times that offer you the opportunity for a fresh start. These small celebrations do that. According to Dan Pink's *When: The Scientific Secrets of Perfect Timing*, "Endings of all kinds — of experiences, projects, semesters, negotiations, stages of life — shape our behavior in four predictable ways. They help us energize. They help us encode. They help us edit. And they help us elevate."[135] So celebrate — to energize your team, to encode what you've learned and accomplished, to edit your project plan, and to elevate those accomplishments that have value for the client.

I encourage you to find inexpensive ways of celebrating that don't necessarily involve a lot of extra food and alcohol. Here are some ideas:

- Take a picnic lunch to the local park and fly kites.
- Have a river in your town? Can you go play at or on the river one day after work?
- Is there a movie that everyone would enjoy? Do a movie night at someone's house or at the office.

It's a shame to spend the time to set up a project with celebration points and then fail to celebrate. Each team will need to find its celebration rhythm and its methods. Get creative. It's not about the money or the alcohol. It's about spending time together doing something fun. But keep in mind that some people on your team have families they want to spend time with too. Depending on the composition of your team, you may celebrate over lunch at the office or include families in a celebratory out-of-office activity. Or you may send a personal note of thanks to everyone on the team.

Procure Resources

Your resources consist of the people that you attract to work on your projects, and the resources that you purchase, often from vendors. Vendors are simply the stakeholders on your project to which you pay money.

Attract the Brightest and Best People for Your Team

To attract the best people to work on your projects, you may need to hunt. I talked about the kinds of natural leaders who might play a valuable role on your project in

Chapter 8. Where are those people? Use the core team that has been developed to date to help you expand your team into the group that can turn your project dreams into reality. Your organization's structure and corporate policies will guide how you go about finding resources. Just know that they may be buried deep in the organization. You probably don't want the people with the big egos who are out there loudly promoting themselves.

Understand the Procurement Process

In many projects, the team, or someone acting on its behalf, will need to contract for goods or services. This may start in the planning phase and continue into project execution. Much of what I cover here is also applicable to the negotiation of the contract that might initiate a project. Understand from the beginning that contracts are legal documents and that much can be at stake. It is critical to take contract management seriously.

Marin County, California, found that out the hard way when it settled a lawsuit in 2013 at a total cost of $33 million. The case stemmed from the Marin Enterprise Resource Integrated Technology (MERIT) project, which was launched in 2004 to replace some legacy systems that weren't functioning well. The project, under the leadership of Deloitte, did not go well and Marin sued. Issues that surfaced in the litigation included problems with understanding deliverable acceptance (remember when I talked about defining what done means and knowing who was able to accept deliverables?), poor project oversight from Marin leadership, and vendor substitutions of resources.[136] It is essential that you think through these contracts carefully when you plan and execute your projects. Here are the four basic steps involved in this process:

1. Identify those items to be procured.

The first step in this process is to understand what resources you need to acquire and then to develop a plan for acquiring them. There are options that run the gamut from a visit to an office supply store to developing a Request for a Proposal or Quote (RFP or RFQ) and going through a formal bidding or procurement process. When you are acquiring people from outside the organization, be especially clear about the skill sets that are needed and how substitutions will be handled, particularly on longer-term contracts. People come and go; what happens when that highly skilled blockchain developer or CFO that you thought you were getting is no longer available?

2. Develop the various procurement documents.

The project manager doesn't typically develop proposal or bid requests. Many organizations have specific guidelines and procedures for acquiring resources, and project management teams should defer to those professionals. Communicate effectively with your procurement department about your timeline for needing resources and know that formal bidding processes will take time.

3. Obtain signed contracts.

There may be delays here, as this is typically not done by the project team. If this is happening mid-project, be sure to allow for delays.

4. Determine and document any requirements under each contract.

This is the step where it becomes essential for the project manager to be involved, even when there is a procurement department. Once a contract has been executed, the project manager needs to understand whether there are any requirements that need to be followed during the project and develop a process for tracking and managing those requirements.

When you determine how contract requirements will be managed, designate someone to be the contract manager. It is essential to understand that contracts are legal documents and may well have requirements that must be followed.

For example, if you have a contract with a temporary staffing agency, does your contract require notice before terminating a crew or crew member? If you have a contract with an architectural or engineering firm, does the contract require your organization to provide progress, specification, or document reviews at various intervals? If you have a contract with a beer keg supplier, does the contract require you to return the kegs within some defined time frame?

There is more to the vendor process that I discuss in chapters 18 and 19.

Think About the Future

The future is changing constantly. Part of the job of executing a project in a complex or chaotic world is being able to sense trends and knowing how to balance the trade-off between executing the planned scope and being flexible enough to make a change. If you change on a dime too frequently, your teams can get whiplash. If you don't change when the circumstances support change, you could lose a valuable opportunity. For this reason, I recommend that organizations develop a change process that works. I outline a four-step method of creating a change management process in Appendix 3.

Scope Management or Uncontrolled Change?

An effective approach to change management affords both agility and control and helps ensure that the constant change around us doesn't result in project chaos. During your project, a time may come when you need to make a change in the scope. This happens for many reasons and particularly in a rapidly changing business environment. But it's essential that you have a way to manage those potential changes.

In a world of rapid change, smart people are always coming up with new and better ideas. The challenge to the team, and the project, is to seize opportunities to save money or improve the project outcome without the inevitable scope creep that can occur if teams are left without guidance, both from management and the client.

You may find that the best storytellers around your organization are good at talking teams into thinking that a particular idea reigns supreme. How many times have you seen people invest in some new venture, only to find out it was a boondoggle? The same applies to organizations.

And then, there are environmental factors that can throw your scope under the bus – such as major disruptions caused by wildfires, pandemics, or hurricanes. As another example, how does your organization (and the projects it is invested in) change when a couple of activist investors are suddenly elected to your board?

You must choose between letting chaos control you or finding a way to navigate the chaos. I once worked for an entrepreneur who changed her mind every other day about what she wanted to do. She gave me more grey hair than five children.

To set our projects up for success, we must be adept at walking the line between needed change and uncontrolled change. No one likes working for the boss who changes his mind about priorities every other day. Change is hard but it's also necessary. As organizations, we must evolve, grow, and sometimes pivot. The challenge is to *manage* the change.

Clearly, leaders are beginning to understand the need for agility. But as we have moved in that direction, many organizations have allowed project managers to select the most appropriate software solution for the individual project. So, some projects are being done with closely monitored Gantt charts, some are being done in Jira or Rally, while others may be using SmartSheet or even Excel, and still others may be using a package like Monday or Wrike. As that has happened, we've lost any ability to understand our project investments without significant manual updates from project managers, who rarely enjoy confessing to unpleasant truths.

We need a way to manage priorities and project investments. A documented change management process, together with the use of focused sprints, can keep your teams from running in circles. Embracing change does not mean embracing chaos. Provide a stable and safe environment in which your teams can thrive.

When Does It Make Sense to Accelerate an Activity?

As you execute projects, you should know what the cost of a month-long delay is on project completion. Occasionally, perhaps a project can finish late without significant impact on the company. But most projects are undertaken to produce benefits that improve the bottom line. If those benefits are delayed by a month, what is the cost to the company? Ten thousand, or a million dollars?

Consider that if one activity is going to delay your

project, it might well make sense to spend the extra dollars to accelerate that activity.

I recommend that you do these cost of delay calculations on all the projects in your organization. Some delays will be more costly than others and project leaders will just have to judiciously choose when to accelerate a particular activity.

An Effective Change Control Process

Imagine that when you arrive at your office every single morning, the contents of your desk have been emptied out and scattered all around and you must spend the first three hours of your workday reorganizing your desk.

That's the feeling when you work on a project team with a boss who changes his/her mind about the project every day. You begin your day by trying to figure out what is going on, where everything is, and how to move forward.

To ensure that teams are given a framework within which to manage scope, it is essential that they have both a clear understanding of where they are ultimately going and a documented change management process.

What is the basic plan? How will we know if we are successful? If a client is involved, the client needs to understand this process, since clients are often the source of many great ideas, only some of which they have the resources to fund.

Who can submit changes? Who approves changes? How are changes evaluated? Without an appropriate change management process, a team can spin mindlessly every time a new idea is introduced. And when the client or the owner is introducing constant change, it can wreak havoc on a team's focus and the project schedule and budget.

An effective change management process can reduce the chaos, and still allow the team to capitalize on change.

Maybe you aren't familiar with Design Thinking. It's a way of solving problems that focuses on the people. It's known for the three Es: empathy, experimentation, and expansive thinking. What does the user want? What does the team need? What does management expect? What have we forgotten to consider?

It doesn't matter whether your client is a Lean, Six Sigma, Kaizen, or Design Thinking organization. All these clients will hire you with the expectation that you can pivot quickly. And if your own company is fighting to stay competitive (and most are), it needs to think creatively and be prepared to pivot.

But constant pivoting leaves project teams grasping for something to hold onto and gasping for breath. Teams need several things: a strong understanding of their guiding star, and a system that includes money management, change control, and some effective business analytics. Here are some characteristics of an effective change management process.

The Process is Clear, Well-Documented, and Fully Communicated

There is no way to have a fair process that no one understands or knows about. It's not easy to create a change management process. There are many questions that you will need to consider. Once you have a change management process established, it will guide you through challenging times.

One aspect of the process that needs clarity is

what constitutes a "change." First, the organization needs a strong focus on the vision for the project. If the recommended change is a departure from that vision in any significant way, it should be reviewed as a totally new project, and not a project scope change.

If the change is simply a rearrangement, elaboration, or clarification of known activities and will not increase the cost or delay the finish, it isn't a change. It's considered staying agile and being able to adapt quickly when needed.

That leaves everything in between – for example, the requests that align with your project vision and that will increase your costs or delay your finish. Your change management process should include a policy on requests that don't change the cost but will cause a significant delay. Sometimes, it is necessary to reprioritize the project portfolio because of unforeseen reasons – the disruption to workplaces and lives caused by the COVID-19 pandemic is an example of a legitimate reason. This is one time when it helps to have a clear understanding of all the critical deadlines throughout your organization. This may allow you to put a substantial amount of work on hold and still move forward in such a way that the project vision can ultimately be realized.

The Process Does Not Play Favorites

A proposed change from someone on the team is given the same level of consideration as a change request from the CEO. This is essential but can be hard to achieve. The change management process must be fair to work well. Senior executives rarely understand the ins and outs of a project, so team members are often better positioned to see opportunities for beneficial changes. Create a process that treats all proposed changes the same way. And make sure everyone understands that the process is designed that way.

When someone has spent their entire life building their own company, it is hard for the project manager (or anyone else) to push back and explain to them that a process needs to be perceived as fair. Perhaps you can explain that team members often see details that the owner cannot possibly know. Therefore, they are well-positioned to spot ways to reduce costs or achieve greater benefits before others in the organization. For this reason, a change process is better if it's perceived as fair.

Create a Change Control Board or Committee

This is particularly helpful when dominant players are prone to changing course frequently. When changes must be approved by a group, it can slow the chaos. The goal here is to have a way to manage change so that change doesn't manage you. Unmanaged change quickly becomes chaos.

Having a group of people who must review change requests slows the process. No one, even the company owner, should be able to simply demand project changes. Yes, that may be hard. You will have to make sure your owner understands the value of focus, and the difficulty of achieving focus when the world is spinning.

Aim for Quantitative Metrics on Which to Evaluate the Request

As discussed in Chapter 6 (on project selection), companies should have a fair process for evaluating the business case for your projects on a regular basis. You might tie your change management process into your business case evaluation. The key is to ensure that all your projects remain aligned with your larger strategy.

To be clear, when I talk about embracing change, pivoting, and change management, it is important to understand that all projects are different. Some are way more experimental and innovative. Some are much more defined. The way you define your scope will determine what your perspective is on change. You can innovate and embrace change on some types of projects and define the details that matter when appropriate.

As you accomplish the work objectives, while keeping an eye on the future, you can adjust and adapt when external or internal factors dictate the need. In the next chapter, I discuss managing the project, which you will be doing at the same time. Perhaps it is helpful to think of execution as moving the train down the track and management as making sure the train stays on the right track. You must do both at the same time.

Chapter 18

Use Hindsight and Foresight to Develop Insight

If you are following the steps outlined so far, you are well on your way to a successful project outcome. This can even be true if you develop insights that cause you to cancel the project early. In this chapter, I cover some basic elements of managing the project (including scope and schedule management), using Checkpoint meetings effectively, money and vendor management, and lessons learned.

Scope and Schedule Management

In the Smart Projex methodology, schedules, as such, aren't created. But that doesn't mean that deadlines aren't managed. Here's an alternative that, along with effective meetings, allows teams to meet the critical deadlines and stay on top of the schedule.

In the activity planning phase, your team committed to meeting a handful of critical fixed deadlines. Perhaps the team identified some target deadlines that it plans to use to guide execution.

I outlined the way that work gets done in Chapter 17 (on execution). By focusing work on a small group of activities and by getting commitment from the team to finish those activities during the sprint, the chance of completing these activities increases. It is essential that everyone, including the client, agrees on what "done" means; if significant time has passed since the definition was created, things have probably changed. Confirm the definition of done before you start work. Make sure you clarify who will sign off on the quality needed and accept the final deliverable.

If you have promised your client a set of deliverables by a certain date, ensure you know what that means. For example, if the deliverable is code, is it in production or staging? If the deliverable is a product usage manual, who needs to review the draft before it goes to print?

Use Deadlines Appropriately

Don't make the mistake of thinking that every deadline is critical. Be selective. Talk to your client about the deadlines that simply cannot be missed. And make sure you communicate the fixed (i.e., critical) deadlines to everyone on your team, including your subject matter experts, peripheral team members, and any project managers of related projects, if they exist.

Manage Scope Change

In the last chapter, I discussed a plan to manage scope change. Hopefully, you have created a change management process because you will be dealing with change. During the execution and management phase, you will receive and evaluate change requests, approve and deny them, and then put the approved changes in place.

Use Checkpoint Meetings Effectively

Checkpoint meetings are one of the most important ways that you will successfully manage your projects. Don't get sloppy about these meetings and start cancelling them without good cause. If you think you don't need these meetings, you may have taken a shortcut on your project management disciplines. The goal is to use this time to reflect backwards, as a team, to develop insights about future work, risks, and problems (such as cost overruns), that need to be addressed. Remember to look at the future as well. Try these seven actions to prepare for and hold these meetings.

1. Review your end game – the what and why.

This is your chance to remind the team of why they are doing this work. They will forget if you don't keep that vision front and center. Pop a surprise question at a meeting and ask someone else to state the vision. And review the objectives – what you said you would accomplish and how you would measure it to ensure that you are still on the right track.

2. Review your accomplishments during the recent sprint.

What did you deliver to the client? Celebrating small wins is a great motivational practice.

3. Identify and document the lessons that were learned.

Use an online database that future teams can easily access to make this work useful, and track your lessons learned at the organization level, not the project level.

4. Review the budget against actual dollars.

Are you well positioned to finish the project within the agreed-upon budget? This is the time to assess whether there are individual activities that are in danger of cost overruns. You may need to advise management or your client about emerging cost concerns. Are there places where you should be cutting back, or where someone is overworking an activity? Is the anticipated cost overrun a true scope increase or a poor estimate?

5. Assess your issues.

Identify any new problems, review outstanding concerns, and designate people to investigate outstanding problems. Hopefully, this is a small task if you have been using your standing meetings wisely.

6. Identify and analyze the project risks.

It is essential that teams make time to identify new risks. Things can change rapidly in the twenty-first century. Before the meeting, have your team reassess the outstanding risks and ensure that you have documented mitigation strategies and identified any trigger events for your top-ranked risks. Set aside time in the meeting to think deeply about whether new risks have emerged. People are busy and this won't happen if you don't make time to stop and think.

7. Plan the work for the next sprint.

Decide which activities you will do in the next sprint and review those activities for clarity. (Remember to review what the "done" statement means, who is in charge, and what quality is desired.) This is your time to get the team to buy into completing these activities, hopefully during the sprint, and ideally within the budget. It is possible you may need to break down activities further at this point, as you continue to learn more about your project. Your goal is to settle on a group of well-defined activities that the team commits to finishing in your next sprint. Perhaps, in choosing activities wisely, you can reduce one of your risks.

Money and Vendor Management

Learn How to Analyze Your Client Relationships

By periodically reviewing the performance on projects, teams are often able to increase efficiencies, better allocate resources, and improve client results at a lower cost.

If your client is paying you on an hourly basis, this rewards inefficiencies. Fewer and fewer clients are willing to do that. You may have to begin offering your clients an alternative billing approach to remain competitive. And your alternative billing approach had better be profitable for your company.

Firms that have systems in place to effectively manage their projects will fare much better than firms that don't. As you learn how to analyze your project performance, you can determine who your most valuable clients are.

Vendors Are Often Critically Important

Managing any relationship with a vendor means understanding the involvement that the vendor wants and needs. It will depend on the resources being acquired.

Would greater involvement with the vendor result in the project objectives being completed more efficiently?

Once the vendor has provided the goods or services called for under the contract, the contract manager needs to confirm that the goods or services meet the contract requirements. Some organizations will want the contract manager to be a member of the project team, while other organizations will have a procurement office that has staff specifically trained for these jobs.

If there is a procurement department, it is still a responsibility of the project manager (unless told otherwise) to understand what is in the contract and ensure that contracts are managed in accordance with the law and the organization's policies and procedures. Project managers should have a basic knowledge of contracting or be prepared to work with someone who does.

When vendors are also clients, it is especially important that teams are clear about roles, responsibilities, and activities in progress. You don't want to put a sales relationship in peril by not following good procedures on the vendor side.

Understand the Impact of People Management on Costs

Money may be one of your most important resources. From understanding the cash flow demands of your clients to protecting the cash flow of your own company, money is a hugely important project need. When project funding is cut, for whatever reason, teams must adjust, and the process can be painful.

If costs are important to your client (and they usually are), it is essential to spend time thinking through what activities are required to accomplish your objectives, and what they will cost.

The Basics of Tracking Money Starts with Estimating

When firms decide to track money, the process begins by creating an estimated cost for each activity that you defined in the work breakdown structure. The trick is to be as thorough as necessary to develop a reliable budget without being so granular that the time spent estimating outweighs the benefits. Planning your budget at the activity level helps, rather than having a budget for every little task, though you may need to think through multiple money items for any one activity. For example, you could have materials costs and labor costs for multiple people on the same activity.

The decision about how to track costs will often require input from your client and/or your management team. Find that sweet spot between something that is so high-level that you won't be able to identify scope creep and so granular that it's not worth the effort. If you have broken your project down into discrete activities, all of which have a clear definition of done, start with creating a budget for each of those activities and then tracking and reviewing the costs for each one.

While the first step may be estimating the costs, one of the next steps is recording the actual costs. Insist that time worked is recorded daily. When a firm is paying a contractor on an hourly basis and the work takes longer than estimated, the project can quickly be thrust into the red. Having a good contract that outlines expectations with your contractors makes sense.

Keeping a close eye on the budget and the actual costs can help ensure that projects stay on track. Understanding the costs associated with each activity may provide data on which team members are working most effectively for the client. Throwing more money at a problem, in and of itself, rarely solves the problem. Cost overruns may be a sign that scope creep is setting in, that people are overworking activities, or that the estimates are flawed. Understand the difference. Few clients want to burn money without results.

In addition to estimating costs, you may decide to record projected income. After all, some projects are done to generate revenue. Understanding the income associated with each project allows a firm to ascertain which clients are most profitable. And understanding how the income relates to your activities may provide scheduling insights.

Connect Cash Flow to Scheduling

The concept of a flexible execution is inconsistent with knowing when the money will be flowing in and out on a project. Thus, compromise is needed. Have you considered the possibility of allowing your teams to execute your projects according to available cash flows? Firms do that when they are forced to because the economy has gone south. Why not do the same at other times?

Understanding the budget and cash flow timing on the key activities, along with appropriate management and client input, better positions the project team to execute in accordance with available cash flow and client needs.

Lessons Learned

This is a subject that is often overlooked – even in massive projects run by so-called experts. What a shame. The insights can be invaluable. As I read the previously mentioned *Dallas Morning News* article which reported that "*After $367.5 million, Texas gets no new child support computer software – just painful lessons*," it was pretty clear that a 12-year project was abandoned after years of numerous problems and disappointments and a failure to learn from those lessons.[137] While there were clearly other factors in this situation, it is nevertheless indicative of the kind of mistake that we make if we wait until the end to focus on lessons learned, or fail to do so at all.

Document Lessons Learned in a Searchable Format

As projects unfold, teams learn new things. They learn what works, what doesn't work, what will drive up costs, and what (or who) will delay results. Set aside time in your Checkpoint meetings to identify and document those lessons learned before they are forgotten. I believe lessons learned are like risks in the sense that it may require deep thought to identify them. Stop the busyness and start thinking deeply to come up with meaningful observations.

When we have team meetings to review lessons learned, we need to be focused on a rational review of the process. Identify what went wrong (or right), and the point in the process where things fell apart (or came together.) Try to name the problem. Dig deeply. Avoid specific discussions about a particular person's failings. Team meetings are not the place for those personnel conversations, which should be conducted by trained HR professionals.

You need to decide how and where you plan to record these lessons, and they should be available across the organization, indexable in a few different ways – including by name, project, people, keyword, etc. You will need to think about that. Selecting a good name to call the lesson, and relevant searchable keywords, will increase the usability of your database, and that's what this is about.

Lessons Learned Means We Learned Lessons

The operative word in the expression "lessons learned" is "learned." We need to actually learn something from our projects and not repeat the same mistakes. The process of uncovering lessons can be difficult, but the rewards can be great.

In his book, *The Culture Code: The Secrets of Highly Successful Groups*, Dan Coyle writes about the Upright Citizens Brigade (UCB), an improv comedy group that uses a well-known and established comedy training method called the Harold. Unlike Second City and other first-tier comedy clubs, UCB is obsessive about using the Harold. I won't try to outline how the Harold works but will simply describe it as a somewhat brutal approach to gathering lessons learned. UCB members would likely agree that, while it's an excruciating process, the resulting familial bonds, trust, and teamwork that are built are worth the pain.[138]

In the military, they use an After Action Review (AAR). It's not a fact-finding mission to assign blame, but a way to learn and improve. Project leaders should be doing the same thing. When companies are innovative, they are constantly conducting experiments to learn more. But are they capturing those lessons so that they can remember them and make the most use of them in the future? Are they truly transforming their teams through this process?

Too often when I review lessons learned registers, the lessons are trite and focused on what a great job some group is doing. That's not the point. The point is to understand what we can and should be doing better. We need to know what's working and what's not working and adapt. This is true *while* we are executing a project *and* at project closure, which I discuss in the next chapter.

Chapter 19

The Gains of Closing Are Lost if You're Dozing

Traditionally trained project managers are taught the importance of project closure, as outlined in this chapter. This essential step protects your relationships with your team, client, and vendors. As tempting as it may be, don't skip this step. I know you are through with the project, the client seems pleased, and the team has moved on to other things, but closure is important. Here are the basics.

Assess the Project Using the Metrics You Defined in the Charter

Remember eons ago when you started the project? You said you were going to accomplish certain objectives. You said that you were going to measure your success with specific metrics. Have you done that? Did the project finish on schedule and within the budget? Don't assume your project was successful because everyone is glad to be finished and the client seems reasonably happy.

I've seen clients that were so tired of thinking about a project that they wanted to move on. They got most of what they wanted. Do you need to direct their attention to something that wasn't done or could have been done better? There may well be lessons your team can or should learn by reexamining your accomplishments, considering what you originally planned. You may never discuss those observations with your client, but you could learn lessons that inform future projects.

Analyze how effectively the project accomplished its objectives. Go back and dig out your original definition of success. Were you successful by those metrics? Try to identify why you were successful or not. You will learn much from that experience that will inform the way you manage future projects, the way you bid on future projects, and the kinds of projects that you take on.

As you gather more specifics on the project performance, you will want to review the original cost estimates, final accounting, scope, constraints, assumptions, and changes, among other details.

Close Out Contracts

Contracts are legal documents. This is the time to audit the contract, ensure that all the contract requirements were met, and that the other party was notified that the engagement is over. Make sure any final payments due under the procurement contracts have been disbursed.

Suppose your contract is for leased meeting space or temporary staff. Don't get stuck paying for another month of rent or labor costs because you didn't properly give notice or cancel your contract.

It is equally important to do a post-engagement (project) review of the contract (or engagement letter) with your client. Memories are short, and you may be surprised to find something in that contract that you had forgotten.

And if you are closing out the project contract, ensure all payments have been made.

Many firms have a standard process for contract closure and a contract manager who performs that function. Failure to ensure that procurement contract requirements have been satisfactorily met, to ensure vendors have been paid, and to notify them that the terms of the contract have been satisfied could subject your firm to penalties or future liabilities and jeopardize ongoing relationships with your vendor.

Have a Face-to-Face Retrospective Meeting with Your Client

To prepare for this meeting, read over the contract with your client and identify talking points. Did you thank your client for the work? What did you originally promise to do for your client? Did you meet your objectives? Don't assume. Confirm that the quality you delivered met your client's needs. Did you meet the critical deadlines on the key deliverables?

As you confirm that you successfully met your objectives and pleased your client, find out if you have received all the payments from your client. Not all clients pay on time. If you haven't received the payments, this would be a good time to ask for your money.

If things didn't work out as well as planned, this meeting will be harder, but it's even more important. You can't improve without knowing what is needed. Be open to the ideas that your client has. Listen actively. Eat crow if you must. And then, when you return to the office or your home, document what you heard. Then, get a good night's rest. Sometimes you must make a concerted effort to have those difficult conversations without letting them ruin days of your life. Some people are more sensitive than others. Some clients are more difficult than others. You may decide that you never want to work with that client again.

Produce Final Accounting

Talk about learning experiences.... There is no substitute for following the money. Where did you underestimate project activities? Are there people on your team who consistently over- or underestimate? Were there places where you could have saved money?

Review and Release Team Members

Don't leave your team wondering what happened. If your project was done in a corporate environment, make sure that HR knows you are no longer using these people and that they can be assigned to other projects. That said, a highly functioning team can be a huge resource and if you've spent months building one, do everything you can to get the team assigned elsewhere to another project.

Write a Performance Appraisal on Each Team Member and Discuss It

Put this appraisal in their personnel file, particularly if you can make some complimentary remarks. If you had a bad experience with a member of the team, consult with your HR department before documenting anything in the file. If appropriate, write a review on LinkedIn, and/or a testimonial that the team member can use on his or her own marketing site. In this project world we live in, we all count on our project leaders to support us as we move on to our next projects. Remember reciprocity.

Celebrate!

The end of a project is a great time to celebrate. This may be an opportunity to produce a simple video or slideshow that shows how successful you were in meeting your project objectives. If most of your team hasn't met the client, consider putting pictures of your happy client in your video. Or perhaps you might invite the client to your celebration. Life in the business world doesn't have to always be about work. Sometimes, we should take time out to celebrate accomplishments, enjoy our friends, and lift our glasses high. Figure 8 summarizes the basic steps to close a project properly. Don't skip this celebratory step.

Figure 8: Project Closing Steps

How to Close a Project

1. Assess Project Success
2. Audit and Close Contracts
3. Review Project with the Client
4. Produce Final Accounting and Closure Documents
5. Review and Release Team

That's the Smart Projex methodology in a nutshell. It offers a concerted focus on many valuable disciplines, developed in the Waterfall approach over the last 100 years, together with the benefits of an Agile methodology, which has evolved over the last 20 years. If you would like more information on the methodology, check out this link: https://smartprojex.com/category/methodology/

Our rapidly changing world demands both project controls and agility. I believe that modern twenty-first-century technologies offer us great opportunities for building decent controls and embracing agility at the same time. In Part 4, I explore some intriguing possibilities.

Part 4
The Future

"Trouble results when the speed of growth exceeds the speed of nurturing human resources."

— *Attributed to Akio Toyoda*

Chapter 20

Can We Make Your Cats Smarter?

As Klaus Schwab, founder and executive chairman of the World Economic Forum, said: "The speed of current breakthroughs has no historical precedent. When compared with previous industrial revolutions, the Fourth [Industrial Revolution] is evolving at an exponential rather than a linear pace. Moreover, it is disrupting almost every industry in every country. And the breadth and depth of these changes herald the transformation of entire systems of production, management, and governance. The possibilities of billions of people connected by mobile devices, with unprecedented processing power, storage capacity, and access to knowledge, are unlimited.... Neither technology nor the disruption that comes with it is an exogenous force over which humans have no control."[139]

What might our future be if we empowered people to their fullest, moved our focus from schedule tracking to delivering real value, and used technology to enhance our decision-making, data tracking, and work efforts? That's the Part 4 discussion. Regardless of what we call it, what is the potential for Smart Projex 2.0 – a software tool that blends the insights that Waterfall offers with the flexibility that Agile offers to manage all work in an organization, using artificial intelligence (AI), blockchain, and a host of other sophisticated technologies?

In this chapter, I do a shallow dive on the opportunities and benefits that AI offers to project management. I'm admittedly no expert on artificial intelligence (or any other technology) and I'll leave those studies to others. I do know that AI gets more real by the week, and ethical issues abound.

For example, Aston University in Birmingham, England, has been awarded £3.06 million for Neu-ChiP, an international project to research the inclusion of human brain stem cells in computer processors with the hope of reducing energy costs and dramatically improving the ability of computers to learn on the job, so to speak.[140]

In 2015, Deloitte published a study that sought to investigate what the business opportunities were for cognitive technologies. This study defined artificial intelligence as "the theory and development of computer systems able to perform tasks that normally require human intelligence."[141] The same study noted: "Cognitive technologies are products of the field of artificial intelligence. They are able to perform tasks that only humans used to be able to do. Examples of cognitive technologies include computer vision, machine learning, natural language processing, speech recognition, and robotics."[142]

According to another Deloitte study, some writers continue to use the terms "artificial intelligence" and "cognitive technologies" interchangeably. They "both refer to technologies that can perform and/or augment tasks, help better inform decisions, and create interactions that have traditionally required human intelligence, such as planning, reasoning from partial or uncertain information, and learning."[143]

Richard Susskind, an independent adviser to national governments and international professional firms, has been writing about the future of law firms and other professions for about twenty years. In his 2017 book, *Tomorrow's Lawyers: An Introduction to Your Future*, he argues that the landscape that lawyers and law firms face is changing rapidly. He advises that we get ready. Change ushers in new languages, new ideas, and many conflicting opinions.[144]

It also presents opportunities for creating software that could dramatically improve the way we plan, do, and manage work in the future.

Basic AI Technologies

I do believe it's helpful to understand some of the basics on AI technologies before I delve into their potential benefits to project management, even in the near term.

Language Technologies

Natural language processing is a branch of AI that allows computers to understand human language; Siri and Alexa are two leading examples. Speech-to-text and text-to-speech technologies convert oral language to the written word, or the reverse. We see that in our ability to dictate texts or emails on our phones. And if you still answer your phone, you've likely heard too many robotic calls with increasingly natural-sounding voices.

Users of Siri, Alexa, or other chatbot or intelligent agent programs alternatively love or hate them – depending on how effectively they are working in the moment. But, as frustrating as they may be right now, these technologies get better by the day.

Vision Technologies

Computers are getting better and better at spotting and analyzing images, as those with their family pictures stored in Apple or Google photos know. And we are seeing leaps in augmented reality and virtual reality technologies, though both are still in their infancy.

Augmented reality (AR) is what you see in your physical world, like the dashboard in your modern car, when you see an overlay of digital images or data that improves your driving experience. Virtual reality (VR) is what Pokémon users are experiencing – their physical world is replaced by digital images and data. According to *Harvard Business Review* authors Michael Porter and James Heppelmann, VR adds simulation to the core capabilities that AR offers, which are visualization, interaction, and instruction.[145]

Machine Learning Technologies

Machine learning is a branch of artificial intelligence that uses algorithms to make smart decisions. It learns on the job, so to speak. Chess players have watched with interest the progression since IBM's Deep Blue beat Garry Kasparov, the reigning chess champion in 1997, to Google's 2017 announcement that AlphaZero had taught itself chess, together with other strategy games. For some time, artificial intelligence was hampered by the need for structured data – meaning that the data fields were carefully identified and labeled. But that is changing quickly.

Deep learning is a specialized type of machine learning that has allowed scientists to move into the unstructured data that surround us 24/7. Imagine software that scans memos and news posts and retrieves the pieces that are significant to the question you are trying to answer. No longer would project managers need to create a database to record their lessons learned. The software would simply be able to analyze the thousands or millions of conversations and documents and retrieve the applicable lessons. And a robot assistant would be able to translate that into spoken language that teams would easily understand as they planned a new project.

Statistical machine learning takes data and fits it to predictive models, while increasingly learning more and more.

What Are the Possibilities?

According to Tom Davenport, professor of information technology and management at Babson College, AI can, broadly speaking, "support three important business activities:

- Automating structured and repetitive work processes, often via robotics or robotic process automation.
- Gaining insight through extensive analysis of structured data, most often using machine learning.
- Engaging with clients and employees, using natural language processing chatbots, intelligent agents, and machine learning."[146]

Projects come with loads of data. AI could help us track and analyze that data, better estimate costs and schedules, identify and analyze risks, and extract the important and urgent. AI can also bring in industry data and organizational data that are not tied to our specific project. We could use AI to develop insights about industry, or competitor shifts that are likely to impact our projects. And we could use visualization tools, such as holograms, to enhance our understandings.

In the near term, we may need to standardize our project language and agree on what data fields are called throughout our organizations. As our machine language processing improves and we no longer require structured data fields, the potential to spot events and trends in the organization and the industry grows. This would allow rapid insights into what is happening in our portfolios.

For example, suppose a large server goes down and will likely be down for several days; how does that impact all the work in your organization, or the project you are leading? Suppose one of your leaders is involved in a serious accident, and cannot work for months; what will that do to your open work? What if one of your competitors announces a product shift that is directly related to the strategy on one of your products? The list is endless.

How Could We Apply This to Smart Projex 2.0?

While there are many opportunities for using AI to improve project and work management, I'll focus on three specific areas of interest: robotic assistants, simulations, and image insights.

Robotic Assistants

The language technologies that I previously discussed, together with some robotics, offer opportunities for creating a "smart" AI-enhanced nonhuman team member that initially might take over some of the boring administrative work that is critical in project management. But as time goes on, this smart team member might begin to offer insights that the team can then debate. Standardizing our project language would go a long way towards making these conversations more effective, robotic assistant or not.

Simulations

As I discussed in Chapter 2 (on analytics), we long to understand what works. What change can we make that will move this project forward the fastest? What impact will there be if this risk materializes? Our competitor has announced a major strategic change. What will that do to our revenues? What will happen to the project schedule if a key resource must be deployed elsewhere? I could go on.

Statistical machine learning could revolutionize project scheduling and risk management, among other things. As neural networks and deep learning (both of which are more advanced forms of machine learning) advance, simulations, recommended changes, and other insights from machines will only get better.

Image Insights

As imaging technologies improve, extracting data from images and creating insights from this data will improve. We will have the capacity to look at an image that represents our entire project portfolio, along with all the other work in the organization. We will be able to overlay the data on where problems, delays, or risks exist, to help us make quick decisions and adjust our focus.

Currently, we see building information modeling (BIM) software programs used on some construction sites. BIM software analyzes images from structures and assesses progress, analyzes components, and can offer insights on spaces that are not accessible to humans. Such software could be used to update project status based on the realities of what has been accomplished.

Imagine what happens when we combine natural language processing, enhanced image processing, and advanced machine learning technologies. The possibilities are more than I can fathom, yet I often ponder the improvements to project management teams that these technologies could offer.

Projects are the vehicle by which companies implement change. Not only will there be increasing change in our organizations, communities, and the world, but shouldn't we rethink how we are making those changes? Isn't there an opportunity to reimagine work management for the future, using what we know about brain science, human behavior, and project management?

In his book *The Undoing Project – A Friendship That Changed Our Minds*, Michael Lewis discusses Tversky's and Kahneman's conclusion that we are now getting close to medical diagnostic software that is more reliable than the diagnostics of the most well-trained doctors. Humans are prone to some biases, not to mention exhaustion and error.[147]

There are currently efforts in the legal and medical worlds to develop software that thinks better than a lawyer or doctor. That may seem scary, as law firms, medical practices, and other businesses continue to hustle for work, and as clients continue to expect more for less.

We are already seeing the point where computers can give sound advice if they are asked the right question. I don't believe we are close to the point of computers being able to effectively guide clients through a *complex* maze of decisions. That still requires people with high intelligence and curiosity. But businesses shouldn't stick their heads in the sand, as such scenarios may be right around the corner.

Whether we can make your cats smarter, or not, the next question is whether we can help them trust each other, even when they don't know each other. In the next chapter, I explore using blockchain to do just that.

Chapter 21

Try Blockchain If You Need Trustworthy Smart Cats

From the difficulty of herding smart cats to the need for metrics that reliably tell us what is happening and the demand for leaders who can build trust, I have repeatedly stressed the concern that it all comes down to whether your team can deliver the results that your client (or your management team) wants. In this chapter, I explore blockchain as a system for recording information that might allow us to better manage work globally in a chaotic and changing world with people that we don't necessarily know. After an overview of the technology, I discuss how it could be incorporated into a work management solution, its limitations, and whether it could solve the problem of trust.

An Overview of Blockchain

For those who are unfamiliar with blockchain, and want a simple definition, it is the technology that Bitcoin (a cryptocurrency) is built on. Blockchain is a highly technical way of linking electronic pieces of data so that the data are preserved and less vulnerable to manipulation.

According to Michael Casey, author of *The Truth Machine*, "Blockchains are a social technology, a new blueprint for how to govern communities."[148] The social part is critical, and Casey believes that the blockchain can rebuild trust in our society.

With the internet, we have increasingly been removing the middleman, and moving towards a peer-to-peer economy. At each stage, technology has had to adapt by providing a trust mechanism; hence, the scoring systems in tools such as Uber, Airbnb, or Google Reviews. As trust issues are resolved through technology, society will move towards a peer-to-peer economy. The blockchain may be the ultimate trust machine.[149]

Ledgers, whether they are bank or investment company ledgers, medical records, or project management logs, have never been an uncontested representation of the truth, but rather, a way of getting closer to the truth. With so many people involved in creating the blockchain ledger, we get closer consensus on what we call truth. That's a powerful idea.

In this new digital world, we are struggling to find a balance between letting private companies control data (think about the Facebook problems) and allowing the government to regulate the way data are controlled (consider the Edward Snowden revelations). And the various governments in our world are all approaching this differently. Casey argues that blockchain offers another choice – but it requires that we reimagine the way that online data are organized.[150]

The blockchain world is ushering in a token economy. In this economy, "we can embed into these 'programmable' forms of money a way to steer communities toward desired common outcomes."[151] For example, we can incentivize advertisers to provide ads that we want to see, instead of those that annoy us. In effect, we can reward people when they behave in positive ways. This could solve the problem of how we manage public resources, such as energy, water, and air.

Improving supply chain management is a key blockchain opportunity. Hyperledger, a venture that includes IBM, Intel, and Accenture, among others, is pursuing "nothing less than a common blockchain/distributed ledger infrastructure for the global economy, one that's targeted not only at finance and banking but also at the Internet of Things, supply chains, and manufacturing."[152]

Could Blockchain Transform How We Do Project Management?

At its core, blockchain is a way of preserving digital assets. You may not have thought of your projects as a collection of digital assets, but some people have done just that.

Suppose we rethink projects as a collection of promises (even if not communicated as such) to deliver something of value. Here are some examples:

- A coder agrees to write a batch of code that will solve a problem, in exchange for a paycheck.
- A steel vendor agrees to deliver 20,000 pounds of steel for the roadway, in exchange for payment.
- A contractor with HR expertise, in exchange for money, agrees to provide a recommendation on a new compensation structure for a company that is making a major organizational change.
- The project manager agrees to produce executive reports that are needed to ensure continued funding of the project in exchange for payment.
- A volunteer agrees to decorate a banquet space for a nonprofit, in exchange for the promise of reimbursement for the actual costs.

In an online world, could these promises to deliver something of value represent digital assets? Suppose we set up these pieces of work as smart contracts?

A smart contract is a digital way to create, verify, and enforce an arrangement between two or more parties. Smart contracts are an effort to remove the middleman (typically a lawyer) and automate the exchange of goods or services. The thinking is that we can set up an automated, digital way to do what the middleman has done by hand in the past.

Thinking about project work from this standpoint, your project plan becomes a series of smart contracts that are executed, and after each contract is closed, payment can be automatically made. This would be incredibly valuable when your project activities are being done by outside contractors. And some say that this gig economy, where contractors play an increasing role, even in companies with large employee forces, is poised to expand.

If the project activities are entered into the blockchain as smart contracts, and resources are tracked in the blockchain, users can quickly spot when, for example, a steel delivery will be delayed. And when the steel is delivered, the system automatically pays the steel vendor. Weather delays can be accounted for more easily, as the software can quickly adjust the schedule. With such a system in place, maybe teams would deliver results before promised dates more frequently?

Blockchain, because of the number of people involved in creating it and the immutability of the chain, provides a digital validation that a transaction has occurred. In the project world, at least for now, I believe we should consider the need for manual security and quality audits before payments are released.

We need to build quality into the project plan. If each activity has a person in charge of approving quality test results, we can have that person or perhaps the project sponsor and/or the project manager validate that the terms of the smart contract were met – thus releasing payment according to the terms of the smart contract. This step of having a quality manager validate the blockchain to release payment can also be combined with a security audit.

Once activities have been completed and payment has been released, project cost reports are immediately updated, providing a much more reliable picture of the project, as it stands.

And when it makes sense to let something like building information modeling software be the final judge on activity completion, we can do that.

When project changes need to occur, they would fall into two categories. First, changes that arise during execution and don't relate to an activity where work has begun would be handled through the change management process that has been established. The second category involves activities that have begun. Once work on an activity is ready to begin, the team's initial action is to develop a smart contract that formalizes the activity scope requirements and cost, and then places it on the blockchain. And that contract on the blockchain cannot be changed. If a change is needed, the contract would need to be replaced with a revised contract that memorializes the new understanding. Regardless, this would be a major step forward in the quest to build clarity in the face of confusion, since smart contracts are specific on the details.

Limitations to Consider

Scalability

Blockchain technology is additive. There is no way to go back into the chain of transactions and delete something. If we are going to move to blockchain, we need to be careful about the data that we put in the tool. While blockchain validates the data, it doesn't validate the quality of the data. Garbage in, garbage out. And with scalability increasingly recognized as a blockchain limitation, there is no reason to load up the blockchain tool with insignificant conversations or negotiations, such as those that might be handled in person, by email, or through chat tools.

I've said for years that all the emailed and chat communications may come back to haunt us. We should pay attention to the science of motivation and use regular and strategic meetings to build better relationships between the actively engaged project team members. I'm not putting out a call for more meetings. I'm advocating for *better* meetings, where problems are solved, commitments are made, information is constructively shared, and decisions are made and documented.

Security

When we read daily news of hacking attempts or spying efforts on credit card companies, hospitals, transportation infrastructure, and credit reporting agencies, it's hard to have confidence in the technologies that undergird our society. We've already seen multiple Bitcoin hacks, and I'm sure there are many that I've not heard about. Debate continues about whether they were inside jobs or true security compromises. Technology problems will continue to impact most everything that connects to the internet. Clearly, the term "cybersecurity" is an oxymoron. And yet, don't we have to focus on improving the security around our tools?

While blockchain may be the most secure technology to date, it relies on individuals to safeguard their keys. What happens when these "private keys" are left lying under desk blotters, or taped to monitors in offices around the world? We're already experiencing the panic when people forget where they stored their keys.

Usage

We operate in a world where much of the developed nations' population still struggles to manage email, online calendars, and to-do lists. Communications, responsibilities, and schedules can overwhelm us. And to further complicate matters, few of us live in a world where we spend our lives in one browser window tab for the entire day. We are back and forth between phones, laptops, desktops, tablets, and multiple software programs and phone apps. For many of us, add the needs of children, housework, pets, families, and community organizations to that list. We juggle multiple projects, operational demands, personal needs, and more than the occasional crisis.

At the end of the day, most of us just want to know what we should do next. And that may be as simple as remembering to pick up the milk on the way home or move some funds to cover the mortgage or rent payment.

If some brilliant minds got together and built a work management tool that incorporates elements of blockchain technology and artificial intelligence, who would use it? And why would they use it? Human nature may be the supreme factor governing usage. Many of the apps that people use today are habit forming. Maybe we should think about building in some addictiveness to something that has real value to our organizations and the people in them. Or maybe we will determine that software with addictiveness properties isn't good for our health.

For larger entities or governments, this kind of work management solution could be run in a permissioned blockchain, which perhaps offers an improved level of security over a shared blockchain. There are clearly many questions that need to be answered. Some questions center on the level of transparency between disparate groups of stakeholders who are working on the same effort. This is particularly true in public-private partnerships, international projects, or legal projects, where the work is being shared by multiple legal entities.

Uncertainty

Because blockchain is such a new technology, there is considerable uncertainty around how it will be regulated, what audit or compliance problems could arise (particularly on government projects), how intellectual property concerns might emerge, which technology providers will emerge as the leaders, and the simple (or not-so-simple) technology decisions that will face developers. Much work needs to be done and this will take time.

Would Blockchain Improve Trust on Project Teams?

Successful project management can, at some point, come down to building trust. Can we trust our colleagues to deliver what they've promised? Will the schedule on the wall work? What do we need to do to meet the final deadline? Are the specs that the client gave us going to change? Will the costs go up? Will the organization lose interest in or funding for this project? Can our client trust us to disclose problems, or will we try to hide them from the client? The need for trust is particularly important in the nonprofit world, where we rely on large numbers of volunteers to execute massive events.

Building trust in our teams and organizations is essential. When we work in organizations where the trust factor is low, it drains our energy and wastes time. In other words, it costs money. But do people innately trust others, or does that trust have to be earned? And can blockchain technology help us build trust? The expression "trust me" — whether issued as a polite request or an order — doesn't work well. Blockchain may well solve that problem and someday transform the way we manage work.

Could the Same Blockchain Tool Change How We Manage Operational Work?

I'll provide a note of explanation here, as this idea is outside of the project management world. In this book's introduction, I first suggested the potential for a software solution that uses the best disciplines from the project management world to manage all operations. This means that a blockchain tool could not only track project contracts but also performance contracts.

Performance contracts are general contracts that organizations, including governments, negotiate to get work accomplished. This work is often basic operational work and can be critically important. In some cases, there is simply no mechanism for following up on these contracts to ensure that the work has been done.

According to an article on the Route Fifty website, "States and local governments have embraced 'performance contracts,' requiring contractors to meet certain objectives. Too often, however, they don't actually check on the success in meeting these goals."153 The article notes several examples. First, San Diego has a tree-trimming contract with a private company. But according to the city's 2019 audit report, "there is not a contract compliance process in place to monitor Contractor performance."[154]

Second, the state of Texas recently released a summary report on 47 contracting audits which notes that about two-thirds showed management and oversight issues.[155] Meanwhile, North Carolina admits that it also has problems keeping up with the oversight on performance contracts.[156]

I talked about product management earlier in the book. There isn't that much difference between the project to create a product, and the operational work to manage that product over the life of the product, *except* that the project is finite, and the product continues indefinitely. So, product management is in effect, a project with no deadline.

Tested project management disciplines, the growing scientific findings on leadership and human behavior, an Agile philosophy, and evolving twenty-first-century technologies offer a pathway to a solution that could dramatically improve the way we work. In the final chapter, I ponder what it might look like and wonder who might build it.

Chapter 22

Who Will Create Our Future?

I began this book with the notion that project management today is like herding smart cats. I expressed my reservation about using a relatively rigid and hierarchical traditional Waterfall approach and argued that we need more agility in a world of rapid change. And yet, we do need some controls on our projects. Well-trained experts have disagreed with me on some of the project management principles that I discuss in this book and perhaps I should listen to them. But I'm pretty convinced of several things that cause me to question the value of the traditional Gantt chart and earned value management approach.

- People, particularly younger ones, want more autonomy and are less interested in locking themselves into a rigid work schedule that lasts for months or years. They are happy to produce results but less interested in necessarily doing it when the Gantt chart reports that they are available. Keep in mind that when you use that approach, the team is asked to report on individual availability during the planning period, which could have been months, or years ago.
- We all need to be thinking more about innovation and delivering value more frequently. Even in a somewhat linear and defined project, we are working in rapidly changing times. How can we ensure that we are capitalizing on a recent change that would benefit the proj-

ect? In this environment, should we stay locked into an approach that requires us to spend time estimating durations on every activity?

- When results of an activity are not easily observed and measured, as the number of windows that have been installed in a new home can be, estimating percent complete on the task is a generally flawed approach. It can be done, perhaps, but it can be misleading to rely on that estimate. And as we think about smart computers and enhanced business intelligence tools, do we truly want that intelligence drawn from flawed data?
- The world is changing rapidly, and technology advances have materialized in such a way that we are at an inflection point. We now have an opportunity to reinvent how we do project management. Should we continue to embrace the tools and processes of the past and let that limit our thinking?

Sometimes, we must accept the fact that what got us here in the past won't get us where we want to be in the future. In this final chapter, I explore the future of an AI-enhanced solution partially built on the blockchain. I offer some tempting scenarios and discuss the challenges that come with this opportunity. But the overwhelming question remains: who will create our future?

There are so many ways to manage a project that it's hard to keep track of them all. Most project managers know a handful. I try to study as many as I can, but the list continues to grow. Some are highly structured methods, while others are more like a set of guiding principles. Many are hybrid models. Most project experts agree that a disciplined and concerted approach to project management does improve results, but how can we move the needle on the current level of 10 percent project waste? And if we did, what would that mean?

According to Antonio Nieto-Rodriguez, globally recognized project management expert and author, "Today, about 70% of projects fail to deliver their objectives. What if we commit to doing much better? If we increase our success ratio from 30% to 60, we would be adding approximately the GDP of China in benefits, impact, value, and social good."[157]

In recent years, there has been an emerging trend to allow project managers to choose the method that works best on their project. One disadvantage of that approach is the lack of comparable portfolio metrics that might improve executive decision-making. Can we build a technology solution that empowers teams to successfully complete all kinds and sizes of projects and delight clients, repeatedly?

With growing transparency and press reporting, it feels to me like problems of mismanagement, fraud, abuse, and unethical behavior are increasingly disclosed. This is coming during a period of massive and rapid technology breakthroughs and massive spending programs all over the world. We may solve the COVID-19 problem, but I believe some level of VUCA (i.e., volatility, uncertainty, complexity, and ambiguity) is here to stay.

There are compelling reasons to reimagine project management and build a work management tool that is partially built on the blockchain and takes advantage of the capabilities that artificial intelligence provides. If we are going to dramatically improve project success rates, we need to evolve our thinking on project management. We must insist on some processes and tools, and some level of effective documentation. Contracts must still be negotiated and monitored, and we need project plans that will help us manage our projects and remain agile.

What Could We Do?

There are many, many ways to approach building a 21st century project management solution but I want to outline three components that could transform project management. These three components, as depicted in Figure 9, could be applied to all kinds of projects – from IT to non-profits, to construction and business projects of all sizes, and even government projects.

Figure 9: Smart Projex Principles

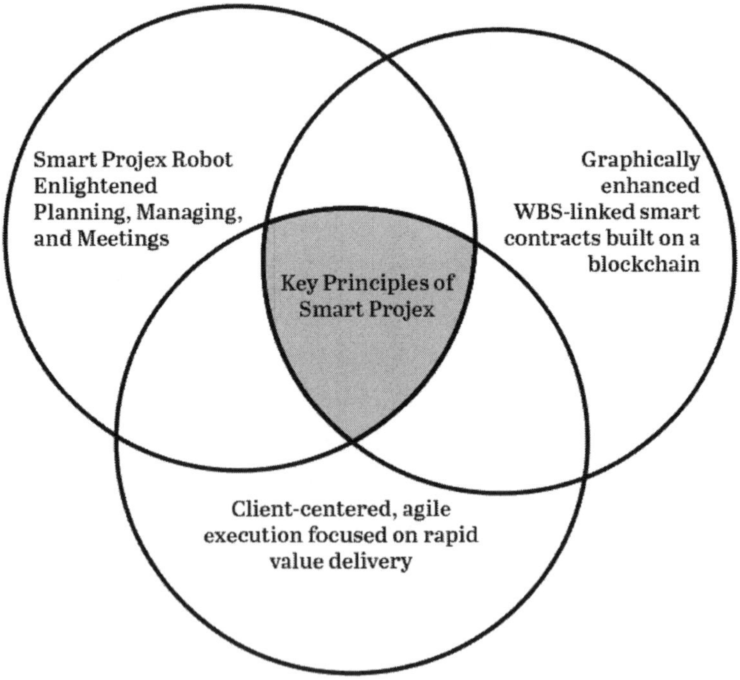

Smart Projex Robot Enlightened Planning, Managing, and Meetings

Graphically enhanced WBS-linked smart contracts built on a blockchain

Key Principles of Smart Projex

Client-centered, agile execution focused on rapid value delivery

To be clear, I believe we need to put people first. Any technology we employ/use should be about enhancing relationships between humans. As I've said, effective teams are one of the most valuable assets a business can create – even if they don't appear on the balance sheet. People are the key to getting your project done. And the more effective and efficient they are, the better they can get your work done. Without people who have the requisite skills and can work together effectively, your project is doomed. But a robot-enhanced team might be like giving everyone on the team steroids or putting cognition-enhancing microchips in their brains.

I have talked about the value of high performing teams and reusing these teams. When we add a smart robot to a team, what does that achieve? There are many enhancements that we can consider as technology improves. I outlined some of those in the last two chapters.

For years, I have promoted a smart start. There is nothing particularly unique about this, except that so many project teams get it wrong and jump straight into execution without laying the groundwork. A robot could be used to remind teams to step back and consider some basics before proceeding further. And the robot could use simulations to speed up the start process, creating schedules much more effectively.

And as teams move through the process of planning, putting the activities into smart contracts will have the effect of forcing teams to slow down and clearly define activity requirements. Sometimes slowing down is the key to moving fast and furiously.

Graphically Enhanced WBS Linked to Smart Contracts Built on a Blockchain

The technological and methodological underpinning of Smart Projex 2.0 is a graphically enhanced work breakdown structure (WBS), which serves as a visual representation of the activities and resulting deliverables that are the essential components of the project scope. Undergirding Smart Projex 2.0 are two connected frameworks. First, the project activities in the WBS are clearly defined and entered as smart contracts on a blockchain during execution. Concrete project assets, such as steel, windows, or pharmaceuticals could also be tracked in the blockchain. Second, several other project factors, some related to these activities and some related to the project itself, are entered on a more traditional database framework during the initial planning process, all the way through closure. Examples of some project factors that we might track outside of the blockchain include risks, lessons learned, issues, and tasks.

Project factors, such as quality specifications, deadlines, procurement contract requirements, risks, issues, decisions, stakeholder preferences, tasks, and a host of other important data points, can be entered into the tool by the robot and inspected by the team during meetings. As AI improves, all these factors could be analyzed by, simulated by, or even thought of by the software.

As the project evolves, teams gain increasing clarity on these activities so that once they are put in the blockchain as smart contracts, it is crystal clear what is needed and when it will be delivered. Project assets, whether that's the steel that must be purchased for a bridge, or a contract to complete a strategic assessment of the HR compensation system's needs, can be tracked in real time through the blockchain. Payments can be automatically made when the work is completed and approved.

Weather delays, risk trigger events, team members logging out with serious sicknesses, and even major industry or competitive events could be factored into the scheduling process and spark management discussions. Users could easily identify deadline concerns, progress, risks, quality needs, and a slew of other project attributes.

Client-Centered Agile Execution Focused on Rapid Value Delivery

The third component of Smart Projex 2.0 centers on how to execute projects and, by extension, how to manage them. The key is to build processes that will help us achieve success. I believe there are four elements:

1. Learn how to properly decompose a project.

Break your project down into the activities that will create the most value for your clients and schedule them so that you are constantly focused on delivering value. This idea can be hard to grasp for people who are working on business projects with a final defined result as the goal. As I have discussed, we need to become more client-centered, and if you can't figure out what that next deliverable is that might help your client, ask them. Ask your robot friend. Stop working for hours on end on something that may not be what is needed. Don't assume that the requirements that were laid out in the beginning are still correct. People change their minds. And new knowledge informs decision-making. Our Smart Projex robot can help us remember the highest-ranked risks, trends, stakeholder concerns, and the gazillion other pieces of project data that matter but that can keep us from focusing on doing the actual work that has value to the client.

2. Effectively conduct meetings.

Use sprints, standing meetings, and Checkpoint meetings to effectively guide execution and deliver value to the client regularly and rapidly. Teams get no credit at the end of a sprint for partially done activities. In Agile development, having a sustainable development process is important. In the nonprofit, business, or government world, different projects will have a different cadence or timeline of priorities. You may not have a fully engaged team at times. Outside contractors and subject matter experts may come and go. You may not have pressing priorities on some but will on others. By using sprints, standing meetings, and Checkpoint meetings, managing those variables is easier.

3. Embrace change, not chaos.

Innovation projects can be planned and executed with more agility while projects needing more structure can be treated that way. We can focus on what we know, experiment, learn, improve, and achieve the benefits that we defined at the outset. We need a way to manage priorities and project investments. A documented change management process, together with the use of focused sprints, can keep your teams from running in circles. Embracing change does not mean embracing chaos. Provide a stable and safe environment where your teams can thrive.

4. Manage what's important.

We need to strike the right balance between planning, doing, and managing. Our AI-enhanced robot friend and interactive dashboards that include scenario planning can help with the planning and managing. But, for now, your people will need to complete the project activities. And many of those activities will include actual conversations with people about needed changes, the intricacies of a new technology, or how to solve a challenging problem. Every project is different. When you started your project, you hopefully focused on figuring out what is important to your client. Some clients are completely budget conscious, others – not so much. There may be times where the risk of a shutdown trumps every other consideration. Have you figured out what is important? Do you know what is most important *now*? Are you ensuring that you deliver what's most important to your client?

What Might This Vision Look Like?

Imagine a world where people who are working together on projects and barely know each other can be trusted to deliver results. Imagine a software tool that tracks project assets and adjusts the schedule in real time. It automatically pays vendors and freelance contractors when supplies and work have been delivered. Imagine having an intelligent digital assistant that alerts teams when problems or opportunities are on the horizon. The assistant "understands" everything that is happening in your organization and can reassess events and alert teams when a project risk increases, even due to operational events.

Imagine being able to look at your entire portfolio of projects and quickly understand which projects are truly creating the most value for your organization. Picture seeing which clients are the most profitable and finding ways to work with them so that they can save money. Imagine being able to analyze your projects in the context of everything in your organization – to better understand when operating demands are surging and likely to significantly impact project deliverables.

Imagine managing all your work, whether operations, projects, products, or tasks that don't seem related to anything, using a work management solution that allows comparisons and insights across the organization. You could more quickly understand when sweeping industry changes or competitor moves might impact the work you are doing. Teams could quickly adapt when activities are blowing up somewhere else in your organization and project schedules, costs, resources, and risks need to be rethought.

This vision could be achieved. Who will do it?

The Russians? In 2017, VEB, a Russian government-owned bank, announced that it was building a project management tool using blockchain technology. According to VEB chairperson Sergey Gorkov, as quoted on *Coin Telegraph*: "When we started to think about how to manage projects efficiently, we realized that there is no platform. We realized that the Blockchain is a good fundamental and qualitative platform for the future."[158]

The Chinese? In Dr. Kai-Fu Lee's best seller, *AI Superpowers: China, Silicon Valley, and the New World Order*, he argues that China is catching up with the US at lightning speed. "Much of the difficult but abstract work of AI research has been done, and it's now time for entrepreneurs to roll up their sleeves and get down to the dirty work of turning algorithms into sustainable businesses."[159]

In the US, efforts are underway at many large companies and in government to incorporate these cutting-edge technologies into various products in a variety of industries. For example, Facebook and Apple are heavily involved in building products that use advanced visual technologies to bring people together and promote better conversations.[160,161] AI efforts have tapped into the work being done at academic institutions or the work that IBM did to develop Watson, with varying degrees of success. According to Tom Davenport, businesses often achieve more success when they start small, rather than shooting for the moon, figuratively speaking.[162]

Clearly, US regulations have made blockchain development more complicated here than in other areas of the world, though that may be changing. We've seen financial services and technology firms approach the use of blockchain more aggressively than some other industries. Yet, Ethereum was set up in Switzerland, because, according to Michael Casey and Paul Vigna, "Swiss law makes it easier to set up the foundations needed to launch coin offerings and issue digital tokens."[163]

I hope that this vision of an AI-enhanced, blockchain-based work management solution materializes and that it is developed by someone who cares about people, science, and the environment. We have learned much from science, especially in recent years, that could greatly inform the development of a new project tool.

MIT professor Sherry Turkle has been researching the impacts of technology on people. According to her book, *Reclaiming Conversation: The Power of Talk in a Digital Age*, there are two big problems that are occurring in the world today as people, particularly young people, move to more online conversations.[164]

First, empathy declines when people stop talking to other people face-to-face. If we can't put ourselves in the shoes of our clients, our bosses, or our teammates, we risk spending time, energy, and money on the wrong activities at the wrong times. The good news is that people are resilient and spending a few days together without phones and computers quickly improves empathy.[165]

The second problem is that even a silent phone positioned near people changes their conversation. People simply aren't as inclined to delve deeply into their conversations when they are waiting on or hoping for a call or a message. According to the research that Turkle cites, people stay on safer subjects, and they don't feel as invested in the conversation when a phone is visible.[166]

While online conversations may be the best that we can do at times, project team conversations are a place where teams need to dig down and find greater efficiencies, discuss risks and lessons learned, and discover solutions to big problems. Doing this in an online chat can deprive participants of complete focus and the honest emotions that arise in complex problem solving.

Professor Turkle writes: "We can also redesign technology to leave more room for talking to each other.... This is our moment to acknowledge the unintended consequences of the technologies to which we are vulnerable, but also to respect the resilience that has always been ours. We have time to make corrections and remember who we are — creatures of history, of deep psychology, of complex relationships, of conversations, artless, risky and face-to-face."[167]

According to Richard Branson, we need to "start putting the well-being of people and the environment at the core of our business."[168] If we haven't learned anything else from the COVID-19 pandemic, it is that we are all dependent on the actions of a few. We needed a few scientists to develop a vaccine. And for it to work, we depended on them to create one that is safe and effective. And now, we depend on people to get it.

Right now, operating the blockchain requires massive amounts of hardware connected to the power grid, and thus enormous energy outlays. But, if we are smart, and focus on sustainable energy sources, we can avoid significant environmental damage from this new technology. If we use technology wisely, we can make it work for us instead of against us. As a species, we humans progress in fits and starts. When my great-grandchildren look back at the long arc of history, will they think we have become better than we are now?

That depends on you. And me. I haven't found a perfect project management tool yet. But I have seen teams accomplish amazing results by applying many of the techniques discussed in this book.

As I said at the beginning, people, not computers, do projects. And people are messy – they argue and disagree, they miss deadlines, they get distracted, and they don't always have the necessary skills. No computer system will change that, and the rapid pace at which people work today aggravates the problem. But we could use a methodology and a technology that supports our teams.

Absent the technology, we can work towards finding a balance between the agility that teams need and the controls that management needs. We could build teams that are characterized by ubuntu, the African belief in a shared humanity, that we exist for others. We can build accountability for results – which includes meeting the critical deadlines and doing that within a budget. We can be leaders who empower our teams through our communications, compensation structures, hiring policies, and decision-making. We can use humor effectively to help our teams perform on a higher level and have more fun. We can help our people pursue their life dreams and, in the process, bring more joy and improved results into our corporate worlds.

We could build a smart, twenty-first-century work management tool that uses a science-based methodology that works easily. We can develop project processes that help ensure that chaos, confusion, and change don't doom our projects. We can set up estimating processes and risk management systems to compensate for the biases that we know exist, though we do need to exercise caution that we don't write those same biases into the algorithms. We could use artificial neural networks to improve estimating and risk management and visual technologies to give us real-time insights into what is happening in our organizations and the larger industry.

It's up to you. I can help you, but I can't do it for you. Change is hard – very, very hard. And it takes a lot of work. There are resources on my website. But you will have to do the hard work. Don't let me down. The future is now. And it depends on you – and how you want to herd your smart cats.

Appendix 1

Smart Projex 1.0 - Software for Herding Smart Cats

In this book I periodically refer to Smart Projex software. Here's the background. Remember that light bulb that went off when I finally figured out why so many of my fellow project managers were struggling? It came down to the difference between complex and complicated projects. Somewhere during that journey, I began spending hours a day, every day, trying to understand what to do about that struggle. The result was Smart Projex 1.0 – working software that offered many of the controls that project managers and executives needed, together with the ability to execute in the face of constant change and ambiguity.

Some project management software is more accurately called task management and/or collaboration software. Smart Projex 1.0 was much more than that. It followed the methodology that is outlined in this book. It encouraged teams to fully define the project scope, activities, and key attributes of the project. That meant asking some hard questions: what, where, why, when, and how. It used a well-defined execution strategy that included risk, issue, change, and cost management. While no project tool substitutes for the human interaction that goes into properly planning, executing, and managing a project, having a tool that manages the data uncovered in the process certainly helps.

While Smart Projex 1.0 aimed to make the data management, collection, and insights easier, make no mistake about it: people, not computers, do projects. And people are human, imperfect, and messy. We should not expect computers to change that. Smart Projex 1.0 allowed the project manager to focus on the soft skills that make project work more rewarding. Instead of spending hours creating status reports, the project manager could more effectively use that time to lead teams and move the project forward.

If the idea of creating Smart Projex 2.0, whatever it is called, interests you, please reach out to me.

Appendix 2

Can You Still Deliver the Planned Benefits?

There are many different approaches to assessing the business case for a project, and many viable benefit realization methods. I'm not suggesting this method of reassessing your business case is perfect. However, in this example of a business case questionnaire, I'm aiming to keep it simple. Here are eight questions that you might consider for each internal project proposal. No one project proposal would score high on every one of these questions.

Topic	Description	Point Scale	Points
Mission	List the ways that this project carries out the mission and/or the objectives of your organization.	Assign 5 points for each way, up to 15 points.	

Topic	Description	Point Scale	Points
Financials	How much will the project increase revenues, net of project costs?	Assign 10 points for double revenues; 9 points for increase by 90%; ... 1 point for increase by 10%.	
Financials	How much will the project reduce costs, net of project costs?	Assign 10 points for 100% cost reduction; 9 points for 90% cost reduction; .... 1 point for 10% cost reduction.	
Financials	For projects that are being done to improve profitability, what is the payback period?	If less than 1 year, assign 5 points; if 1 - 2 years, assign 4 points; if 2 - 3 years, assign 2 points; if 3 - 4 years, assign 1 point.	

Topic	Description	Point Scale	Points
Customers	How widespread is the customer satisfaction on this project?	Assign 5 points if many customers will benefit from this project; 3 if only a few will benefit; and 1 if only one customer will benefit from this project.	
Legal	Is this project required by law?	Assign 5 points for yes.	
Teamwork	Will this project help the organization develop a highly functioning team that will be beneficial in the future?	Assign 5 points if yes.	

Topic	Description	Point Scale	Points
Environmental	Will this project ultimately result in environmental improvements in the community?	Assign 5 points if the project substantially improves the environment; 3 if there is only a modest improvement; 1 if the project is an environmentally sound project that will have only a minor impact on the environment.	
Total			

Once each potential project is evaluated using these metrics, you can rank the projects, with higher scores suggesting a better project investment.

This process doesn't consider the need to separately compare projects that effectively compete against each other to accomplish the same outcomes. Therefore, in the project selection phase, you need to understand those competing projects and rank them separately.

Appendix 3

How Can You Create a Change Management Process?

This example reviews the four basic steps that you can include in any change management process. You can think of these steps as the four "R's" of a change management process: Request, Review, Resolve, and Revise.

Before I explain the steps, there is one key requirement for making this process work effectively. You must define the "who" and the "how" for every step. The "how" is unique to your organization. There may be variances depending on the size of the project, but in general, you should have a defined set of processes for managing project change. The "who" will likely vary from project to project, depending on the size of your organization.

Create a consistent and fair process for how changes are requested, reviewed, resolved, and revised to ensure that people feel heard and appreciated.

1. **REQUEST** a change to the project, if warranted.

The question that you want to ask yourself here is: how hard do you want to make it for the people around you to suggest changes? Normally, I would err on the side of making it easier, rather than harder, to submit a change request. Not every organization is the same.

If you have spent considerable time scoping the project in the beginning, you may decide to make it harder to submit changes. On the other hand, if this is a fluid project where you anticipated changes at every phase, you might make it easy to submit changes. It's your call.

The "Who" – In most cases, I recommend that anyone connected to the project be allowed to submit a change request. Great ideas can come from project change conversations, and you might be surprised by who has the great ideas.

The "How" – There should be a legitimate process for submitting changes. It can be as simple as sending an email to the project manager. Or there can be a specific form where requests are logged in. The goal is to provide a simple structure for receiving change requests, so that teams continue to move forward instead of moving in circles. At a minimum, the request should contain a description of the proposed change and the reason the change is needed or the benefits from making the change.

2. **REVIEW** the impact of the proposed change.

Once a change has been proposed, someone needs to do an unbiased review. Not all change requests will be approved. Much of the review process will depend on what kind of project you are working on. For example, a construction project will need a rigid process that often begins with the customer. Signed change orders will be important. A new product design project may be much more fluid and planned in phases that anticipate change requests. Regardless, there can be a step-by-step process that works.

The "Who" – Once a change request has been submitted, someone needs to evaluate the impact of the proposed change. Often, the project manager will take on this task, but it can be assigned to someone who might be more qualified. In most cases, and unless the project size is large, I suggest having one person on your team who is responsible for reviewing all change requests.

Exceptions might include a change initiative that involves multiple functional areas and subject matter experts or a very complex project. In these cases, you may want to have the team (or a subset) review all change requests, to get the intellectual expertise needed for a fair review.

Typically, the client is not involved in the details of the review process. They are a major part of the request, and you will need to confirm your understanding of the revised scope. After all, the client hopefully knows what it wants and why.

The "How" – It is important to think about the total impact, so consider how the change will impact the scope, schedule, financials, risks, and the team. It is important that the process is unbiased. Here is a simple step-by-step review process that can be modified or adapted to your needs.

Project change review form – Typically, I recommend that you have some type of change review form that can be used to structure the review. You may choose to have the person who submitted the request be the one to complete part of this form. This puts some burden on the person with the idea to think it through before the people on the team are bounced around in discussions.

Then, someone needs to analyze the request. Here are some areas that you may wish to capture on that form and analyze. Some will require actual data crunching. Others are more subjective.

1. *Description of proposed change and reason the change is needed*
This should have been captured in the request.
2. *Proposed changes to scope inclusions and exclusions*
You should confirm your understanding of this with the client.
3. *Anticipated change in Complexity*
Try to understand what activities are needed to implement this change and estimate the aggregate Complexity of the change.
4. *Anticipated impact on the finish date*
Consider any impact on the team, given other workloads, vacation schedules, etc.
5. *Anticipated impact on budget*
Consider that there may be some changes that reduce costs or eliminate scope.
6. *Any impact on risks*
At this point, at a minimum, new risks should be defined, documented, and discussed.

Review the change proposal with your team for input. Some organizations may choose to skip this step, or combine this conversation with the planning conversation, to minimize the time spent in meetings. Your defined process should specify whether team reviews are important at this stage.

Make a recommendation decision but recognize that the decision-maker(s) may not be bound by your recommendation.

3. **RESOLVE** whether the proposed change should be approved or not.

It's decision time. Once a decision has been made, you need a method for communicating the decision. In the case of approved projects, you may wish to wait until the project has been re-planned.

The "Who" – Every organization is different. The decision on whether to approve the change may be made by the customer, the project sponsor, the company owner, or a change management board – depending on the nature of the project request.

The "How" – The "how" is relatively simple if you have appropriately defined the "who" and you have a strong review process in place.

4. **REVISE** the project plan.

No change management process is complete without a revision step, where approved changes are incorporated into the project plan.

The "Who" – Once a decision is made to change the project plan, someone must be responsible for revising it. Depending on the aggregate Complexity of the change, this may be a job for the entire team.

The "How" – The approach is like what you went through when you planned the project. You need to:

- Break down the project using your revised scope
- Completely define the new activities
- Delete activities, if appropriate
- Revise the budget
- Reassess the risks
- Review the impact on the schedule of this change and determine the revised planned completion date
- Disseminate the revised project details to your team

Occasionally I have seen a situation where a team missed the boat when they analyzed a proposed change. When the approved project change was fully planned out, the impact on the schedule and/or costs turned out to be much greater or varied significantly from what was anticipated.

Should that happen, I recommend creating an "issue" (yes, you should have a log for dealing with issues) for any significant variance between what was proposed in the "Review" step, and what emerged from the "Revise" step. As to what constitutes significant, that is your call. That "variance" should be defined and the person(s) who can approve the variance should be named. In some cases, you may choose a tiered approach. For example, the project sponsor can approve variances under five percent. Larger variances must go back to whatever change approval committee has been created.

Sound simple? It's not. But you must start somewhere.

Endnotes

1 Video chat with Pamela Merritt, author of *The Way of Cats*, on Aug. 20, 2020. https://www.wayofcats.com/blog/books

2 Benoit Hardy-Vallee, "The Cost of Bad Project Management," *Gallup Business Journal* (2012), https://news.gallup.com/businessjournal/152429/Cost-Bad-Project-Management.aspx.

3 Hardy-Vallee, "The Cost of Bad Project Management."

4 Project Management Institute, "Ahead of the Curve: Forging a Future-Focused Culture," *Pulse of the Profession* (2020), https://www.pmi.org/learning/library/forging-future-focused-culture-11908.

5 "Project Management Institute," https://www.projectmanagement.com/.

6 Ben Gilbert, "Amazon CEO Jeff Bezos Says Multibillion-Dollar Failures are Actually a Good Thing: 'If the Size of Your Failures isn't Growing, You're Not Going to be Inventing at a Size That Can Actually Move the Needle,'" *Business Insider* (2019), https://www.businessinsider.com/jeff-bezos-says-multi-billion-dollar-failures-necessary-for-amazon-growth-success-2019-4.

7 Gilbert, "Amazon CEO Jeff Bezos Says Multibillion-Dollar Failures are Actually a Good Thing."

8 Jeff Sommer, "Robert Shiller: A Skeptic and a Nobel Winner," *The New York Times* (2013), https://www.nytimes.com/2013/10/20/business/robert-shiller-a-skeptic-and-a-nobel-winner.html.

9 Colin Mayer, "Reinventing the Corporation," *Journal of the British Academy* 4 (2016), https://www.thebritishacademy.ac.uk/documents/1613/03_Mayer_1825.pdf.

10 Klaus Schwab, "The Fourth Industrial Revolution: What it Means and How to Respond," World Economic Forum (2016), https://www.weforum.org/agenda/2016/01/the-fourth-industrial-revolution-what-it-means-and-how-to-respond/.

11 Schwab, "The Fourth Industrial Revolution: What it Means and How to Respond."

12 Schwab, "The Fourth Industrial Revolution: What it Means and How to Respond."

13 Clayton M. Christensen, *The Innovator's Dilemma: When New Technologies Cause Great Firms to Fail*, The management of innovation and change series (Boston, Massachusetts: Harvard Business Review Press, 2013), p. 20.

14 Chris Bradley, "Surprise: Those 'Great' Companies Generally Turn Out to be Meh ... or Duds," (2017), https://www.marketwatch.com/story/great-companies-are-more-likely-to-do-really-badly-over-time-than-really-well-2017-07-12.

15 Jay Greene, "Microsoft Won't Sell Police its Facial-Recognition Technology, Following Similar Moves by Amazon and IBM," *Washington Post* (2020), https://www.washingtonpost.com/technology/2020/06/11/microsoft-facial-recognition/.

16 Dana Mattioli, "Amazon Scooped Up Data From Its Own Sellers to Launch Competing Products," *Wall Street Journal* (2020), https://www.wsj.com/articles/amazon-scooped-up-data-from-its-own-sellers-to-launch-competing-products-11587650015?mod=djemalertNEWS.

17 Robert T. Garrett, "After $367.5 Million, Texas Gets No New Child Support Computer Software – Just Painful Lessons," *Dallas Morning News* (2019) https://www.dallasnews.com/news/politics/2019/05/17/after-367-5-million-texas-gets-no-new-child-support-computer-software-just-painful-lessons/.

18 "Beyond Agility," *Pulse of the Profession* (2021), https://www.pmi.org/-/media/pmi/documents/public/pdf/learning/thought-leadership/pulse/pmi_pulse_2021.pdf?v=151f8a8e-c074-44ba-a933-91eb32e172bf&sc_lang_temp=en.

19 Robert S. Kaplan and Anette Mikes, "Managing Risks: A New Framework," *Harvard Business Review* (June 2012), https://hbr.org/2012/06/managing-risks-a-new-framework.

20 Daniel H. Pink, *When: The Scientific Secrets of Perfect Timing* (New York: Riverhead Books, 2018).

21 "Teddy Bear Madness," Calleam Consulting, Ltd. (2018), https://calleam.com/WTPF/?p=8540.

22 Gabriella Demczuk, "Inside the Race to Rescue a Health Care Site, and Obama," *The New York Times* (2013), https://www.nytimes.com/2013/12/01/us/politics/inside-the-race-to-rescue-a-health-site-and-obama.html.

23 Kathleen Hall, "Government Pulls Plug on Ailing £11bn NHS IT Programme," *Computer Weekly* (2011), https://www.computerweekly.com/news/2240105673/Government-pulls-plug-on-ailing-11bn-NHS-IT-programme.

24 Open Door Technology, "The Standish Group Report 83.9% of IT Projects Partially or Completely Fail," Open Door Technology (2019), https://www.opendoorerp.com/the-standish-group-report-83-9-of-it-projects-partially-or-completely-fail/#:~:text=According%20to%20Standish%20only%2016.2,and%2For%20lacking%20-promised%20functionality.

25 *Applying Continuous Improvement to High-End Legal Services*, Clifford Chance (2014), https://www.cliffordchance.com/content/dam/cliffordchance/About_us/Continuous_Improvement_White_Paper.pdf.

26 *Applying Continuous Improvement to High-End Legal Services.*

27 "TED Talks Worth Talking About | Ken Robinson on Bring on the Learning Revolution," Vialogue (2010), https://vialogue.wordpress.com/2010/05/26/ted-talks-worth-talking-about-ken-robinson-on-bring-on-the-learning-revolution/.

28 Gurpreet Dhillon and Mário Caldeira, "A Bumpy Road to Success (or Not): The Case of Project Genesis at Nevada DMV," *International Journal of Information Management* 28, no. 3 (2008), https://www.sciencedirect.com/science/article/abs/pii/S0268401208000388?via%3Dihub (p. 222-28).

29 Dhillon and Caldeira, "A Bumpy Road to Success (or Not): The Case of Project Genesis at Nevada DMV."

30 W. Chan Kim and Renée Mauborgne, *Blue Ocean Strategy: How to Create Uncontested Market Space and Make the Competition Irrelevant* (Boston: Harvard Business Review Press, 2015).

31 Panos A. Chatzipanos and Theofanis Giotis, "Cognitive Biases as Project & Program Complexity Enhancers: the Astypalea Project," Paper presented at PMI® Global Congress 2014, Project Management Institute (2014), https://www.pmi.org/learning/library/cognitive-biases-complexity-enhancers-projects-1454.

32 Scott D. Anthony, "The Planning Fallacy and the Innovator's Dilemma," *Harvard Business Review* (2012), https://hbr.org/2012/08/the-planning-fallacy-and-the-i.

33 Roger Buehler, Dale Griffin, and Michael Ross, "Exploring the 'Planning Fallacy': Why People Underestimate Their Task Completion Times," *Journal of Personality and Social Psychology*, 67, no. 3 (1994), https://web.mit.edu/curhan/www/docs/Articles/biases/67_J_Personality_and_Social_Psychology_366,_1994.pdf.

34 D. Westen et al., "Neural Bases of Motivated Reasoning: An FMRI Study of Emotional Constraints on Partisan Political Judgment in the 2004 U.S. Presidential Election," *Journal of Cognitive Neuroscience* 18, no. 11 (2006), https://doi.org/10.1162/jocn.2006.18.11.1947, https://www.ncbi.nlm.nih.gov/pubmed/17069484.

35 Michael Lewis, *The Undoing Project: A Friendship that Changed our Minds* (New York: W.W. Norton & Company, 2017), p. 40-42.

36 Daniel H. Pink, *Drive: The Surprising Truth About What Motivates Us* (New York, NY: Riverhead Books, 2011).

37 Michael O'Brochta, "Why Bad Projects Are So Hard to Kill," PM *World Journal*, VI, no. III (2017), https://pmworldlibrary.net/wp-content/uploads/2017/03/pmwj56-Mar2017-OBrochta-why-bad-projects-are-hard-to-kill-featured-paper.pdf.

38 Ting-Peng Liang et al., *Escalation of Commitment in Software Projects: A Neural Science Perspective* (2016), https://aisel.aisnet.org/amcis2016/ITProj/Presentations/22.

39 Chatzipanos and Giotis, "Cognitive Biases as Project & Program Complexity Enhancers: the Astypalea Project."

40 John N. Parker et al., "Using Sociometers to Advance Small Group Research," *Sage Journals* (2018), https://journals.sagepub.com/doi/10.1177/0049124118769091.

41 Robert D. Putnam, 2020, http://robertdputnam.com/.

42 Tony Hsieh, *Delivering Happiness: A Path to Profits, Passion, and Purpose* (New York: Business Plus, 2010).

43 Namni Goel et al., "Circadian Rhythms, Sleep Deprivation, and Human Performance," *Progress in Molecular Biology and Translational Science* Vol. 119 (2013), https://www.sciencedirect.com/science/article/pii/B9780123969712000075.

44 Brené Brown, *The Gifts of Imperfection: Let Go of Who You Think You're Supposed to Be and Embrace Who You Are* (Center City, Minn.: Hazelden, 2010), p. 26.

45 Ben Horowitz, *The Hard Thing About Hard Things: Building a Business When There Are No Easy Answers* (New York, NY: HarperCollins Publishers, 2014), p. 274.

46 Jocko Willink and Leif Babin, *Extreme Ownership: How U.S. Navy SEALs Lead and Win* (New York, NY: St. Martin's Press, 2017).

47 Daniel Coyle, *The Talent Code: Greatness Isn't Born. It's Grown. Here's How.* (New York, NY: Bantam Dell, 2009).

48 Coyle, *The Talent Code: Greatness Isn't Born. It's Grown. Here's How.*, p. 32.

49 Coyle, *The Talent Code: Greatness Isn't Born. It's Grown. Here's How.*, p. 44.

50 Coyle, *The Talent Code: Greatness Isn't Born. It's Grown. Here's How.*

51 Hsieh, *Delivering Happiness: A Path to Profits, Passion, and Purpose*, p. 160.

52 Liz Wiseman, *Multipliers: How the Best Leaders Make Everyone Smarter* (New York, NY: HarperBusiness, 2017).

53 Wiseman, *Multipliers: How the Best Leaders Make Everyone Smarter.*

54 Wiseman, *Multipliers: How the Best Leaders Make Everyone Smarter.*

55 Wiseman, *Multipliers: How the Best Leaders Make Everyone Smarter.*

56 Dalai Lama, Desmond Tutu, and Douglas Abrams, *The Book of Joy: Lasting Happiness in a Changing World* (New York: Avery; Penguin Random House, 2016), p. 14.

57 Lama, Tutu, and Abrams, *The Book of Joy: Lasting Happiness in a Changing World*, p.74.

58 Lama, Tutu, and Abrams, *The Book of Joy: Lasting Happiness in a Changing World*, p.248.

59 Lama, Tutu, and Abrams, *The Book of Joy: Lasting Happiness in a Changing World*, p. 19.

60 Lama, Tutu, and Abrams, *The Book of Joy: Lasting Happiness in a Changing World*, p. 220.

61 Lama, Tutu, and Abrams, *The Book of Joy: Lasting Happiness in a Changing World*, p. 178.

62 Paul C. Light, "A Cascade of Failures: Why Government Fails, and How to Stop It," Brookings Institute (2014), https://www.brookings.edu/research/a-cascade-of-failures-why-government-fails-and-how-to-stop-it/.

63 Simon Sinek, *The Infinite Game* (New York: Portfolio/Penguin, 2019).

64 Thomas J. Peters and Robert H. Waterman, *In Search of Excellence: Lessons from America's Best-Run Companies* (New York: Harper & Row, 1982), p. 35.

65 Sinek, *The Infinite Game.*

66 Simon Sinek, *Start With Why: How Great Leaders Inspire Everyone to Take Action* (New York: Portfolio, 2009).

67 Sinek, *Start With Why: How Great Leaders Inspire Everyone to Take Action..*

68 Sinek, *Start With Why: How Great Leaders Inspire Everyone to Take Action*, p. 86.

69 Sinek, *Start With Why: How Great Leaders Inspire Everyone to Take Action.*

70 Colin L. Powell and Tony Koltz, *It Worked for Me: In Life and Leadership* (New York: Harper, 2012), p. 34.

71 Powell and Koltz, *It Worked for Me: In Life and Leadership*, p. 24.

72 Joanne Lipman, *That's What She Said: What Men Need to Know (and Women Need to Tell Them) About Working Together* (New York, NY: William Morrow; Harper Collins Publishers, 2018).

73 Stephen Turban, Dan Wu, and Letian (LT) Zhang, "Research: When Gender Diversity Makes Firms More Productive," *Harvard Business Review* (2019), https://hbr.org/2019/02/research-when-gender-diversity-makes-firms-more-productive.

74 Reuters, "Don't Be Silent: How a 22-year-old Woman Helped Bring Down the Tokyo Olympics Chief," (CNN, 2021), https://www.cnn.com/2021/02/18/sport/momoko-nojo-tokyo-olympics-spt-intl/index.html.

75 Turban, Wu, and Zhang, "Research: When Gender Diversity Makes Firms More Productive."

76 Lipman, *That's What She Said.*

77 Lipman, *That's What She Said.*

78 Lipman, *That's What She Said*, p. 50.

79 Lipman, *That's What She Said.*

80 Resmaa Menakem, *My Grandmother's Hands: Racialized Trauma and the Pathway to Mending Our Hearts and Bodies* (Las Vegas, NV: Central Recovery Press, 2017).

81 Jeffrey L. Seglin, "The Right Thing; When Fear of Firing Deters Hiring," *The New York Times* (1999), https://www.nytimes.com/1999/04/18/business/the-right-thing-when-fear-of-firing-deters-hiring.html.

82 Adrian Gostick and Chester Elton, *The Best Team Wins: The New Science of High Performance* (New York: Simon & Schuster, 2018), Kindle loc. 224-27.

83 Daniel Goleman, *Leadership: The Power of Emotional Intelligence* (Northampton, MA: More than Sound, LLC, 2011).

84 Goleman, *Leadership: The Power of Emotional Intelligence.*

85 Travis Bradberry and Jean Greaves, *Emotional Intelligence* 2.0 (San Diego, CA: TalentSmart, 2009).

86 Bradberry and Greaves, *Emotional Intelligence* 2.0.

87 David Honigmann, "Vision in Verse from Boardroom Bard," *Financial Times* (2009), https://www.ft.com/content/6ab26a24-124e-11de-b816-0000779fd2ac.

88 Honigmann, "Vision in Verse from Boardroom Bard."

89 Donald T. Phillips, *Lincoln on Leadership: Executive Strategies for Tough Times* (New York: Warner Books, 1992), p. 91.

90 Eric Bergman, "LinkedIn & Amazon Eliminate Slide-Driven Presentations" (2014), http://www.presentwithease.com/Blog/Blog/files/eliminate-ppt-presentations.html.

91 Kerry Patterson, *Crucial Conversations: Tools for Talking When Stakes Are High* (New York: McGraw-Hill, 2012), p. 12.

92 Patterson, *Crucial Conversations: Tools for Talking When Stakes are High.*

93 Matt Egan, "Workers Fear Humans Implanted with Microchips Will Steal Their Jobs" (2020), https://www.cnn.com/2020/09/18/business/jobs-robots-microchips-cyborg/index.html.

94 Greg Yanke, "Tying the Knot with a Robot: Legal and Philosophical Foundations for Human-Artificial Intelligence Matrimony," *AI & Society* 36 (2021), https://doi.org/10.1007/s00146-020-00973-5.

95 Patrick Lencioni, *The Advantage: Why Organizational Health Trumps Everything Else in Business* (San Francisco: Jossey-Bass, 2012), p. 77.

96 Patrick Lencioni, *Silos, Politics, and Turf Wars: A Leadership Fable About Destroying the Barriers That Turn Colleagues into Competitors* (San Francisco, CA: Jossey-Bass, 2006).

97 Lencioni, *The Advantage: Why Organizational Health Trumps Everything Else in Business.*

98 Lencioni, *Silos, Politics, and Turf Wars.*

99 Lencioni, *The Advantage: Why Organizational Health Trumps Everything Else in Business.*

100 Lencioni, *Silos, Politics, and Turf Wars.*

101 Charles Duhigg, *The Power of Habit : Why We Do What We Do in Life and Business*, 1st ed. (New York: Random House, 2012).

102 Simon Sinek, *Leaders Eat Last: Why Some Teams Pull Together and Others Don't* (New York, New York: Portfolio/Penguin, 2014), p. 24.

103 Sinek, *Leaders Eat Last: Why Some Teams Pull Together and Others Don't.*

104 Robert Slater, *29 Leadership Secrets from Jack Welch* (New York: McGraw-Hill, 2003), p. 77-78.

105 Gostick and Elton, *The Best Team Wins - The New Science of High Performance.*

106 Brené Brown, *Braving the Wilderness: The Quest for True Belonging and the Courage to Stand Alone* (New York: Random House, 2017).

107 Slater, 29 *Leadership Secrets from Jack Welch*, p. 14.

108 Leah Weiss, *How We work: Live Your Purpose, Reclaim Your Sanity, and Embrace the Daily Grind* (New York, New York: Harper Wave; Harper Collins Publishers, 2018).

109 Claudia Irigoyen, "The FBI Virtual Case File System," Centre for Public Impact (2017), https://www.centreforpublicimpact.org/case-study/fbi-virtual-case-file-system/.

110 Horowitz, *The Hard Thing About Hard Things: Building a Business When There Are No Easy Answers.*

111 "Beyond Agility."

112 Adam M. Grant, *Originals: How Non-Conformists Move the World* (New York: Viking; Penguin Random House LLC, 2016)..

113 Grant, *Originals: How Non-Conformists Move the World.*

114 Grant, *Originals: How Non-Conformists Move the World.*

115 Grant, *Originals: How Non-Conformists Move the World*, p. 125.

116 Brené Brown, *Dare to Lead: Brave Work, Tough Conversations, Whole Hearts* (New York: Random House, 2018).

117 Atul Gawande, "Slow Ideas - Some Innovations Spread Fast. How Do You Speed the Ones that Don't?," *The New Yorker* (2013), https://www.newyorker.com/magazine/2013/07/29/slow-ideas.

118 Richard Branson, *Business Stripped Bare: Adventures of a Global Entrepreneur* (London: Virgin Books, 2009).

119 Julia Sklar, "'Zoom Fatigue' is Taxing the Brain. Here's Why That Happens," *National Geographic Magazine* (2020), https://www.nationalgeographic.com/science/2020/04/coronavirus-zoom-fatigue-is-taxing-the-brain-here-is-why-that-happens/.

120 Light, "A Cascade of Failures: Why Government Fails, and How to Stop It."

121 Malcolm Gladwell, *The Tipping Point: How Little Things Can Make a Big Difference* (Boston: Back Bay Books, 2002).

122 Weiss, *How We Work: Live Your Purpose, Reclaim Your Sanity, and Embrace the Daily Grind.*

123 "Humor, Laughter, and Those Aha Moments," *On the Brain: The Harvard Mahoney Neuroscience Institute Letter* (2010), https://hms.harvard.edu/news/humor-laughter-those-aha-moments.

124 Christensen, *The Innovator's Dilemma: When New Technologies Cause Great Firms to Fail*, p. 41.

125 Brown, *Dare to Lead: Brave Work, Tough Conversations, Whole Hearts.*

126 Calleam Consulting Ltd., *An Illustration of Ineffectual Decision Making: A Case Study on the Denver International Airport Baggage Handling System* (Calleam Consulting Ltd., 2008), http://calleam.com/WTPF/wp-content/uploads/articles/DIABaggage.pdf.

127 *An Illustration of Ineffectual Decision Making.*

128 *An Illustration of Ineffectual Decision Making.*

129 *An Illustration of Ineffectual Decision Making.*

130 *An Illustration of Ineffectual Decision Making.*

131 *An Illustration of Ineffectual Decision Making.*

132 *An Illustration of Ineffectual Decision Making.*

133 *An Illustration of Ineffectual Decision Making.*

134 Greg McKeown, *Essentialism: The Disciplined Pursuit of Less* (New York: Crown Business, 2014).

135 Pink, *When: The Scientific Secrets of Perfect Timing*, p. 146.

136 "Why Do Projects Fail? Marin County," University of British Columbia's Sauder School of Business - Continuing Business Studies unit (2013), http://calleam.com/WTPF/?p=4886#:~:text=Lack%20of%20quality%20control%20and,direct%20causes%20of%20the%20failure.

137 Garrett, "After $367.5 Million, Texas Gets No New Child Support Computer Software – Just Painful Lessons."

138 Daniel Coyle, *The Culture Code: The Secrets of Highly Successful Groups* (New York: Bantam, 2018).

139 Schwab, "The Fourth Industrial Revolution: What it Means and How to Respond."

140 “Stem Cell AI — ‘Brain on a Chip’ Project Aims to Revolutionize Computing Power,” Aston University (2021), https://eurekalert.org/pub_releases/2021-01/au-sca012621.php.

141 David Schatsky, Ragu Gurumurthy, and Craig Muraskin, “Cognitive Technologies: The Real Opportunities for Business,” *Deloitte Review*, Issue 16 (2015), https://www2.deloitte.com/us/en/insights/deloitte-review/issue-16/cognitive-technologies-business-applications.html.

142 Schatsky, Gurumurthy, and Muraskin, “Cognitive Technologies: The Real Opportunities for Business.”

143 *Bullish on the Business Value of Cognitive: Leaders in Cognitive and AI Weigh in on What’s Working and What’s Next*, Deloitte (2017), https://www2.deloitte.com/content/dam/Deloitte/us/Documents/deloitte-analytics/us-da-2017-deloitte-state-of-cognitive-survey.pdf.

144 Richard E. Susskind, *Tomorrow’s Lawyers: An Introduction to Your Future* (Oxford, United Kingdom: Oxford University Press, 2017).

145 Michael E. Porter and James E. Heppelmann, “Why Every Organization Needs an Augmented Reality Strategy,” in *HBR’s 10 Must Reads On AI, Analytics, and the New Machine Age* (Boston: Harvard Business Review Press, 2019), p. 84.

146 Thomas H. Davenport, *The AI Advantage: How to Put the Artificial Intelligence Revolution to Work* (Cambridge, MA: The MIT Press, 2018).

147 Lewis, *The Undoing Project: A Friendship that Changed Our Minds*.

148 Michael Casey and Paul Vigna, *The Truth Machine: The Blockchain and the Future of Everything* (New York: St. Martin’s Press, 2018), p. 14-15.

149 Casey and Vigna, *The Truth Machine: The Blockchain and the Future of Everything*, p. 7.

150 Casey and Vigna, *The Truth Machine: The Blockchain and the Future of Everything*, p. 39.

151 Casey and Vigna, *The Truth Machine: The Blockchain and the Future of Everything*, p. 93.

152 Casey and Vigna, *The Truth Machine: The Blockchain and the Future of Everything*, p. 167.

153 Katherine Barrett and Richard Greene, "The Poor Performance of Performance Contracts" (2020), https://www.routefifty.com/management/2020/07/poor-performance-performance-contracts/167090/.

154 *Performance Audit of the City's Right-of-Way Tree Maintenance Program* (2019), https://www.sandiego.gov/sites/default/files/19-018_tree_trimming_maintenance.pdf.

155 Lisa R. Collier, A *Summary of Results from Contracting Audits* (2020), http://www.sao.texas.gov/Apps/SummaryReports/Home/Index/CN.

156 Barrett and Greene, "The Poor Performance of Performance Contracts."

157 Antonio Nieto-Rodriguez, "2021 and beyond.... 5 Disruptive Trends in Project Management" (2020) https://www.linkedin.com/pulse/2021-beyond-disruptive-trends-project-management-nieto-rodriguez/?trackingId=67VeCbG36NBE5ILQvPlXmg%3D%3D.

158 Joshua Althauser, "Russian Ministry Partners with VEB to Pilot Blockchain Project" (2017), https://cointelegraph.com/news/russian-ministry-partners-with-veb-to-pilot-blockchain-project.

159 Kai-Fu Lee, AI *Superpowers: China, Silicon Valley, and the New World Order* (Boston: Houghton Mifflin Harcourt, 2018).

160 Jacob Kastrenakes, "Tim Cook Says Apple Wants to Use AR to Make Conversations Better" (2021), https://www.theverge.com/2021/4/5/22367715/tim-cook-augmented-reality-apple-car-hints-interview.

161 Alex Heath, "The People With Power at Facebook as Its Hardware, Commerce Ambitions Expand" (2021), https://www.theinformation.com/articles/the-people-with-power-at-facebook-as-its-hardware-commerce-ambitions-expand.

162 Davenport, *The AI Advantage: How to Put the Artificial Intelligence Revolution to Work.*

163 Casey and Vigna, *The Truth Machine: The Blockchain and the Future of Everything*, p. 262.

164 Sherry Turkle, *Reclaiming Conversation: The Power of Talk in a Digital Age* (New York: Penguin Press, 2015).

165 Turkle, *Reclaiming Conversation: The Power of Talk in a Digital Age.*

166 Turkle, *Reclaiming Conversation: The Power of Talk in a Digital Age.*

167 Sherry Turkle, “Stop Googling. Let’s Talk,” *The New York Times*

(2015), https://www.nytimes.com/2015/09/27/opinion/sunday/stop-googling-lets-talk.html?_r=0.

168 Branson Business Stripped Bare: *Adventures of a Global Entrepreneur* p. 292.

Bibliography

Althauser, Joshua, "Russian Ministry Partners with Veb to Pilot Blockchain Project." 2017, https://cointelegraph.com/news/russian-ministry-partners-with-veb-to-pilot-blockchain-project.

Anthony, Scott D. "The Planning Fallacy and the Innovator's Dilemma." *Harvard Business Review* (2012), https://hbr.org/2012/08/the-planning-fallacy-and-the-i.

Aston University, "Stem Cell AI — 'Brain on a Chip' Project Aims to Revolutionize Computing Power." 2021, https://eurekalert.org/pub_releases/2021-01/au-sca012621.php.

Barrett, Katherine, and Richard Greene, "The Poor Performance of Performance Contracts" (2020), https://www.routefifty.com/management/2020/07/poor-performance-performance-contracts/167090/.

Bergman, Eric, "LinkedIn & Amazon Eliminate Slide-Driven Presentations." 2014, http://www.presentwithease.com/Blog/Blog/files/eliminate-ppt-presentations.html.

Bradberry, Travis, and Jean Greaves. *Emotional Intelligence* 2.0. San Diego: TalentSmart, 2009.

Bradley, Chris, "Surprise: Those 'Great' Companies Generally Turn out to Be Meh ... Or Duds." 2017, https://www.marketwatch.com/story/great-companies-are-more-likely-to-do-really-badly-over-time-than-really-well-2017-07-12.

Branson, Richard. *Business Stripped Bare: Adventures of a Global Entrepreneur.* London: Virgin Books, 2009.

Brown, Brené. *Braving the Wilderness: The Quest for True Belonging and the Courage to Stand Alone.* New York: Random House, 2017.

———. *Dare to Lead: Brave Work, Tough Conversations, Whole Hearts.* New York: Random House, 2018.

———. *The Gifts of Imperfection: Let Go of Who You Think You're*

Supposed to Be and Embrace Who You Are. Center City, Minn.: Hazelden, 2010.

Buehler, Roger, Dale Griffin, and Michael Ross. "Exploring the 'Planning Fallacy': Why People Underestimate Their Task Completion Times." *Journal of Personality and Social Psychology* Vol. 67, no. 3 (1994): 366-81, https://web.mit.edu/curhan/www/docs/Articles/biases/67_J_Personality_and_Social_Psychology_366,_1994.pdf.

Calleam Consulting Ltd. *An Illustration of Ineffectual Decision Making: A Case Study on the Denver International Airport Baggage Handling System*, 2008, http://calleam.com/WTPF/wp-content/uploads/articles/DIABaggage.pdf.

———. "Teddy Bear Madness." 2018, https://calleam.com/WTPF/?p=8540.

———. "Why Do Projects Fail? Marin County." University of British Columbia's Sauder School of Business - Continuing Business Studies unit, 2013, http://calleam.com/WTPF/?p=4886#:~:text=Lack%20of%20quality%20control%20and,direct%20causes%20of%20the%20failure.

Casey, Michael, and Paul Vigna. *The Truth Machine: The Blockchain and the Future of Everything.* New York: St. Martin's Press, 2018.

Chatzipanos, Panos A., and Theofanis Giotis, "Cognitive Biases as Project & Program Complexity Enhancers: The Astypalea Project." Paper presented at PMI® Global Congress 2014, Project Management Institute, 2014, https://www.pmi.org/learning/library/cognitive-biases-complexity-enhancers-projects-1454.

Christensen, Clayton M. *The Innovator's Dilemma: When New Technologies Cause Great Firms to Fail.* The Management of Innovation and Change Series. Boston: Harvard Business Review Press, 2013.

Clifford Chance. *Applying Continuous Improvement to High-End Legal Services.* (2014). https://www.cliffordchance.com/content/dam/cliffordchance/About_us/Continuous_Improvement_White_Paper.pdf.

Collier, Lisa R. A *Summary of Results from Contracting* Audits. (2020), http://www.sao.texas.gov/Apps/SummaryReports/Home/Index/CN.

Coyle, Daniel. *The Culture Code: The Secrets of Highly Successful Groups*. New York: Bantam, 2018.

———. *The Talent Code: Greatness Isn't Born. It's Grown. Here's How.* New York: Bantam Dell, 2009.

Davenport, Thomas H. *The AI Advantage: How to Put the Artificial Intelligence Revolution to Work.* Cambridge: The MIT Press, 2018.

Deloitte. *Bullish on the Business Value of Cognitive: Leaders in Cognitive and AI Weigh in on What's Working and What's Next*, 2017, https://www2.deloitte.com/content/dam/Deloitte/us/Documents/deloitte-analytics/us-da-2017-deloitte-state-of-cognitive-survey.pdf.

Dhillon, Gurpreet, and Mário Caldeira. "A Bumpy Road to Success (or Not): The Case of Project Genesis at Nevada Dmv." Vol. 28, no. 3 (2008): 222-28,https://www.sciencedirect.com/science/article/abs/pii/S0268401208000388?via%3Dihub.

Duhigg, Charles. *The Power of Habit : Why We Do What We Do in Life and Business.* New York: Random House, 2012.

Egan, Matt, "Workers Fear Humans Implanted with Microchips Will Steal Their Jobs." 2020, https://www.cnn.com/2020/09/18/business/jobs-robots-microchips-cyborg/index.html.

Garrett, Robert T. "After $367.5 Million, Texas Gets No New Child Support Computer Software – Just Painful Lessons." *Dallas Morning News*, 2019, https://www.dallasnews.com/news/politics/2019/05/17/after-367-5-million-texas-gets-no-new-child-support-computer-software-just-painful-lessons/.

Gawande, Atul. "Slow Ideas - Some Innovations Spread Fast. How Do You Speed the Ones That Don't?" *The New Yorker*, 2013, https://www.newyorker.com/magazine/2013/07/29/slow-ideas.

Gilbert, Ben. "Amazon Ceo Jeff Bezos Says Multibillion-Dollar Failures Are Actually a Good Thing: 'If the Size of Your Failures Isn't Growing, You're Not Going to Be Inventing at a Size That Can Actually Move the Needle'." *Business Insider* (2019), https://www.businessinsider.com/jeff-bezos-says-multi-billion-dollar-failures-necessary-for-amazon-growth-success-2019-4.

Gladwell, Malcolm. *The Tipping Point: How Little Things Can Make a Big Difference.* Boston: Back Bay Books, 2002.

Goel, Namni, Mathias Basner, Hengy Rao, and David F. Dinges. "Circadian Rhythms, Sleep Deprivation, and Human Performance." *Progress in Molecular Biology and Translational Science* Vol. 119 (2013): Pages 155-90, https://www.sciencedirect.com/science/article/pii/B9780123969712000075.

Goleman, Daniel. *Leadership: The Power of Emotional Intelligence.* Northampton, MA: More Than Sound, LLC, 2011.

Gostick, Adrian, and Chester Elton. *The Best Team Wins: The New Science of High Performance.* New York: Simon & Schuster, 2018.

Grant, Adam M. *Originals: How Non-Conformists Move the World.* New York: Viking/Penguin Random House LLC, 2016.

Greene, Jay. "Microsoft Won't Sell Police Its Facial-Recognition Technology, Following Similar Moves by Amazon and IBM," *Washington Post*, 2020, https://www.washingtonpost.com/technology/2020/06/11/microsoft-facial-recognition/.

Hardy-Vallee, Benoit. "The Cost of Bad Project Management." *Gallup Business Journal* (2012), https://news.gallup.com/businessjournal/152429/Cost-Bad-Project-Management.aspx.

Harvard Medical School. "Humor, Laughter, and Those Aha Moments." *On the Brain: The Harvard Mahoney Neuroscience Institute Letter*, 2010, https://hms.harvard.edu/news/humor-laughter-those-aha-moments.

Heath, Alex, "The People with Power at Facebook as Its Hardware, Commerce Ambitions Expand." 2021, https://www.theinformation.com/articles/the-people-with-power-at-facebook-as-its-hardware-commerce-ambitions-expand.

Horowitz, Ben. *The Hard Thing About Hard Things: Building a Business When There Are No Easy Answers.* New York: HarperCollins Publishers, 2014.

Hsieh, Tony. *Delivering Happiness: A Path to Profits, Passion, and Purpose.* New York: Business Plus, 2010.

Irigoyen, Claudia, "The FBI Virtual Case File System." Centre for Public Impact, 2017, https://www.centreforpublicimpact.org/case-study/fbi-virtual-case-file-system/.

Kaplan, Robert S., and Anette Mikes. "Managing Risks: A New Framework." *Harvard Business Review* June (2012), https://hbr.org/2012/06/managing-risks-a-new-framework.

Kastrenakes, Jacob, "Tim Cook Says Apple Wants to Use AR to Make Conversations Better." 2021, https://www.theverge.com/2021/4/5/22367715/tim-cook-augmented-reality-apple-car-hints-interview.

Kim, W. Chan, and Renée Mauborgne. *Blue Ocean Strategy: How to Create Uncontested Market Space and Make the Competition Irrelevant.* Boston: Harvard Business Review Press, 2015.

Lama, Dalai, Desmond Tutu, and Douglas Abrams. *The Book of Joy: Lasting Happiness in a Changing World.* New York: Avery/Penguin Random House, 2016.

Lee, Kai-Fu. *AI Superpowers: China, Silicon Valley, and the New World Order.* Boston: Houghton Mifflin Harcourt, 2018.

Lencioni, Patrick. *The Advantage: Why Organizational Health Trumps Everything Else in Business.* San Francisco: Jossey-Bass, 2012.

———. *Silos, Politics, and Turf Wars: A Leadership Fable About Destroying the Barriers That Turn Colleagues into Competitors.* San Francisco: Jossey-Bass, 2006.

Lewis, Michael. *The Undoing Project: A Friendship That Changed Our Minds.* New York: W.W. Norton & Company, 2017.

Liang, Ting-Peng, Nai-Shin Yen, Yuwen Li, and Shen-Mou Hsu. *Escalation of Commitment in Software Projects: A Neural Science Perspective.* (2016), https://aisel.aisnet.org/amcis2016/ITProj/Presentations/22.

Light, Paul C., "A Cascade of Failures: Why Government Fails, and How to Stop It." Brookings Institute, 2014, https://www.brookings.edu/research/a-cascade-of-failures-why-government-fails-and-how-to-stop-it/.

Lipman, Joanne. *That's What She Said: What Men Need to Know (and Women Need to Tell Them) About Working Together.* New York: Harper Collins Publishers, 2018.

Mattioli, Dana. "Amazon Scooped up Data from Its Own Sellers to Launch Competing Products." *Wall Street Journal*, 2020, https://www.wsj.com/articles/amazon-scooped-up-data-from-its-own-sellers-to-launch-competing-products-11587650015?mod=djemalertNEWS.

Mayer, Colin. "Reinventing the Corporation." *Journal of the British Academy* 4 (2016): 53-72, https://www.thebritishacademy.ac.uk/documents/1613/03_Mayer_1825.pdf.

McKeown, Greg. *Essentialism: The Disciplined Pursuit of Less.* New York: Crown Business, 2014.

Menakem, Resmaa. *My Grandmother's Hands: Racialized Trauma and the Pathway to Mending Our Hearts and Bodies*. Las Vegas: Central Recovery Press, 2017.

Nieto-Rodriguez, Antonio, "2021 and Beyond.... 5 Disruptive Trends in Project Management." 2020, https://www.linkedin.com/pulse/2021-beyond-disruptive-trends-project-management-nieto-rodriguez/?trackingId=67VeCbG36NBE5ILQvPlXmg%3D%3D.

O'Brochta, Michael. "Why Bad Projects Are So Hard to Kill." PM *World Journal* Vol. VI, no. III (2017), https://pmworldlibrary.net/wp-content/uploads/2017/03/pmwj56-Mar2017-OBrochta-why-bad-projects-are-hard-to-kill-featured-paper.pdf.

Office of the City Auditor, City of San Diego, CA. *Performance Audit of the City's Right-of-Way Tree Maintenance Program*. (2019), https://www.sandiego.gov/sites/default/files/19-018_tree_trimming_maintenance.pdf.

Open Door Technology, "The Standish Group Report 83.9% of It Projects Partially or Completely Fail." 2019, https://www.opendoorerp.com/the-standish-group-report-83-9-of-it-projects-partially-or-completely-fail/#:~:text=According%20to%20Standish%20only%2016.2,and%2For%20lacking%20promised%20functionality.

Parker, John N., Edgar Cardenas, Alexander N. Dorr, and Edward J. Hackett, "Using Sociometers to Advance Small Group Research." 2018, https://journals.sagepub.com/doi/10.1177/0049124118769091.

Patterson, Kerry. *Crucial Conversations: Tools for Talking When Stakes Are High*. New York: McGraw-Hill, 2012.

Peters, Thomas J., and Robert H. Waterman. *In Search of Excellence: Lessons from America's Best-Run Companies*. New York: Harper & Row, 1982.

Phillips, Donald T. *Lincoln on Leadership: Executive Strategies for Tough Times*. New York: Warner Books, 1992.

Pink, Daniel H. *Drive: The Surprising Truth About What Motivates Us*. New York: Riverhead Books, 2011.

———. *When: The Scientific Secrets of Perfect Timing*. New York: Riverhead Books, 2018.

Porter, Michael E., and James E. Heppelmann. "Why Every Organization Needs an Augmented Reality Strategy." *In HBR's 10 Must Reads on AI, Analytics, and the New Machine Age*. Boston: Harvard Business Review Press, 2019.

Powell, Colin L., and Tony Koltz. *It Worked for Me: In Life and Leadership.* New York: Harper, 2012.

Project Management Institute, https://www.projectmanagement.com/.

———. "Ahead of the Curve: Forging a Future-Focused Culture." *Pulse of the Profession,* 2020, https://www.pmi.org/learning/library/forging-future-focused-culture-11908.

———. "Beyond Agility." *Pulse of the Profession*, 2021, https://www.pmi.org/-/media/pmi/documents/public/pdf/learning/thought-leadership/pulse/pmi_pulse_2021.pdf?v=151f8a8e-c074-44ba-a933-91eb32e172bf&sc_lang_temp=en.

Putnam, Robert D., 2020, http://robertdputnam.com/.

Reuters. "Don't Be Silent: How a 22-Year-Old Woman Helped Bring Down the Tokyo Olympics Chief." CNN, 2021, https://www.cnn.com/2021/02/18/sport/momoko-nojo-tokyo-olympics-spt-intl/index.html.

Schatsky, David, Ragu Gurumurthy, and Craig Muraskin. "Cognitive Technologies: The Real Opportunities for Business." *Deloitte Review* Issue 16 (2015), https://www2.deloitte.com/us/en/insights/deloitte-review/issue-16/cognitive-technologies-business-applications.html.

Schwab, Klaus, "The Fourth Industrial Revolution: What It Means and How to Respond." World Economic Forum, 2016, https://www.weforum.org/agenda/2016/01/the-fourth-industrial-revolution-what-it-means-and-how-to-respond/.

Seglin, Jeffrey L. "The Right Thing; When Fear of Firing Deters Hiring." *The New York Times*, 1999, https://www.nytimes.com/1999/04/18/business/the-right-thing-when-fear-of-firing-deters-hiring.html.

Sinek, Simon. *The Infinite Game.* New York: Portfolio/Penguin, 2019.

———. *Leaders Eat Last: Why Some Teams Pull Together and Others Don't.* New York: Portfolio/Penguin, 2014.

———. *Start with Why: How Great Leaders Inspire Everyone to Take Action.* New York: Portfolio, 2009.

Sklar, Julia. "'Zoom Fatigue' Is Taxing the Brain. Here's Why That Happens." *National Geographic Magazine* (2020), https://www.nationalgeographic.com/science/2020/04/coronavirus-zoom-fatigue-is-taxing-the-brain-here-is-why-that-happens/.

Slater, Robert. 29 *Leadership Secrets from Jack Welch.* New York: McGraw-Hill, 2003.

Sommer, Jeff. "Robert Shiller: A Skeptic and a Nobel Winner." *The New York Times*, 2013, https://www.nytimes.com/2013/10/20/business/robert-shiller-a-skeptic-and-a-nobel-winner.html.

Susskind, Richard E. *Tomorrow's Lawyers: An Introduction to Your Future.* Oxford: Oxford University Press, 2017.

Turban, Stephen, Dan Wu, and Letian (LT) Zhang. "Research: When Gender Diversity Makes Firms More Productive." *Harvard Business Review* (2019), https://hbr.org/2019/02/research-when-gender-diversity-makes-firms-more-productive.

Turkle, Sherry. *Reclaiming Conversation: The Power of Talk in a Digital Age.* New York: Penguin Press, 2015.

———. "Stop Googling. Let's Talk." *The New York Times*, 2015, https://www.nytimes.com/2015/09/27/opinion/sunday/stop-googling-lets-talk.html?_r=0.

Vialogue, "Ted Talks Worth Talking About | Ken Robinson on Bring on the Learning Revolution." 2010, https://vialogue.wordpress.com/2010/05/26/ted-talks-worth-talking-about-ken-robinson-on-bring-on-the-learning-revolution/.

Weiss, Leah. *How We Work: Live Your Purpose, Reclaim Your Sanity, and Embrace the Daily Grind.* New York: Harper Collins Publishers, 2018.

Westen, D., P. S. Blagov, K. Harenski, C. Kilts, and S. Hamann. "Neural Bases of Motivated Reasoning: An FMRI Study of Emotional Constraints on Partisan Political Judgment in the 2004 U.S. Presidential Election." [In eng]. *Journal of Cognitive Neuroscience* Vol. 18, no. 11 (2006): 1947-58, https://doi.org/10.1162/jocn.2006.18.11.1947. https://www.ncbi.nlm.nih.gov/pubmed/17069484.

Willink, Jocko, and Leif Babin. *Extreme Ownership: How U.S. Navy Seals Lead and Win.* New York: St. Martin's Press, 2017.

Wiseman, Liz. *Multipliers: How the Best Leaders Make Everyone Smarter.* New York: HarperBusiness, 2017.

Yanke, Greg. "Tying the Knot with a Robot: Legal and Philosophical Foundations for Human-Artificial Intelligence Matrimony." *AI & Society* 36 (2021): 417-27, https://doi.org/10.1007/s00146-020-00973-5.

Acknowledgements

No good book is produced without the help of a lot of great people and Herding Smart Cats is no exception. I offer my profound gratitude to:

Jeff Seglin, whose graciousness years ago when I was in graduate school and navigating my father's death, led me to contact him about finding a good editor, and then, reading one of the later drafts in the hopes of understanding whether I should burn the manuscript or press onward. He was kind enough to read the book and offer encouragement.

Kate Victory Hannisian, my gifted editor, of Blue Pencil Consulting, for making this happen. She displayed an incredible ability to understand what I was trying hard to say, even before I could put it into words. Since her first manuscript review, Kate has inspired me with her elegant prose and though-provoking suggestions, always designed to help "connect the dots for the reader."

Leigh Silverstein, my marketing colleague, without whom nothing I do would ever be known. Somehow, with skills ranging from programming to photoshop, she manages to help me avoid the worst of my perfectionist tendencies and introverted nature. My apologies for any mistakes.

Harini Rajagopalan, my talented graphic designer, for her patience and skills in helping me move from uncertainty to clarity, and her smiling imperturbability when I frequently proposed yet another idea.

Pam Merritt, author of The Way of Cats, for her invaluable guidance on the way she believes cats think and feel. Developing this metaphor with her was truly a joy.

Joshua Golub, owner of Finite Wisdom, who helped me build Smart Projex 1.0, and for his unwavering support for over a decade.

Antonio Nieto-Rodriquez, a globally recognized project management expert, for inviting me to participate in his online community of experts seeking to explore how projects can turn around a world in crisis and for reading the final manuscript.

Thomas Walenta, a vastly more experienced project manager, who read an early draft and, in a labor of love, returned it to me with hundreds of comments and annotations, and almost apologized for being what Adam Grant calls a disagreeable giver. He gave me the confidence and encouragement to go forward even when he disagreed with some of my thoughts.

Many other readers, whose names appear in the Praise section, for comments and conversations, and those who didn't have time to read a draft but sent me encouraging messages. Writing and self-publishing your first book is a roller-coaster ride. Getting a positive nudge from someone who owes you nothing can push you up the next hill.

Tom Morkes, of Insurgent Publishing, who periodically had to move the Herding Smart Cats train back on the track.

And finally, to my sometimes-supportive family, all of whom kept me laughing and positive, and taught me more about conflict resolution, leadership, organization, management, and takeout dining, than any course or school.

Kate Moore Davenport, my stepdaughter and goddaughter, for walking into my hospital room, at age seven, carrying my eight-hour-old son. If I thought that I was in charge, I quickly learned that I was never going to be in charge – and isn't that the first lesson in project management? Isn't raising four youngsters all born within 41 months a project? And for her wife, Emily Balogh, and our many conversations on building and selling new technology products.

John Davenport, my oldest son, for helping me understand that not everyone is interested in planning, for urging me not to take life too seriously, for occasionally encouraging my wordsmithing struggles, and for not spilling his brother's blood.

Stephen Davenport, my youngest son, for conversations around business and boundaries, and helping me understand how schools think about projects, and for his wife, Madison, for her encouragement and our many conversations about human resources.

Sarah Davenport Quinn, my oldest daughter, for naming her firstborn after me, and her husband Taylor Quinn, for our many faith and entrepreneurial conversations.

Maria Davenport, my youngest daughter, who was kind enough to read a very early draft and continues to share her thoughts on how medical professionals manage projects and clinical trials, or perhaps should manage them.

Brad Davenport, my husband, and soul mate, for reading countless blogs, emails, and book drafts, despite having no interest in project management. I wish I had his writing talents. I can't thank him enough for helping me understand how older lawyers think about managing work (often projects) and being my counselor in perplexity, which has been a near-constant state for me since I began my project management journey.

And lastly, for my growing brood of grandchildren, who make life worth living, give me hope for the future, inspire me to continue to push this conversation, and remind me of God's grace and goodness.

About the Author

Suzanne S. Davenport has worked for years with project teams struggling to successfully complete projects. Over ten years ago, she created Smart Projex, working project management software that helped teams move project ideas from conception to reality, and provided the kinds of project and portfolio metrics that executives need to make solid business decisions. To do this, she went back to first principles and questioned everything she had been taught and thought she knew about project management. She used the software as a stepping-stone to the creation of a methodology that works on all kinds of projects and offers agility and accountability. She continues to experiment with and promote this methodology.

She enjoys herding smart cats and readily admits that she learned much about what works and what doesn't work from watching her own five children learn to communicate, collaborate, experiment, fail, and grow; and by brainstorming with her husband, a retired litigator, about the ways that attorneys work on cases.

Davenport holds an undergraduate degree from East Carolina University, an MBA from Virginia Commonwealth University, and multiple project management certifications. When she is not herding smart cats, she might be pondering current events, business trends, or her faith in God.

She believes there is a huge opportunity for reimagining work and project management software by incorporating twenty-first-century technologies like blockchain, smart contracts, voice technologies, and artificial intelligence, and drawing upon what we have learned through advanced scientific studies about project management, work management, change, biases, and human behavior.

Davenport publishes extensively on her own blog: http://www.smartprojex.com/smartblog/, as well as on Medium: https://medium.com/@SMARTPROJEX and LinkedIn: http://www.linkedin.com/in/suzannesdavenport.